SUPPLY CHAIN RISK

Supply Chain Risk

Edited by
CLARE BRINDLEY

160401

ASHGATE

Published by
Ashgate Publishing Limited
Gower House
Croft Road
Aldershot
Hampshire GU11 3HR
England

Ashgate Publishing Company
Suite 420
101 Cherry Street
Burlington, VT 05401-4405
USA

Ashgate website: http://www.ashgate.com

British Library Cataloguing in Publication Data
Supply chain risk
  1.Business logistics 2.Risk management
  I.Brindley, Clare
  658.5'03

Library of Congress Cataloging-in-Publication Data
Supply chain risk / [edited] by Clare Brindley.
      p. cm.
  Includes bibliographical references and index.
  ISBN 0-7546-3902-9
1. Business logistics. 2. Risk management. I. Brindley, Clare.

  HD38.5.S89624 2004
  658.7--dc22

                                                                2004007279

ISBN 0 7546 3902 9

Reprinted 2005

Printed and bound in Great Britain by MPG Books Ltd, Bodmin, Cornwall

Contents

PART I: RESEARCH FRAMEWORKS

PART II: TECHNIQUES AND APPLICATIONS

List of Figures

List of Tables

List of Diagrams

List of Contributors

Dan Andersson, Researcher Dept of Management and Economics, Linköpings Universitet, Linköpings, Sweden.

Dr. Clare Brindley, Acting Head of Department of Business and Management, Manchester Metropolitan University, UK.

Dr. Simon A. Burtonshaw-Gunn, Managing Consultant, BAE SYSTEMS and Hon Research Fellow, Manchester Metropolitan University, UK.

Jukka Hallikas, Researcher in Industrial Management, Lappeenranta University of Technology, Lappeenranta, Finland.

Robert Lindroth, Lecturer at Lund University and ex-Visiting Researcher Stanford University. Undertaking a PhD focusing on risk sharing models.

Prof. Steve A. Melnyk, Professor of Operations Management, The Eli Broad Graduate School of Management, Michigan State University, USA.

Arben Mullai, Researcher, Lund University, Sweden.

Dr Andreas Norrman, Research Fellow, Department of Industrial Management and Logistics, Lund University, Sweden.

Ulf Paulsson, Assistant Professor, Dept. of Industrial Management and Logistics, Div. of Engineering Logistics, Lund University, Sweden.

Dr. Gary L. Ragatz, Associate Professor of Supply Chain Management in the Eli Broad Graduate School of Management at Michigan State University.

Prof. Bob Ritchie, Professor in Risk Management, University of Central Lancashire, UK.

Dr. Michael E. Smith, Department of Management and International Business, Western Carolina University USA

Dr Veli-Matti Virolainen, Lappeenranta University, Finland.

Dr. George A. Zsidisin, Assistant Professor, Department of Marketing and Supply Chain Management, The Eli Broad Graduate School of Management, Michigan State University.

Foreword

Often the ripple effect of research is taken as a given – it is assumed it just happens without really a stream of consciousness. This book is testament to the ripple effect and an illustration that it does occur, thanks to enthusiasm and a lot of hard work!

Looking back it is difficult to pinpoint one key catalyst that led to this book, rather it was a series of ripples in the pond. Firstly, John Morris (Manchester Metropolitan University – MMU) presented a paper at IPSERA in 1999 and met up with George Zsidisin, Michigan State University. A couple of months later Andreas Norman (Lund University) emailed Clare Brindley after coming across a paper written by Clare and colleagues at MMU. Realising there were a number of us interested in supply chain risk, Clare decided to organise a seminar at MMU in October, 2001. Over the three days of the seminar George Zsidisin, Andreas Norrman, Robert Lindroth, Paul Björnsson, Ulf Paulsson, Clare Brindley, John Morris, Simon Burtonshaw-Gunn and Bob Ritchie, discussed their research on risk and the supply chain. Industry speakers came from AGCO Ltd, BAE Systems, HJ Lea Oakes and Rolls Royce and Bentley Motor Cars Ltd.

The key outcome of the seminar was the establishment of an international research network focusing on risk and the supply chain – ISCRIM was born! Lund University colleagues established the ISCRIM web page (http://www.tlog.1th.se/) and the ISCRIM newsletter under the editorship of Ulf Paulsson. It was also decided that due to the diversity of perspectives on risk and the supply chain ISCRIM members should publish a book. The next seminar was held at Lund University in 2002 and with new members added, further ideas for the book were developed.

As the ISCRIM network meet again at Manchester Metropolitan University in October 2003 the book has come to fruition. Thanks must be given to Caroline Robinson and Kerri Faulkner, MMU, for their patience and professionalism in helping to put the book together. We hope that ISCRIM members, fellow academics, practioners and students enjoy the book and it inspires the readers to create their own ripples!

Dr Clare Brindley
Founder of the ISCRIM Network

PART I
RESEARCH FRAMEWORKS

Chapter 1

Introduction

Dr. Clare Brindley and Prof. Bob Ritchie

Introduction

Supply chain operations, their management and the incidence or risk are not new phenomena, although they may have taken on a new level of significance. The reality of the supply chain has a long and important history, as any form of bartering or exchange of goods, would represent a supply chain in its simplest form. Medieval communities and economies were developed around such simple models of the supply chain, typically operating in a localised marketplace. Presumably many of the structures, processes and systems evident in today's supply chains were in existence then, albeit in a rudimentary form. This text addresses these issues in the context of present day supply chains and more specifically the uncertainties and risks that pervade supply chains and the effectiveness of managing these.

There are a number of developments which have caused primary stakeholders such as organizations, markets, consumers and governments to address supply chain issues and their management with increasing urgency. Three key developments illustrate the nature and scale of the impact and the consequential responses of these stakeholders:

1. Information and Communication Technology (ICT) developments have revolutionized the availability and exchange of information between all stakeholders in the supply chain. Consequently, competitive advantage has become more short-lived as entry barriers and niche markets have rapidly been eroded, through increased information and knowledge to all stakeholders.
2. ICTs have facilitated the development of global competition, impinging on almost every marketplace and organization size (Ritchie and Brindley, 2000). Product markets as well as service markets have been affected. Arguably services are more amenable to on-line delivery, although the impact of on-line promotional, ordering and payment systems for products has revolutionized many areas of retailing. It should be recognized that this enhancement of global competition has required many other developments (e.g. government policies and actions to reduce trade barriers) in addition to ICT innovations.
3. Interactions and relationships within the supply chains themselves have

resulted both as a consequence of ICT developments and the increasing competition in the marketplace. The supply chain itself has now become a significant weapon in the competitive arsenal, capable of delivering reduced costs, higher quality, faster and more reliable delivery and other dimensions of added value to the consumer. Such changes have the capacity to enhance the performance of the individual members in the supply chain and the supply chain membership as a whole.

The consequences of these three primary developments and the associated responses of members of the supply chain and indeed, parallel competitive supply chains clearly signal a potential increase in both uncertainty and risk. Added to this rapidly changing context is the increasing complexity of structures, strategies and systems emerging in response to the new competitive challenges. These provide further sources of uncertainty and risk. It is important to note that the identified sources of uncertainty and risk pervade every stage in the supply chain and not just the final stage of the product/service delivery to the consumer. In essence, the aims of this text are: the examination of the issues of increasing uncertainty and risk in the context of the supply chain, investigation of the sources and reasons for the increase, assessment of the potential approaches to managing such risks and the evaluation of the consequences for the performance of the individual member organization and the supply chain as a whole.

Risk management within supply chains is one of the most significant challenges facing every organization by virtue of the fact that all organizations are a member of at least one and more probably, multiple supply chains. There is an absence of research and texts on the specific dimension of risk management in supply chains, although many studies on supply chain management in general make reference to the issue. The authors contributing to this text are all actively researching different dimensions of the risk management phenomenon which reflect the multi-functional and multi-disciplinary nature of the issues involved. The collection of papers seeks to provide the initial platform for further research and development in this field. The authors recognize that as with any emerging field of study there is a need for improving the clarity of definitions, frameworks and models etc. and would see this text as providing the basis for this.

This introductory chapter seeks to establish some of the key definitions employed throughout the text, whilst recognizing that particular papers may explore these in greater depth. Initially, we seek to define the terms Supply Chain and Supply Chain Management. Secondly, a working definition of the terms Uncertainty and Risk are developed and their association with risk management in the supply chain context is outlined. The term risk is then integrated within the definition of business performance to establish the need to balance risk, effectiveness and profitability. This provides the basis for the discussion on metrics later in the chapter. Finally, some of the key strategies and tactics within risk management are identified and reference is made to where these are developed further in later chapters.

The Supply Chain

The difficulty with the term the supply chain is that there are almost an infinite number of definitions, most of which are not inconsistent with each other but rather choose to focus on particular perspectives or attributes. Christopher (1992) provides a reasonably generic definition, describing a supply chain as a network of organizations that are involved, through upstream (i.e. supply sources) and downstream (i.e. distribution channels) linkages, in the different processes and activities that produce value in the form of products and services in the hands of the ultimate consumers. This definition conceives of a multiple set of organizations operating upstream and downstream with often multiple organizations operating at each stage in the chain (e.g. alternative competing suppliers). More recent studies (e.g. Ritchie and Brindley, 2001) have suggested the inclusion of information flows and financial flows, reflecting the developments in ICTs mentioned earlier. They have also recognized the increasingly important dimension of relationships.

Within this generic supply chain definition there are further subsets. For example, the limited or *basic supply chain* typically focuses on the linkages between a single organization and its immediate supplier and/or immediate customer, although not always the final consumer. A large proportion of the research in the field focuses on these dyadic linkages or relationships. The term the *extended supply chain* encapsulates those organizations working further up or down the supply chain from the immediate suppliers and customers. This may involve multiple organizations at each of the successive stages. The *ultimate supply chain* refers to the complete set of stages from initial raw material through to final consumer, incorporating all the associated services that contribute to the ultimate added value received by the consumer.

Supply chains may be considered from a variety of perspectives, structural, systems, strategic and relationship. The *structural perspective* has probably been the most enduring though even this is undergoing radical transition with developments of more amorphous structures with multi-faceted relationships replacing the previous linear structures and often uni-directional relationships (e.g. Ritchie and Brindley, 2001). An alternative perspective is the *systems perspective* which focuses on the efficiency of the system in terms of the transition of resources from raw materials through to consumption (e.g. Cooper et al, 1997). In many respects this systems perspective fits with the application of logistics, seeking to ensure maximum efficiency in processing, storage, transportation and communications. The *strategic perspective* concerns itself primarily with developing and sustaining competitive advantage, often through positioning of the organization in relation to its supply chain members and seeking to maximize the value added to the eventual consumer (e.g. Porter, 1985). More recent developments in the field of supply chains suggest a new *relationship perspective* (e.g. Ritchie and Brindley, 2001), one that focuses on building and managing relationships at both the strategic and operational level. Each of these perspectives is mutually compatible, providing different insights into the same set of issues, often suggesting differing solutions which in themselves may not necessarily be incompatible.

Supply Chain Management

The differing perspectives of the supply chain outlined in the previous section, indicate the range of activities and decisions that represent the roles and responsibilities of supply chain management. For example, logistics at the strategic level (e.g. single source supplier) and the operational level (e.g. progress chasing particular orders) are an essential element of supply chain management, although by no means the only ones. The sharing of commercial information, cooperation in product development and the full integration of key manufacturing processes, are all examples of strategic dimensions of supply chain management. The commitment to enhancing customer value and satisfaction represents a further dimension, one which may be shared by all members of the ultimate supply chain, as this should collectively enhance the aggregate performance of the supply chain. This all-embracing commitment to generating value to the consumer and the members of the supply chain is being termed *supply chain orientation*. All of these management activities and others are underpinned or will result in changes in the relationships between the members of the chain. Terms such as co-operation, collaboration and partnering are becoming increasingly prevalent in the literature associated with the management of supply chains. Supply chain management is therefore, a multi-disciplinary and multi-functional set of activities, which deals not only with the more physical and tangible attributes and activities (e.g. logistics) but equally the more behavioral and intangible dimensions (e.g. relationship building and management).

Emerging from this brief description of the supply chain and supply chain management, should be the recognition that the nature, scale and rapidity of these changes. This has significant consequences for the risk exposure of the organizations within the supply chain and their management, in terms of new and additional sources of uncertainty and risk.

Uncertainty and Risk

Attempts at defining the terms uncertainty and risk have spawned a large variation of approaches, evidence the broad themes emanating from various academic disciplines, for example in the 1920s risk became popular in the economics fields (Dowling and Staelin, 1994, p.119). This is illustrated by the study of gambling being seen as a useful way to test economic theories such as risk taking (Clotfelter and Cook, 1989). The associated dimension of risk perceptions has its antecedents in economics and behavioral decision theory according to Forlani and Mullins (2000). Subsequently, the concept of risk has formed part of management, environmental, insurance and psychological studies, each focusing on a particular aspect but normally, contextualized within the area of decision making i.e. the individual or organization is faced with making a decision. Most studies have focused on the individual rather than the group decision maker.

Commonalities in these paradigms relate to their definition of risk, which link to the issues of unpredictability, decision-making and potential loss. For example, Sitkin and Pablo (1992, p.9) define risk as 'the extent to which there is uncertainty about whether potentially significant and/or disappointing outcomes of decisions will be realized.' Similarly, MacCrimmon and Wehrung (1986) identified three components of risk: the magnitude of loss, the chance of loss and the potential exposure to loss. The variation in how these 'losses' may be perceived is why, for March and Shapira (1987), risks are taken or not. Technically, risk may be defined as the probability of incurring a loss (Knight, 1921), although in reality this is a somewhat imbalanced definition given that most risky decisions in business are taken on the basis of generating a potential gain (Blume, 1971), whilst recognising that this may not be certain (i.e. few if any business or investment decisions would be undertaken solely to avoid losses).

Uncertainty is defined as the absence of information (Rowe, 1977) concerning the decision situation and the need to exercise judgment in determining or evaluating the situation, alternative solutions, possible outcomes etc. At the extreme level, uncertainty could be categorized as the total absence of information or knowledge that the problem or decision situation exists. However, uncertainty typically reflects the ambiguity surrounding the decision, possibly in terms of the precise nature of the situation, its causes, possible solutions and the reaction of other stakeholders to the implementation of the solution. An important tenet of the field of risk management is the integration and interaction of the terms risk and uncertainty, within the commonly used term of risk itself. Indeed, common usage of the term risk within the business context is deemed to incorporate both the uncertainty and risk dimensions. This inclusive approach will also be utilized throughout the text.

The composition of the decision-making unit will influence the nature of the strategies that evolve in terms of their risk and potential financial performance. Research into the risk behavior of individuals and groups in the context of business decisions has been relatively limited. Newall's (1977) study of industrial buyers suggested that risk-taking behavior was unlikely to vary irrespective of whether the group was large or small or indeed was an individual. However, Valla (1982) did suggest that the size and composition of the decision taking unit, the interpersonal relationships and the decision processes employed may all influence the propensity to take risky decisions.

Other important issues discussed in the text include those of risk perception and propensity. These relate to an individual's, or in some cases a group's, preparedness to take risks. A preparedness, that may depend on the uncertainty of outcomes (due for example to imperfect knowledge or experience) and or the potential scale of losses or gains. McCarthy (2000) suggested that the personal attributes of age, gender, and ethnicity effect risk perception. A view supported by the work of MacCrimmon and Wehrung (1990) which established that the factor of age influences risk propensity and risk taking. As there can be a diversity in the decision making unit in terms of composition, then it is important to understand the differences and the impact that these can make in terms of perception and preparedness to take risks.

Risk and Risk Management

An outline model of risk determination within the business context constructed by Ritchie and Marshall (1993) suggested the following key elements:

Aggregate Business Performance $= f$ (Profitability * Risk)

where

Risk $= f(E_r, I_r, O_r, P_r, DM_r)$

The risks generated from particular variables are:

E_r = environmental variables
I_r = industry variables
O_r = organizational variables
p_r = problem specific variables
DM_r = decision-maker related variables

Figure 1.1 Model of Risk Determination

This simplified model indicates that these variables influence financial performance as well as the risk inherent in the business. Each of the first four variables will determine the risk *extant* or inherent in the given situation due to a combination of the contextual parameters and the specific problem parameters. The behavior of the decision maker may change the total risk exposure, as the quality of the decision may *induce* risk into the situation to a greater or lesser degree. For example, the decision to invest in a standby generator may not reduce the probability of a power supply failure and the dislocation of production but will reduce the scale of the consequences should such an event occur. In essence this is an example of *risk management*. Ritchie and Marshall (1993, pp.167-168) defined risk management at the strategic level as responding to '...secular shifts in demand due to product obsolescence, changes in technology and industry-wide patterns of demand/supply [which] are the major sources of risk that organizations seek to address and resolve through corporate strategy'.

Risk and Risk Management in the Supply Chain

Reference to the Model (Figure 1.1) in the previous section provides a means of classifying the types of risks encountered in the supply chain. The first three groups of characteristics primarily define the context within which the decisions are taken.

1. *Environment characteristics:* Changes in the constituent elements of the competitive environment generates risk exposure for all organizations operating within the environment. Developments in generic technologies, economic trade groupings, politics and national cultures may potentially generate heightened risk exposure for the business organization.
2. *Industry characteristics:* Changes within a particular industry context will pose risks for the organizations operating within or relating to the industry. These changes may be driven by the industry's response to the wider environmental developments, resulting in new product/service development, changes in competitive strategies or possible new structural arrangements (e.g. re-configuration of the supply chain structure and membership).
3. *Organizational characteristics:* The organization may potentially change a number of dimensions (e.g. structure, culture, operations, systems etc.) either re-acting to changes in the competitive environment or taking precipitate actions to address anticipated risks. In either event, the changes and perhaps more importantly the process of implementing such changes poses risks for the organization.

The degree of influence of the individual organization over the risks emanating from these three sources is limited, especially those from the environment and the industry. The term *Systematic Risks* has been coined in the risk literature to represent those risks that are in a sense unavoidable risk, generated from the environment within which the decision takes place and where few, if any, organizations have the ability to modify their environment in any significant way. In the context of the supply chain and its management, the adoption of a marketing approach may enable the organization to adapt and be more responsive to its environment and thus, reduce the level of systematic risk exposure. For example, the application of effective environmental and market scanning processes or the introduction of an effective policy of relationship marketing may simultaneously make the organizations more aware and responsive to its environments and ensure that sound relationships are in place, to ameliorate some of the potential threats and risks from the environment. Marketing has traditionally played a major role in the information communication and analysis between the organization and its environment. The processes of market research, competitor analysis, consumer behavior studies and market forecasting are all well established roles. This knowledge and understanding of the market, the consumer and the environment also contributes to the development of more effective and efficient communications strategies. The development of relationship marketing has consolidated much of this earlier work, recognizing the importance of close relationships to ensure effective understanding and communications.

Returning to the earlier Model (Figure 1.1) and the two remaining determinants of risk exposure, the problem specific characteristics and the decision maker characteristics, these generally represent factors which the organization may have more influence over.

4. *Problem Specific:* It is difficult to generalize about such factors as they will vary between distinct decisions. Those posing the highest risk exposure are likely to be concerned with the strategic and longer term decision making. Such decisions typically involve not only the highest risk exposure but may also have the most severe consequences. For example, the strategic decision to reconfigure the supply chain by seeking to sell direct to the final consumer and eliminating the downstream distributors may prove potentially attractive in profit terms but poses significant risks if the marketplace fails to respond or the distributors respond to protect their competitive position through price cutting.

5. *Decision Maker:* Increasing attention has been given to understanding the particular attributes of individuals and groups involved in decision making and how they may be developed to improve their risk handling capabilities. Some of these issues are referred to in a number of the later chapters.

The term *Unsystematic Risks* has been used to describe those risks that emanate from the strategies and decisions of the organization itself and may often be organization-specific. The key differentiating feature with systematic risk is that these unsystématic risks are considered to be manageable by the organization itself and are often generated as a result of its own decisions. Company-specific risks may not only be generated by threats (e.g. financial constraints) but also by potential opportunities. The strategies that seek to penetrate new markets, launch new technologies or to compete more aggressively with existing competitors are all likely to increase the level of unsystematic risk for the organization. The key issue for the organization is one of balancing these increased risks with the potential opportunities to improve the financial performance and the overall corporate performance.

The final feature to mention in relation to this initial model of supply chain risk and its management is the interdependency of the five sets of factors. Whilst conceptually it is relatively simple to isolate and deal with each of the five sets of factors, the reality is far more complex. This complexity has two primary dimensions. Firstly, the sheer number of variables that may have an impact on the particular decision and the nature of their potential to enhance risk exposure is difficult to assess. Secondly, the complex nature of the interactions of these variables and recognition that these are in a dynamic state of flux as well as being subject to the deliberate responses of consumers and competitors means that, the nature and scale of the risks may vary considerably during the decision making process itself. Add to this the recognition of the general uncertainty surrounding any such decisions provides a more realistic picture of the decision making position for decision makers seeking to manage the risks in the supply chain.

Measuring Corporate Performance

The measurement of corporate performance may be addressed from a number of different although not mutually exclusive perspectives. Different stakeholders may seek different balances between short-term and long-term performance, profitability and liquidity and the level of risk inherent in the business itself. Stainer and Stainer (1998) identify eight different categories of stakeholder together with their expectations from the business. In addition to the normal participants in the supply chain (i.e. shareholders, suppliers, creditors, employees and customers) they included competitors, government and society. A basic tenet of performance for most if not all these stakeholders concerns both profit performance and the risks associated with achieving this performance. The importance of these two performance elements (Mathur and Kenyon, 1997) is suggested by the consequences of failure, which would be the liquidation of the business and the loss of the shareholders investment and potential benefits to all other stakeholders. The primacy of this narrower measure of performance is challenged on the basis that '[i]nstead of an organization's bull's eye being dividends and share price growth for shareholders, it should relate to the ultimate outcome of a better society for all' (Stainer and Stainer, 1998, p.7). Whilst recognising the thrust of this argument for a wider definition of corporate performance measures (Marsden, 1997) and the desire for a more long-term perspective rather than the short-termism often implied by the financial performance measures, it is evident that financial performance measures remain the predominant measure of corporate performance. Therefore, the two key elements employed in the present text to measure corporate performance are profitability and risk.

Outline Structure of Text

The text is divided into two sections, the first section provides an exploration of the conceptual issues in the field whilst the second focuses on the application aspects. In the first section, the chapter by Norrman and Lindroth extends the ideas introduced in this chapter by providing a framework that categorizes research and managerial issues within supply chain risk management. The framework can be used to position different managerial actions or research contributions and its inclusion supports the premise that the field is an embryonic one. The groundwork laid in this first chapter is extended in the next by Ritchie and Brindley who justify and develop a contingency framework. This framework is designed to categorize the sources of risk within the supply chain and to examine the potential consequences for risk management. Chapter 4 by Hallikas and Virolainen adopts a network approach and debates another set of definitional aspects of the supply chain. They introduce a transaction cost-based framework for risk analysis and discuss the impacts of relationships, specifically that a network of ties is essential to manage risk. Chapter 5 postulates that the increasing incidence of disintermediation within existing supply chains poses further threats, uncertainties and risks for all organizations irrespective of size or position and hence, it is the customer that is a key part of the supply chain and can help ameliorate risks as well as creating specific risk issues. Paulsson's Chapter provides a timely review of journal publications about supply chain risk. The chapter identifies the unit of analysis, type of risk, management process and direction of the supply chain researched by academics and in doing so encapsulates the complex, multi-faceted nature of supply chain risk management.

The first chapter in Section 2 by Burtonshaw-Gunn examines the distinctive nature of the supply chain within the UK construction industry, identifying the key management parameters and reflecting the risk and uncertainty factors within these. This is followed by a discussion on the client/contractor relationship existing within this industry examining the strengths and weaknesses of this in strategic terms and the case for changing to a more collaborative arrangement through the use of supply chain partnering. The essence of the risk management is the development of strategic relationships and of critical importance is the commitment to three key themes – mutual objectives, problem resolution and dedication to continuous improvement. Zsidisin and Smith's chapter present a case study of the purchasing organization of a US aerospace supplier that illustrates how Early Supplier Involvement (ESI) can be used to reduce the probability and affect of an adverse supply incident. Chapter 4 discusses a framework for the analysis of risks in marine transport involving packaged dangerous goods. Transport is an essential constituent element of the distribution system (supply chain/logistics). Large quantities of different types of dangerous goods, ranging from agriculture and pharmaceutical products to extremely toxic and severe marine pollutant products, are carried by water and risk management is essential. In Chapter 10 Andersson and Norrman explore the issue of outsourcing using a case study of a Swedish shipping organization. They conclude that in the case of outsourcing advanced logistics both the shipper and the provider increase their need to assess and mange risk. The final chapter in this section by Zsidisin et al, focuses on how business continuity planning as a response to supply chain risk. The concluding chapter draws together the themes presented in the text and provides a platform for further research.

References

Blume, M.E. (1971), 'On the assessment of risk', *Journal of Finance,* Vol.26, No.1, pp.1-10.
Christopher, M.L. (1992), *Logistics and Supply Chain Management*, Pitman, London.
Clotfelter, C.T. and Cook, P.J. (1989), *Selling Hope*, Harvard University Press, Cambridge, Mass.

Cooper, M.C., Lambert, D.M. and Pugh, J.D. (1997), 'Supply Chain Management: More than a new name for logistics', *The International Journal of Logistics Management*, Vol.8, No.1, pp.1-14.

Dowling, R.G. and Staelin, R. (1994) 'A model of perceived risk and intended risk-handling activity', *Journal of Consumer Research*, Vol.21, No.1, pp.119-125.

Forlani, D. and Mullins, J.W. (2000) 'Perceived risks and choices in entrepreneurs' new venture decisions', *Journal of Business Venturing*, Vol.15, No.4, pp.305–322.

Knight, F.H. (1921), *Risk, Uncertainty and Profit*, Houghton Mifflin Company, Boston and New York.

MacCrimmon, K.R. and Wehrung, D.A. (1986), *Taking Risks: The Management of Uncertainty*, Free Press, New York.

MacCrimmon, K.R. and Wehrung, D.A. (1990), 'Characteristics of risk taking entrepreneurs', *Management Science*, Vol.36, pp.422-435.

March J.G. and Shapira Z. (1987), 'Managerial perspectives on risk and risk taking' *Management Science*, Vol.33, No.11, pp.1404-1418.

Marsden, C. (1997), 'Corporate Citizenship', *Faith in Business*, Vol.1, No.4, pp.3-15.

McCarthy, B. (2000), 'The cult of risk taking and social learning: a study of Irish entrepreneurs', *Management Decision*, Vol.38, No.8, pp.563-575 .

Newall, J. (1977), 'Industrial buyer behaviour', *European Journal of Marketing*, Vol.11, No.3, pp.166-211.

Porter, M.E. (1985), *Competitive advantage: creating and sustaining superior performance*, Free Press, New York.

Ritchie, R.L. and Brindley, C.S. (2000), 'Will ICT's Change the Balance of Global Competitive Advantage? Ascendancy of the SME in International Business' *Proceedings 27th Annual Conference UK Chapter, Academy of International Business*, Glasgow.

Ritchie, R.L. and Brindley, C.S. (2001), 'The Information – Risk Conundrum', *Journal of Marketing Intelligence and Planning*, Vol 19, No.1, pp.29-37.

Ritchie, R.L. and Marshall, D.V. (1993), *Business Risk Management*, Chapman and Hall, London.

Rowe, W.D. (1977), *Anatomy of Risk*, Wiley, New York.

Sitkin, S.B. and Pablo, A.L. (1992), 'Reconceptualizing the determinants of risk behaviour', *Academy of Management Review*, Vol.17, No.1, pp.9-38.

Stainer, A. and Stainer, L.(1998), 'Business performance – a stakeholder approach', *International Journal of Business Performance Management*, Vol.1, No.1, pp.2-12.

Valla, J.P. (1982), 'The concept of risk in industrial buyer behaviour', Presented at workshop on organisational buyer behaviour, *European Institute for Advanced Studies in Management*, Brussels, December 9-10.

Chapter 2

Categorization of Supply Chain Risk and Risk Management

Dr. Andreas Norrman and Robert Lindroth

Introduction

Recently, the interests of uncertainty, risks and vulnerability related to Supply Chain Management have increased, both in industry (e.g. a lot of practitioner conferences on the topic) and among academics (e.g. Smelzer and Siferd, 1998; Zsidisin and Ellram, 1999; Hallikas et al, 2000; Ritchie et al, 2000; Svensson, 2000, Lindroth and Norrman, 2001; Johnson, 2001; Lamming et al, 2001; Christopher et al, 2002). However, as the terms 'risk' and 'uncertainty', as well as the term 'Supply Chain Management' (SCM) are very 'broad' in their definitions, many different issues could be and have been, discussed within the field of 'supply chain risk management.'

There are not many explicit definitions of supply chain risk management available yet. This chapter will rely on the following definition as it is developed in parallel with the categorization framework that will be presented: 'Supply chain risk management is to collaboratively with partners in a supply chain apply risk management process tools to deal with risks and uncertainties caused by, or impacting on, logistics related activities or resources' (Norrman and Lindroth, 2002). Another definition, launched by Professor Martin Christopher, is 'Supply chain risk management is the management of external risks and supply chain risks through a co-ordinated approach among the supply chain members to reduce supply chain vulnerability as a whole'.
(http://www.som.cranfield.ac.uk/som/executive/conferences/content.asp?id=52).

However, the purpose of this chapter is not to find or promote one definition but to introduce a framework that can be used to categorize issues within supply chain risk management: both research areas and managerial issues. The framework could be used to position and relate different issues to each other, e.g. what part of supply chain risk management different researchers are dealing with, how different types of uncertainty or risk related to logistics and SCM are addressed and what managerial responses to risk and uncertainty companies are focusing on. Firstly, the general framework will be introduced and then its different dimensions will be discussed in detail, before we show how it could be used.

Three Dimensions of Supply Chain Risk Management

Logistics and Supply Chain Management risks could include a number of different issues. To structure these, we have chosen three dimensions:

1. the 'logistics' unit of analysis
2. the type of risk/uncertainty and
3. the stage of the risk management process (Lindroth and Norrman, 2001).

The first dimension addresses the level of complexity of the unit analyzed or addressed. The more business functions or companies along the supply chain that are focused, the more complex the problems will be. The second dimension deals with the type of risk or uncertainty of interest; they can be very different in nature and consequently they may not be treated together, in the same study or managerial approach. The third and final dimension in the framework addresses the level of the risk management activities. These dimensions can be put together into a conceptual framework (Figure 2.1) that can be used for categorizing different supply chain risk management issues.

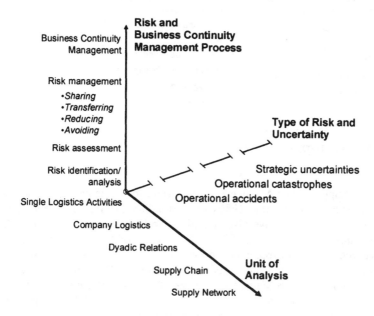

Figure 2.1   A Framework for Assessing and Positioning Supply Chain Risk Issues

The Logistic Unit of Analysis

The scope of the 'industrial setting' that is addressed within supply chain risk management differs among practitioners as well as between researchers. To start, the terms Supply Chain Management (SCM) and logistics management are not equal but closely related. Many argue that SCM has its roots in 'logistics' but is actually an extension of the scope of logistics. The most used definition of *logistics* is 'Logistics management is that part of the Supply Chain Management process that plans, implements, and controls the efficient, effective forward and reverse flow and storage of goods, services, and related information between the point of origin and the point of consumption in order to meet customers' requirements' (CLM, 2003). By this definition, a first glance of activities usually handled within logistics management is given. A more extensive list is given in Figure 2.2.

Example of logistics activities

- Traffic and transportation
- Warehousing and storage
- Industrial packaging
- Material handling
- Inventory control
- Order processing
- Customer service levels
- Demand forecasting

- Procurement
- Distribution communications
- Plant and warehouse site location
- Return goods handling
- Parts and service support
- Salvage and scrap disposal

Figure 2.2 Logistics Activities

Source: Coyle et al, (1992, p.18)

The concept of Supply Chain Management (SCM) has been increasingly discussed among logisticians since the mid-1980s (e.g. Houlihan, 1985; Jones and Riley, 1985) and lately companies have also started to work according to its principles. Recently, a *Supply chain* has been defined as 'a set of three or more entities directly involved in the upstream and downstream flows of products, services, finances, and/or information from a source to customer' (Mentzer et al, 2001). *Supply Chain Management* is defined as 'the systemic, strategic coordination of the traditional business functions and the tactics across these business functions within the supply chain, for the purpose of improving the long-term performance of the individual companies and the supply chain as a whole' (Mentzer et al, 2001). SCM could be seen as an extension in scope to the multiple company context of what is called logistics management in the single company context.

When looking at logistics and SCM, some researchers and managers have a narrower unit of analysis, while others take a more holistic view. The same is true for supply chain risk management. A more narrow approach would be to focus on, for example, risks with dangerous transports, on how to best protect and secure a plant or warehouse or to look at demand uncertainty for a single product. Others look outside a specific functional unit and into the whole company or enterprise (compare the approach 'Enterprise-wide Risk Management' (EWRM) used by many major consultancy firms, (see e.g. Deloach, 2000). Many focus on suppliers and supply risks – a dyad – while others try to adopt a comprehensive approach encompassing the entire supply chain or network.

Supply chain risk management could deal with risks for a single company, or even the impact on a single logistics activity. The focus is to understand and try to avoid, devastating ripple effects which disasters or even minor business disruptions can have on the supply chain. In this sense, SCRM is a broader perspective than normal 'risk management'. Therefore, from a supply chain perspective the unit analyzed should represent a buyer-seller relationship (a dyad) or a supply chain of three or more companies. Hence, the rippling effect for the companies in the same supply chain would be considered. Some examples from such 'supply chain rippling effects' are:

1. Hurricane Floyd flooded a Daimler Chrysler plant, producing suspension parts in Greenville, North Carolina (USA). As a result, seven of the Company's other plants across North America had to be shut down for seven days.
2. The Foot and Mouth Disease in the UK in 2001 impacted the agricultural industry more than its last outbreak 25 years ago. The reason for this was that former local and regional supply networks had become national and international and that the industry was much more consolidated (Jüttner et al, 2002). Also, many other industries were impacted: luxury car manufacturers e.g. Volvo and Jaguar had to stop deliveries due to a lack of high quality leather.
3. Toyota was forced to shut down 18 plants for almost 2 weeks following a fire in February 1997 at is brake-fluid proportioning valve supplier (Aisin Seiki). Costs caused by the disruption were estimated at $195 million and the sales loss was estimated at 70,000 vehicles (~ $325 million) (Convirium).
4. Ericsson in Sweden lost many months of mobile phone production and major sales of consumer products with a short 'market window' in 2000 due to a minor fire at sub-supplier Philips Components in US. Business Interruption Cost was later evaluated to be about $200 million.
5. Rapidly weakening demand coupled with locked-in supply agreements made Cisco undertake a $2.5 billion inventory write off in the second quarter of 2001.

The Type of Risk or Uncertainty

It is important to know what people address and mean by the 'risk' they are discussing. A first step is to understand what risk and uncertainty is. Starting from the beginning, the word risk derives from the Arabic word *'risq'* meaning *'given from Allah'*. This indicates that risk is something external decided by God. Hazards, closely related to risks, has its roots from 3500 BC referring to the Arabic word for *dice* (maybe a slightly more optimistic view on hazards and more related to chance and opportunity than what is common today). Finally, the Greek word 'risicum' meant to '*challenge a cliff or rock'*, apparently related to the Greek archipelago. This seems to be more proactive than the Arabic view.

Deloach (2000) defines *business risk* as 'the level of exposure to uncertainties that the enterprise must understand and effectively manage as it executes its strategies to achieve its business objectives and create value.' A more standard definition of *risk* is 'risk is the chance, in quantitative terms, of a defined hazard occurring. It therefore combines a probabilistic measure of the occurrence of the primary event(s) with a measure of the consequences of that/those event(s)' (The Royal Society, 1992, p.4). Risk is hence a quality that reflects both the range of possible outcomes and the distribution of respective probabilities for each of the outcomes. This 'quantitative definition' could be expressed as Risk = Probability (of the event) * Business Impact (or Severity) of the event. This risk is most commonly referred to as 'Expected value' (Doherty, 2000) and often illustrated in a risk map or matrix (Figure 2.3). While risks can be calculated, uncertainties are genuinely unknown.

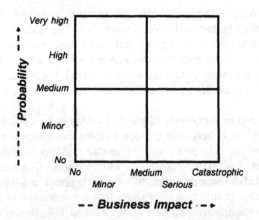

Figure 2.3 Risk Map or Matrix

As soon as the 'quantitative definition' is left for a broader and more business oriented perspective, the term also gets fuzzier. Many categorizations of risks in general terms have been made, a few examples will be given below of how business risks in general have been classified. Hiles and Barnes (2001, p.31) divides the population of risks an organization can be exposed to into five core groups:

1. *Strategic:* the risk of plans failing or succeeding, e.g. marketing strategy, changes in consumer behavior or political/regulatory changes.
2. *Financial:* the risk of financial control failing or succeeding.
3. *Operational:* the risk of human error or achievement, e.g. design mistakes, unsafe behavior, employee practices risk, sabotage.
4. *Commercial:* the risk of relationships failing or succeeding, e.g. business interruption due to loss of key executive, supplier failure or lack of legal compliance.
5. *Technical:* the risk of physical assets failing/being damaged or enhanced, e.g. equipment breakdown, infrastructure failure, fires, explosion, pollution, etc.

Hiles and Barnes (2001) underline that these risk groups are not mutually exclusive, by exemplifying that e.g. human factors (prime drivers of operational risks) are significant in many strategic and financial risks.

Deloach (2000, p.50) divides sources of uncertainty in a business into three risk categories:

1. *Externally-driven or environmental risk* arises when there are external forces that can affect a firm's performance, or makes its different choices obsolete or ineffective. This is related, for example, to competitors, customer needs, technological innovations, political, legal, regulatory, financial markets, catastrophes, etc.
2. *Internally-driven or process risk* arises when business processes do not achieve the objectives they where designed to achieve. This is related, for example, to operations, empowerment, information processing and to some financial issues related to price, liquidity and credit.
3. *Decision-driven or information risk* arises when information used to support business decisions is incomplete, out of date, inaccurate, late or simply irrelevant to the decision making process. This is related to process/operational issues such as pricing, contracting and measurements; business reporting and environment/strategic issues.

Deloach (2000) also underlines that risk is dynamic and that risk categories are interrelated: some risk events could be sources or drivers of other risk events.

Jüttner et al, (2002) has also observed that the uses of the term 'risk' can be confusing, and they argue that risk should be separated from *risk (and uncertainty) sources* and *risk consequences* (equal to the term risk impact). Risk sources are the environmental, organizational or supply chain-related variables that cannot be predicted with certainty and which impact on the supply chain outcome variables. Jüttner et al, (2002) suggest organizing risk sources relevant for supply chains into three categories: external to the supply chain, internal to the supply chain, and network related. External risk sources are exemplified by 'political risk', 'natural risks', 'social risks', 'industry/market risk' (e.g. volatility of customer demand). Internal risk sources range from labour (e.g. strikes) or production (e.g. machine failure) to IT-system uncertainties. Network-related risks arise from interaction between organizations within the supply chain, e.g. due to insufficient interaction and cooperation. Risk consequences/impact are the focused supply chain outcome variables like costs or quality but also health and safety, i.e. the different forms in which the variance becomes manifest.

Supply chain risks are risks that are related to the logistics activities in companies' flows of material and information. Consequently, it is only a part of all business risk. The supply chain perspective also implies a perspective not only including your own company but on a chain of at least three entities: customer, suppliers, sub-suppliers. In our framework for supply chain risk management we try to distinguish between different types of risk and uncertainty by the three categories operational accidents, operational catastrophes and strategic uncertainty. For all of those, there might be internal as well as external driven risks. With a logistics/SCM perspective, our interest will of course be on operations related logistics and SCM activities and resources and less on business risks related only to financial, legal, currency, etc (unless it does affect other parties in the supply chain). An operational accident (such as fires and truck accidents), could generally be said to have higher probability but less impact than an operational catastrophe (e.g. earthquakes, floods etc.) that are very rare but could have disastrous consequences. However, both categories are operational to their nature. Related to the classifications above, our operational risk would be *operational risks* and *technical risks* according to Hiles and Barnes (2001) and according to Deloach (2000) mainly *internally-driven process risk* and to some extent *externally-driven risk*. The operational risks are focused on disruptions and risk sources are either connected to operational processes or resources related to logistics, or the business impacts will focus on operational process or resource related to logistics.

The more strategic uncertainties are generally unknown and thus more difficult to address. In the referred classifications they would be strategic and commercial (Hiles and Barnes, 2001) and externally-driven environmental risk (Deloach, 2000). Risk sources for strategic uncertainties could hence, be both external and internal to the supply chain – e.g. volatile demand, bottlenecks in supply, unclear future rules and regulations, technology shifts etc.

The Stages of the Risk Management Process

Many authors agree that there is a process for managing or handling risks and the content of each step provided are often quite similar. However, the names of the different steps suggested differ. The risk management process is focused on understanding the risks and minimizing the impact of them by addressing for example, probability and direct impact. The stages of the risk management process discussed can differ from risk identification/analysis (or estimation) via risk assessment (or evaluation) to different ways of risk management. Risk management is the making of decisions regarding risks and their subsequent implementation, and flows from risk estimation and risk evaluation (The Royal Society, 1992, p.3). To 'manage' risk could mean to avoid, reduce, transfer or share risks.

Another perspective on this issue is how to mitigate the consequences from an accident if it does happen, to take care of the situation in a way that minimizes business impact. This is normally referred to as Business Continuity Management (BCM) and relates to those management disciplines, processes and techniques which seek to provide the means for continuous operations of essential functions under all circumstances (Hiles and Barnes, 2001, p.379). BCM aims at getting interrupted businesses restarted again. In many ways risk management and BCM are overlapping and some argue that to develop Business Continuity Plans is the risk management action to take for risks of low probability (such as fires and floods) but whose potential impact is a business failure (Charters, 2001, p.136). There are certain differences and consequently, we have put BCM as a later and more refined process step than risk management in our framework (although there could be arguments for merging those). We keep them separate, since risk management is more focused on how to reduce risks and uncertainties, whereas BCM is focusing on how to handle the incidents once they appear.

Supply Chain Risk Analysis and Assessment

Risk analysis/identification can be seen as a fundamental stage in the risk management process. It follows that by identifying a risk, decision-makers become aware about events that may cause disturbances. In order to assess supply chain risk exposures, the company must identify not only direct risks to its operations but also the potential causes or sources of those risks at every significant link along the supply chain (Christopher et al, 2002). Hence, the main focus of supply chain risk analysis is to recognize future uncertainties in order to enable pro-active management of risk related issues.

There are many methods for risk identification and analysis. An important tool is risk mapping, to use a structured approach and map risk sources, thereby understanding their potential consequences. Two commonly used techniques for researching factors and causes contributing to accidental events include the Fault Tree Analysis (FTA) and the Event Tree Analysis (ETA). Both are logic diagrams that represent the sequences of failures that may be propagated through a complex system. FTA examines all potential events leading up to the critical event and is a graphical diagram that shows how a system can fail. The analysis starts with top events, then the necessary and sufficient hazardous events, their causes and contributing factors are identified together with their logical relationships using a 'backward logic.' The ETA is also a graphical logical diagram but goes the other way. It focuses on events that could occur after some critical event and identifies and quantifies possible outcomes following initiating events by looking at potential consequences (e.g. Mullai and Paulsson, 2002 and Ellis, 2002). For both techniques quantitative data such as probabilities for events could be used to get an idea of the final probability. Deloach (2000) proposes a similar tool called a 'risk driver map', where potential threats are mapped.

Besides risk analysis, there is a need to protect the company and the supply chain against identified risk factors and to choose suitable management actions to the situation – it is important to assess and prioritize risks. One common method is to compare events by assessing their probabilities and consequences and put them in a risk map (Figure 2.3 earlier). In theory and when historical events are assessed this could be a quite straightforward and quantitative task but in business this could be a subjective process relying on specialists' judgements. The results of this work could then be used for prioritising actions.

Risk Management

Risk management is defined as the process whereby decisions are made to accept a known or assessed risk and/or the implementation of actions to reduce the consequences or probability of occurrence. Generally used actions for risk management are, for example, to avoid, reduce, transfer, share or even take the risk. By avoiding we mean to eliminate the types of event that could trigger the risk. To reduce, applies both to the reduction of probability and the consequence. Examples of how to reduce the impact could be to have extra inventory, multiple sources, back-up sites/resources identified, sprinklers in buildings, having risk managers and emergency teams appointed, parallel systems or to diversify. Probability could be reduced by improving risky operational processes, both internally and in cooperation with suppliers and to improve related processes, e.g. supplier selection. Risk could also be transferred to insurance companies – but also to supply chain partners by moving inventory liability, changing delivery time of suppliers (just-in-time deliveries) and to customers (make-to-order manufacturing), or by outsourcing activities. Furthermore, contracts can be used to transfer commercial risks. Finally risks could be shared, both by contractual mechanisms and by improved collaboration. According to Lambert and Cooper (2000) and Mentzer et al, (2001) a key component for Supply Chain Management is to share both risks and rewards between the members of the supply chain.

Business Continuity Management

A concept, sometimes seen as part of Risk Management and sometimes vice versa, is Business Continuity Management (BCM). It is defined as '... the development of strategies, plans and actions which provide protection or alternative modes of operation for those activities or business processes which, if they were to be interrupted, might otherwise bring a seriously damaging or potentially fatal loss to the enterprise' (Hiles and Barnes 2001, p.xvii). Business Continuity Management includes Crisis management (overall processes to manage the incident), Disaster recovery (recovery of critical systems, applications, data and networks), Business recovery (recovery of critical business processes) and Contingency planning (recovery from impact external to the organization) (CMI, 2002).

Developing action plans is important in Business Continuity Planning (BCP) is a term often used. BCP is to plan to ensure continued operations in case of a catastrophic event. It goes beyond disaster recovery planning since it includes the actions to be taken, resources required and procedures to be followed to ensure the continued availability of essential services, programs and operations in the event of unexpected interruptions. BCP has previously been most related to computers and information technology-related disasters, especially before Y2K but the approach has since then moved towards more applications in other business contexts.

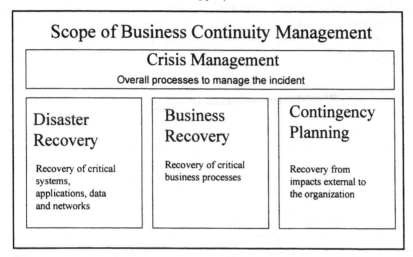

Figure 2.4 Scope of Business Continuity Management

Source: Chartered Management Institute, (2002)

The first activities in developing Business Continuity Plans are to identify the risks and assess their probability and impact – the steps are hence identical to risk management (see Figure 2.4 above). Part of this is to understand what will be affected (Damage Potential Analysis). Then strategies and plans for how to recover should be developed that could be implemented, both before the incident (similar to risk management strategies) and after the incident. Post-incident strategies are implemented to maintain partial or total product supply and could for manufacturing and logistics include (Musson, 2001):

1. Use of spare capacity within the organization.
2. Shutdown of marginal product lines and transfer of key products to those production facilities.
3. Assistance from competition.
4. Outsourcing to subcontractors, job shops, etc.
5. Re-labelling of competitors' products (after consideration of all legal implications).
6. Establishment of temporary facilities when production capabilities can be established with 'off the shelf' or second hand equipment.

The main reason for taking a supply chain approach to risk management and Business Continuity Management is the fact that companies are increasingly interconnected due to the increased integration and decrease of buffers between companies. However, according to a study by the CMI (2002) only about 30 per cent of all companies studied developed BCP jointly with suppliers. Only nine per cent of companies that have outsourced activities (not only logistics) insist on their outsource suppliers to have Business Continuity Plans (BCP). This seems to be an area to develop further.

The Supply Chain Risk Management Framework

As shown in the discussion above, each dimension of the framework, or even each specific segment of a dimension, could include many specific areas of research issues or managerial actions. Although supply chain risk management, in our opinion, is about the holistic view, we also know that progress in research as well as in management sometimes is better reached by focusing on specific issues or actions. For this reason we argue that something can be a part of supply chain risk management although it does not fully cover all aspects of our definition.

The definition, 'Supply chain risk management is to collaboratively with partners in a supply chain apply risk management process tools to deal with risks and uncertainties caused by, or impacting on, logistics related activities or resources' (Norrman and Lindroth, 2002) is illustrated by the framework as the most important concepts are covered: *the supply chain approach* and the use of *the risk management process*. Further the framework helps us understand that there are risk and uncertainties of different nature that have to be handled differently.

The framework can be used to position different managerial actions or research contributions. Some examples of managerial actions are exemplified in Figure 2.5.

Finally, Ulf Paulsson shows in Chapter 6 how the framework can be used to position different research contributions, he has analyzed the content of 80 different journal articles.

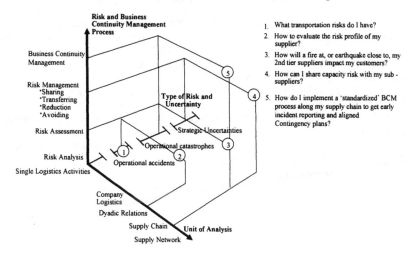

1. What transportation risks do I have?
2. How to evaluate the risk profile of my supplier?
3. How will a fire at, or earthquake close to, my 2nd tier suppliers impact my customers?
4. How can I share capacity risk with my sub-suppliers?
5. How do I implement a 'standardized' BCM process along my supply chain to get early incident reporting and aligned Contingency plans?

Figure 2.5 Using the Framework to Categorize Various Managerial Actions

References

Charters, I. (2001), 'Risk evaluation and control: II. Practical guidelines for risk assessment' in Hiles, A. Barnes, P. (eds) (2001), *The Definitive Handbook of Business Continuity Management*, J. Wiley and Sons, Chichester. pp.131-138.

Christopher, M., McKinnon, A., Sharp, J., Wilding, R., Peck, H., Chapman, P., Jüttner, U. and Bolumole, Y. (2002), *Supply Chain Vulnerability*, Cranfield University.

CLM, (2003), Council of Logistics Management, www.clm1.org/aboutus/aboutus_policy.asp#definitions Accessed on 29th October.

CMI – Chartered Management Institute, (2002), Business Continuity and Supply Chain Management. Report available at www.thebci.org/2809-01%20Bus%20 Continuity% 20Summ.pdf. Accessed on 29th October.

Converium: www.converium.com 'Suppliers' Extension or Contingent Business Interruption Insurance' by Jason Mortimer. (http://www.converium.com/web/converium/ converium.nsf/2a1b7a462af6c00185256ad2000da28c/30c4e3ebc211d4f9c1256 ad5004334b5? OpenDocument &Highlight=0,toyota).

Coyle, J.J., Bardi, E.J. and Langley, C.J. (1992), *The Management of Business Logistics*, West Publishing, St. Paul.

Cranfield School of Management, (2003), http://www.som.cranfield.ac.uk/som/executive/conferences/content.asp?id=52. Accessed on 29th October.

Deloach, J.W. (2000), 'Enterprise-wide Risk Management', *Strategies for linking risk and opportunities*, Financial Times/Prentice Hall, London.

Doherty, N.A. (2000), 'Integrated Risk Management – Techniques and Strategies for Managing Corporate Risk', McGraw-Hill, New York, USA.

Ellis, J. (2002), 'Risk in Dangerous Goods Transport: An Analysis of Risk in Road, Rail, and Marine Transport', *Chalmers University of Technology*, Göteborg, Sweden.

Hallikas, J., Virolainen, V-M., Tuominen, M. (2000), 'Risk analysis and Assessment in Network Environment – a Dyadic Case Study', *Preprints of 11th International Working Seminar on Production Economics*, pp.255-270.

Hiles, A. and Barnes, P. (eds), (2001), *The Definitive Handbook of Business Continuity Management*, J. Wiley and Sons, Chichester.

Houlihan, J.B. (1985), 'International Supply Chain Management', *International Journal of Physical Distribution and Materials Management*, Vol.15, No.1, pp.22-38.

Johnson, M.E. (2001), 'Learning from Toys: Lessons in Managing Supply Chain Risk from the Toy Industry', *California Management Review*, Vol.43, No.3, pp.106-124.

Jones, T.C. and Riley, D.W. (1985), 'Using inventory for competitive advantage through Supply Chain Management', *International Journal of Physical Distribution and Materials Management*, Vol.15. No.5, pp.16-26.

Jüttner, U., Peck, H. and Christopher, M. (2002), 'Supply Chain Risk Management: Outlining an Agenda for Future Research', in Griffiths J., Hewitt, F. and Ireland, P. (eds) *Proceedings of the Logistics Research Network 7th Annual Conference*, pp.443-450.

Lambert, D.M. and Cooper, M.C. (2000), 'Issues in Supply Chain Management', *Industrial Marketing Management*, No.29, pp.65-83.

Lamming, R.C., Caldwell, N.D., Harrison, D.A. and Phillips, W. (2001), 'Transparency in supply relationships: Concept and practice', *Journal of Supply Chain Management*, Fall 2001, Vol.37, No.4, pp.4-10.

Lindroth, R. and Norrman, A. (2001), 'Supply Chain Risks and Risk Sharing Instruments – An Illustration from the Telecommunication Industry', *Proceedings of the Logistics Research Network 6th Annual Conference*, Heriot-Watt University, 13th-14th September, pp.297-307.

Lonsdale, C. (1999), 'Effectively managing vertical relationships: a risk management model for outsourcing', *Supply Chain Management: An International Journal*, Vol.4, No.4, pp.176-183.

Mentzer, J.T., DeWitt, W., Keebler, J.S., Min, S., Nix, N. W., Smith, C.D. and Zacharia, Z. G. (2001), 'Defining Supply Chain Management', *Journal of Business Logistics*, Vol. 22, No.2, pp.1-25.

Mullai, A. and Paulsson, U. (2002), 'Oil Spills in Öresund – Hazardous Events, Causes and Claims', *Lund University*.

Musson, M. (2001), 'Business continuity strategies for manufacturing and logistics', in Hiles, A., Barnes, P. (eds). *The Definitive Handbook of Business Continuity Management*, J. Wiley and Sons, Chichester. pp.163-169.

Norrman, A. and Lindroth, R. (2002), 'Supply Chain Risk Management: Purchasers' vs. Planners' Views on Sharing Capacity Investment Risks in the Telecom Industry', *Proceedings of the 11th International Annual IPSERA Conference, Twente Univesity, 25th-27th March*, pp.577-595.

Ritchie R., Brindley C.S., Morris J. and Peet S. (2000), 'Managing risk within the supply chain', *The 3rd Worldwide Research Symposium on Purchasing & Supply Chain Management/9th International IPSERA Conference Proceedings*, Canada, 24th - 26th May 2000, pp.606-617.

Smeltzer, L.R. and Siferd, S.P. (1998), 'Proactive supply management: the management of risk', *International Journal of Purchasing and Materials Management*, Vol.34, No.1, pp.38-45.

Souter, G. (2000), 'Risks from Supply chain also demand attention', *Business Insurance*, Vol. 34, No.20, pp.26-28.

Svensson, G. (2000), 'A conceptual framework for the analysis of vulnerability in supply chains', *International Journal of Physical Distribution and Logistics Management*, Vol.30, No.9, pp.731-750.

The Royal Society, (1992), 'Risk: Analysis, Perception and Management', *The Royal Society, London.*

Walker, G. (1988), 'Strategic Sourcing, Vertical Integration, and Transaction Costs', *Interfaces,* Vol.18, No.3, May-June, pp.62-73.

Zsidisin, G. and Ellram, L.M. (1999), 'Supply Risk Assessment Analysis', Practix, *Best Practices in Purchasing and Supply Chain Management,* June, pp.9-12.

Chapter 3

Risk Characteristics of the Supply Chain – A Contingency Framework

Prof. Bob Ritchie and Dr. Clare Brindley

Introduction

Risk pervades every dimension of our lives, personal and professional. In every element of our daily routine we encounter and manage risk to a greater or lesser extent successfully. Each of these encounters with risk is different and we probably employ different approaches to handling these. There are arguably, however, a series of common rules or steps that we might take in handling such decisions, usually based on our previous experiences of something similar – in other words a *Contingency Approach*. Supply chains also exhibit risk in a variety of dimensions and rely on decision makers, individuals or groups, to take appropriate decisions to manage these effectively on behalf of the other partners in the chain. Risk in the supply chain is not a new phenomenon. Business organizations have always been exposed to the failure of a supplier to deliver the right quantity, at the right time, to the agreed quality and at the agreed price. Different organizations have developed different strategies and tactics to manage these risks and have typically been successful in doing so, although not universally so as business cases such as Enron demonstrate. What has changed to make risk management in supply chains worthy of greater attention? There are arguably three key developments which enhance the case for increased attention to the management of risk in supply chains:

1. Strategies and structures relating to supply chains are evolving more rapidly in the search for competitive advantage.
2. Technological changes provide opportunities to alter the shape and the relationships within supply chains.
3. Increased exposure to global competitive pressures means that most business organizations are exposed to new and additional risks that may impact more rapidly and with more severe consequences than previously.

These characteristics arguably lead to each individual supply chain being unique in certain respects. Equally, this uniqueness may require unique approaches to the management of the risks involved. The approach taken in this chapter is to argue that despite each supply chain being unique, exposed to unique risks and requiring unique solutions, there is significant value in seeking to map the common or shared characteristics onto a Framework. This chapter seeks to justify and establish such a *Contingency Framework.*

Initially the key sets of factors influencing risk in the supply chain will be examined to illustrate the nature of their impact on the risk exposure to the members of the supply chain itself. The meaning of the terms risk and uncertainty in the context of the supply chain will be assessed leading to a working definition of these terms for the Framework. The nature of the Contingency Framework proposed, is itself examined to illustrate the contribution it may make. The key dimensions of the *Supply Chain Risk Management Framework* are identified and developed throughout the remainder of the chapter.

Supply Chain Revolution

Discussions on risk and risk management often fail to fully recognize the dynamic and reactive nature of risk and the associated decision processes in business in general (see Ritchie and Brindley, 2000). Moreover, recent developments in technologies, business structures and competitive practices have tended to enhance this dynamism, accelerate the rate of change and magnify the scale of the commercial consequences (see Mentzer et al, 2001). Consideration of risk in the supply chain provides a good example of this dynamism and the consequences being experienced in many aspects of a business organization's activities.

Risks within the supply chain may be categorized along a particular continuum (see Diagram 3.1). Paulsson and Norrman (2003) identified three points on this continuum as Operational Disturbance, Tactical Disruption and Strategic Uncertainty. These descriptors are essentially related to differences in the type of risk rather than seeking to necessarily imply that one is more significant or prevalent than the others. Similarly, Kleindorfer and Wassenhove (2003) divided the risk types into two 'supply-demand co-ordination risk' and 'disruption risk.' In essence, what is being proposed is that there are different types of supply chain risk and these may require different approaches to management and resolution, an issue that we explore later in the chapter.

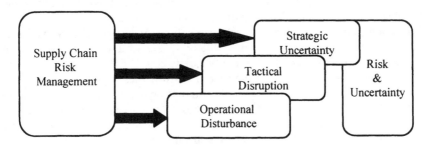

Diagram 3.1 Supply Chain Risk Continuum

Whilst it may be helpful in a contextual sense, to separate the different types of supply chain risks, it is important to recognize the interdependence of these types in practice. For example, decisions to minimize the risk of operational disturbance through single sourcing may in itself increase the exposure to tactical disruption. Similarly, actions taken to improve the performance (i.e. enhanced efficiency and profitability) of the supply chain through making it leaner and more agile may consequently increase risk exposure to tactical disruption and strategic uncertainty. There have been and continue to be significant developments which have an impact at all three levels of Supply Chain Management outlined in Diagram 3.1. Key features of these developments in the supply chain and the implications for risk include:

1. The commercial negotiations with a supplier of goods or services are essentially an interactive process with both parties seeking a resolution on parameters such as price, quality, delivery etc. Whilst there may be the ultimate desire to seek a resolution, each party will be seeking to satisfy their particular objectives and in so doing may alter the risk presented to the other party. For example, the supplier may experience increased perceptions of risk if the customer seeks a resolution at lower prices, higher minimum quality standards, or shorter timescales. Alternatively, the customer may experience increased risk if they lack confidence in the ability of the supplier to meet the agreed delivery times and quality standards (see Nix, 2001). Arguably, these dimensions have always been present in commercial transactions. However, the general increase in competitive pressures has focused increased attention on every dimension of the transactions between partners to generate new or to sustain existing competitive advantage. Consequently, the perceptions of risk by both parties may simultaneously increase.

2. The anticipated reactions of partners in the supply chain to particular proposals are also likely to alter the risk perceived by both parties. Gauging the likely reactions in advance is and has always been an essential ingredient of the commercial negotiation process (see Ward and Smith, 2003; and Min, 2001). The nature of this negotiation process is itself changing. The accessibility to a greater volume of higher quality information for both parties may ensure, that not only is this now a better informed negotiation but potentially a more sophisticated one based on knowledge and understanding. Although this may change the risk perceptions of the parties involved it is difficult to conclude whether this will be to the advantage or detriment of each individual partner (Ritchie and Brindley, 2001).

3. The interaction and reactions between the two parties will increasingly have much wider implications, both within and outside of the supply chain. Within the supply chain itself, suppliers further up the supply chain are likely to experience some impact of agreements reached by partners further downstream. Competitive pressures from the ultimate consumer in the marketplace in terms of price, availability, quality, design etc. will subsequently feed through the successive stages in the supply chain. Faced

with such significant changes it would not be unexpected for each member of the supply chain, at least initially, to seek to sustain or recover their position in terms of satisfying their commercial objectives and to simultaneously reduce their risk exposure. This 'disturbance' to the system may arguably cause only a short-term dislocation of the relationships and agreements in the supply chain before 'settling down' to a new position of 'equilibrium' in which all the partners' requirements are 'satisfied.' On the other hand, a localised 'disturbance' in the supply chain may have amplified and long-term consequences for the whole structure and pattern of relationships in the supply chain. This latter scenario is one that many researchers have identified as the more likely in the current climate of technological change and global competition. For example, Kleindorfer and Wassenhove (2003) identified two categories of supply chain risk, 'supply-demand co-ordination risk' and 'disruption risk.' The former suggests risk management approaches concerned with supply chain design and contracting arrangements, whilst the latter suggests approaches designed to minimize exposure to disruption and minimizing the consequences should such events occur. Apart from the impact on existing members of the supply chain, it is possible that competitors at each stage in the chain may observe the dislocation in the structure and relationships and seek to offer alternative solutions, e.g. offer enhanced services and guarantees at equivalent or lower prices.

4. The sustainability of the previous risk management solutions is increasingly being exposed. Classic risk management solutions such as the maintenance of buffer stocks, built-in slack in delivery lead times; excess profit margins to cover returns due to poor quality are less viable in a world of JIT, MRP and ISO9000 where the requirements are built in to the contractual arrangements.

5. A final feature of the supply chain in terms of risk is that the whole context in which decisions are being taken, is continuously evolving and changing. Underpinning many of the changes identified above are fundamental changes in technology. The impact of Information and Communication Technologies (ICTs) has generated and will continue to generate significant changes in the supply chain. This is not only in basic products and services but possibly more significantly the structure and relationships within the supply chains involving business to business (B2B) and business to consumer (B2C) linkages (Ritchie and Brindley, 2000). ICTs may be viewed as reducing the entry and exit barriers in many markets, often on a global basis. They may change the methods of communicating with the final consumer, altering marketing communication channels, consumer ordering and purchasing methods, product/service delivery channels and the process of sustaining customer relationships. All of these changes have potential consequences not only for the structure and processes of the whole supply chain but equally the risk exposure (i.e. increased likelihood of detrimental change combined with the increased scale of the negative consequences of such changes) and the perception of more rapid and possibly unexpected impacts.

What has been described is a situation in which many of the commercial practices and negotiations continue as previously. However, we are beginning to witness some fundamental changes in the nature of these, both in terms of the quality of information available to support the negotiations and in the imperatives to seek solutions which provide competitive advantages, no matter how short-lived these may be in the new global marketplace. These developments in the negotiation processes are taking place against a backcloth of more radical changes in supply chain structures and relationships, primarily responding to the opportunities facilitated by new technologies and the pressures these may simultaneously generate on all partners in the supply chain. An increased sense of vulnerability to the rapid changes taking place is likely to enhance perceptions of riskiness. However, counter-balancing this is the recognition that such changes also create opportunities for organizations (i.e. risk taking is about acceptance of risk on the basis that there will be a commercial advantage that will outweigh such risks), a point emphasized by Ritchie and Marshall (1993) as fundamental to any approach to risk management.

Uncertainty and Risk in the Supply Chain

A reasonable proposition, which few would refute, is that managing the supply chain process involves elements of uncertainty and elements of risk. The differentiation between these terms has classically been defined as one in which uncertainty reflects the decision situation in which there exists lack of information, knowledge and understanding of the likely outcomes, including the associated probabilities and consequences of each (Rowe, 1977). In the extreme form this may be represented by total lack of awareness or total ignorance of the decision situation existing. Risk on the other hand may be defined as complete knowledge of the potential outcomes to a given situation, the objective probability of the occurrence of each and their consequences (Knight, 1921; Warren, 1992). This definition of risk reduces the decision process to one of choice between given outcomes on the basis of the decision taker's utility preferences. However, this is a somewhat simplistic representation of the term risk and the consequent behavior patterns in Supply Chain Management.

The reality for most decision makers, irrespective of the stage in the supply chain, is that they face complex decision situations, which comprise elements of uncertainty. Such uncertainty is not just a function of the potential outcomes in the marketplace but also the potential reactions of other members within the supply chain itself and possibly more importantly, the competitive actions of those operating within parallel supply chains. The term risk is commonly used to represent those decision situations which incorporate uncertainty as well as those in which there is some knowledge and understanding of the outcomes. In short, decision makers face a spectrum of situations in terms of risk and uncertainty, the degree of uncertainty varying from situation to situation, with often no evident methods for determining this in advance.

Viewing risk in isolation from the other performance dimensions of an organization provides a somewhat distorted view of the reality of the context in which decision makers operate. Diagram 3.2 illustrates conceptually some of the key performance dimensions that contribute directly or indirectly to the profit performance. Paralleling the more tangible dimensions of performance are the risks related individually and collectively with these dimensions. The individual risks aggregate to provide the risk profile for the business as a whole corresponding to the aggregate performance.

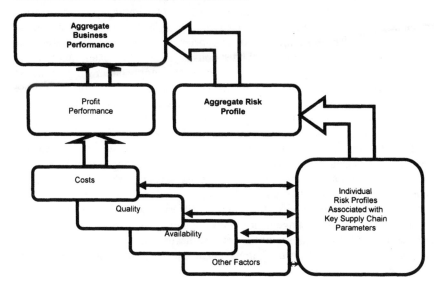

Diagram 3.2 Supply Chain Parameters – Risk and Business Performance

The relationships involving risk and uncertainty and the supply chain may be summarized in the following formulation :

Aggregate Business Performance = f (Profit)*(Risk) = f (Quality, Availability, Cost.....) * (Risks associated with Quality, Availability, Cost......)

In essence, the term business performance may be defined in a number of ways e.g. efficiency and profitability (Child, 1975); employee satisfaction (Dewar and Werbel, 1979). The terms *effectiveness* and *efficiency* are terms that would encapsulate many of these varied definitions and reflect business performance. The profitability of the organization is employed here as the metric which encapsulates both efficiency and effectiveness. However, we would argue that aggregate business performance is not solely concerned with profit performance but also the level of business and personal risk that the management is prepared to accept in achieving this performance. Excellent levels of profitability in the short term may be achieved at the expense of increased risk exposure in the longer term, e.g. significant discounting of prices may increase sales volume and total profit in the short term but may consequently expose the business to greater risks if these become accepted or expected in the longer term. The primary sources of risk in the typical supply chain relate to a number of factors or parameters. Chief amongst these are quality, product/service availability and cost though there may be other parameters which become relatively more important in specific sectors.

The classification of risks into *endogenous risks*, those that are inherent within the situation itself and *exogenous risks*, those that impinge on the situation from outside are a further means of classifying the risks in a given situation. In order to classify risks into these two categories it is necessary to define the boundaries of the decision situation under consideration. For example, defining the unit of analysis as a single organization within the supply chain would result in the categorisation of those risks within the organization as endogenous and those emanating from the rest of the supply chain partners as exogenous. If we widen the scope in terms of the unit of analysis to the immediate partners in the supply chain then the classification of risks would again change. Classifying risks into the two categories simply indicates the source of the risk and does not indicate the nature, scale or manageability, although by implication endogenous risks may be perceived to be more manageable than those exogenous risks emanating from outside of the defined risk situation.

The definition of the supply chain and the differing contexts and perspectives this may present for risk management within the supply chain are dealt with in an earlier chapter. For the purposes of the present discussion the scope will focus on the single organization within the supply chain and its immediate partners, both upstream and downstream.

Aggregate Business Performance = f (Risk Management) = f (Risks associated with Quality, Availability, Cost......)

Where: Risk Management incorporates activities such as risk assessment, diagnosis, evaluation, avoidance, amelioration...etc.

The final dimension postulates the relationship between the risks inherent in the supply chain and the role that risk management may perform, through activities such as prior identification of risks and taking actions to resolve these. The quality of the risk management processes and activities will have a direct impact on the aggregate business performance, through changes in the financial performance and the risks associated with this.

Why a Contingency Framework?

Decisions involving risk may be classified according to their particular characteristics. For example, the decision to take an umbrella in relation to the risk of getting wet would employ a different set of decision cues, information resources and processing arrangements than say the decision to overtake the car in front on the way to work. Both of these situations would probably have a common set of characteristics (e.g. decision cues, information collection, information processing, probability assessment and outcome evaluation) though the nature of the characteristics would vary between the two situations. The time frame in which the former decision of taking the umbrella would differ from that of overtaking the car in front, as might the consequences of taking the wrong decision. We are faced with a dilemma in terms of posing the question: Is every decision involving risk unique to a given situation and hence, there is no value in seeking to draw out common characteristics, distil evidence of behavior and proffer advice? Alternatively, is there sufficient commonality for us to draw together evidence from the wide variety of risk taking situations and to somehow generalise the characteristics and proffer general advice and guidance on how to handle such situations? These two extreme positions may be viewed respectively as the *situational* and the *generic* approaches. Both approaches offer differing insights into the aspect of risk and the associated decision processes.

However, both have their limitations from a research perspective. An alternative third approach is the *contingency* approach, which is positioned somewhere in between the other two approaches whilst recognizing that there are common sets of characteristics. The contingency approach accepts that there are likely to be variances according to particular decision contexts, in other words the characteristics and their behavior are likely to be *contingent* on the context. This chapter develops and employs a contingency approach to risk within the context of the supply chain and its management. More specifically, it seeks to establish a Contingency Framework of context, process, support systems and behavioral characteristics for decisions associated with risk in the supply chain and its effective management.

Developing any framework that seeks to group or categorize certain characteristics of particular business phenomena requires some prior definition on the purpose of the Framework. We have postulated three types of Framework ranging from the *situational* through *contingency* to *generic*. The situational framework develops from the premise that each decision situation is unique in terms of the context, variables, participants, structures and processes. Hence, there may be limited scope or advantage in transferring experience, knowledge and expertise from one decision situation to another. At the other extreme, the generic framework would subscribe to the view that many of the variables and parameters are fairly common from one decision to another. Hence, there is value in seeking to transfer experience, knowledge and expertise gained from one setting to another. In simplistic terms neither of these frameworks may provide the necessary insight to understanding risk within the supply chain setting. The situational approach would suggest little scope for transferring knowledge and the generic may provide little guidance on how to adapt generic principles and rules to specific settings. The Contingency Framework in many respects provides a middle ground in relation to this spectrum of frameworks and one that provides greater utility to the decision maker. The approach adopted in such a framework is the '*if* a particular set or pattern of variables/parameters occur *then* the decision maker may apply certain pre-defined approaches to resolving the risks involved.' The reason for adopting such an approach in relation to the supply chain context is primarily explained by the characteristics outlined in the previous section. The dynamic, interactive and evolutionary nature of supply chain relationships suggests that a contingency approach to constructing a risk framework may be more suitable than a generic approach seeking to establish common risk characteristics and responses or the situational approach which simply suggests that every supply chain is different and needs to be treated as a one-off decision case in terms of risk resolution. Mentzer et al, (2001, p.7), emphasizes the complexity of supply chains, recognizing 'the potential for countless alternative supply chain configurations' and that 'any one organization can be part of numerous supply chains'.

Dimensions of the Framework

Developing any framework which seeks in some way to characterize the particular situations, requires the determination of the particular dimensions to be employed. In relation to risk within the supply chain there are a number of key sets of characteristics or dimensions that will determine the nature of the risks involved, providing guidance on how these risks might be conceptualized, measured and resolved. The key sets of characteristics considered are: Contextual, Structural/Process, Decision Support, Human.

It is argued that these four dimensions (illustrated in Diagram 3.3) should enable the classification of most decision situations relating to supply chain risk management. The nature of each of these dimensions will be explored in the following sections, before integrating these as a whole.

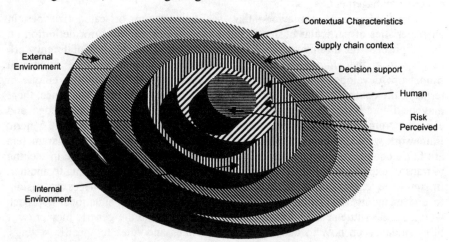

Diagram 3.3 Supply Chain Risk – Contingency Framework

Contextual Characteristics

The contextual characteristics seek to define the principle variables in the decision setting that may influence both the inherent risk in a given situation and the risk perception. The subset of these dimensions have been determined as: External Environment, Supply Chain Context, Internal Environment

The External Environment represents the general backcloth within which the supply chain is operating and against which decisions have to be taken. General trends in the political, social, economic and technological arena both at international, national, regional and sub-regional levels may all characterize the nature of the risks facing all of the businesses and supply chains operating within this context. Some of these dimensions may have a greater impact on individual supply chains and possibly particular members within the chain than others e.g. operating in particular countries may increase political risk exposure. Makhija and Stewart (2002) concluded that managers operating in planned economies, where they did not face the same personal consequences (e.g. loss of employment or income) as those operating in free market economies were more prepared to take risky decisions. Within this broader arena of the External Environment the individual Supply Chain Context itself may provide further scope for risk variability. A well established, effective and efficient supply chain is unlikely to face the same pressures to change as those, which are newly formed and struggling to find an effective and efficient mode of operation or are not prepared to adapt and innovate. These external variables represent only one dimension of the context, the internal environment encompassing the objectives of the organization, strategies, resources and culture are all factors which may influence both perception of risk and the preparedness to undertake particular types of decision to manage these.

Structural and Process Characteristics

The structure of the supply chain and its constituent elements represent important characteristics influencing the risk inherent in the decision situation. In many respects this relates to the degree of stability in terms of structure as well as processes and relationships. A multitude of examples (e.g. Mentzer et al, 2001; and Ritchie and Brindley, 2000) illustrate that for many businesses the prospect is instability, radical change and new partnerships in their supply chains. The nature of the responses to changes in the structure, processes and behavior of the partners in the supply chain present an important set of variables that will characterize the nature of risk and the potential approaches to risk resolution and management. Frequent and rapid changes may militate against the development of robust relationships and processes, fostering a sense of instability and mistrust, which itself is likely to engender perceptions of greater vulnerability to risk. Examples of these structural/process characteristics include:

1. How stable and enduring are the existing members and communication channels in the supply chain?

2. What are the pressures within the sector to achieve single sourcing at the expense of multiple sourcing arrangements?
3. Are there pressures towards disintermediation to improve effectiveness and efficiency i.e. dropping or skipping particular stages in the supply chain such as eliminating the warehousing function or the steel stockholder? (Ritchie and Brindley, 2000)
4. What pressures are there to forge new associations within existing supply chain partners or new partners to provide new product/service opportunities?
5. Does the process involve groups or individual decision makers? What has been their relationship and to what extent is there a presence of confidence and trust?
6. Is the approach one that focuses on the individual decision in hand or is there a more strategic and holistic appreciation of the consequences for other decisions both currently and prospectively?
7. Does the process operate in an open system, with partners sharing information?
8. Is there an expectation that partners to the decision will operate in a rational and logical manner? What would be the consequences of operating in alternative modes?
9. How does the decision process and the role of players within this adapt to new situations such as changes in technology, new partnerships, changes in key individuals in existing partnerships?
10. Can the decision structures and processes adapt to the more revolutionary changes that may take place from time to time?
11. Is the decision process a series of disjointed and dysfunctional activities with little coherence or cohesion between parties or over time?

This set of questions illustrates the diversity of characteristics relating to supply chain structure and process. Indeed, the majority of the research case material associated with supply chains and their management relates primarily to structural and process developments.

Decision Support

Whist the external environment, the supply chain environment and the internal environment all prescribe the context within which decisions will be taken, the specific problem requiring resolution will be represented within the organization as a decision. The way in which the decision is characterized may have important consequences for the risk perceived, the process of taking the decision and the preparedness to take risks. For example, the level or significance attached to the decision (e.g. strategic v operational) is likely to produce differential approaches to the decision processing and also the person(s) responsible for assessing the risk and taking the risk. Closely associated with the level of decision is the significance of consequences both negatively and positively (e.g. the potential to place firm at risk of survival and the associated strategic benefits of improved effectiveness and efficiency in the supply chain.

The significance may also correlate with the time-relatedness of the decision and its potential impact on future decisions (e.g. supplier choices and pricing decisions may pre-empt future choices and price changes). Evidence suggests (Ritchie and Marshall, 1993) that the further into the future the potential impact of the consequences then the lower the risk perceived and the more prepared the decision maker is to take risks.

The degree of interdependence of the decision with other decisions within the organization and with other external partners is another facet that may generate a greater sense of risk exposure the more inter-connected the decision. In many situations the decision is dictated by others in the supply chain, either up-stream or down-stream, in which case the organization itself may experience significant exposure together with a sense of lack of influence to resolve any risks. Associated with this latter point is the source of the cues that prompt the decision process. For example, is the organization reactive and pressurized by others into taking the decision or is the organization more proactive in this context. The initiator of the action is often assumed to have lower perceptions of risk than those on whom the decision is imposed. The imperative nature or urgency of the decision and whether there is scope for delaying is another factor that may influence risk perception, given the belief that such delay is likely to enhance the quality of the information available and hence, resolve to some degree the risk perceived. Divisibility of any decision in terms of breaking it down into discrete parts, which may be handled relatively independently over time or between different parties, is another approach to handling risk and complexity in decisions.

A further set of characteristics relates to the nature of the decision support mechanisms and facilities available to the decision maker(s), which may enhance their ability to identify, measure, resolve and manage the risks involved. Examples of these might include:

1. Availability of particular facilities to enable the decision maker(s) to construct a logical or conceptual model of the decision situation (e.g. spreadsheet or other modelling software that may permit testing alternative solutions).
2. Metrics or measurement systems to assess the outcome of potential solutions integrating the risk dimension.
3. Information resources, search engines and the quality of these.
4. Availability of information exchange and/or knowledge transfer both inter-organizational (i.e. between the partners in the supply chain), or intra-organizational (i.e. between members of the same organization).
5. Capacity of the supply chain and its organizational infrastructure to achieve organizational learning for the supply chain as a whole.

Human Characteristics

Much of the early work in the field of risk focused on the dimension of individual risk taking behaviors (e.g. Kogan and Wallach, 1964; and Slovic, 1972), though this was often isolated from behavior in organizational contexts. Researchers have increasingly devoted attention to risk behavior within the context of organizational decisions. This research into risk and decision taking behavior of individuals and groups, includes:

1. *Risk perceptiveness and preparedness* (Appelbaum et al, 1998, p.120), for example, identify four dimensions that relate to individual risk perception and preparedness which they express as 'fear of failure; fear of success; fear of what others will think; and the fear of uncertainty.' They concluded that most people in organizations focused more on what they might lose instead of what they might gain.
2. *Gender and age influences* (e.g. MacCrimmon and Wehrung, 1990; Forlani and Mullins, 2000) identified differences in both risk perceptions and the preparedness to take risks on the basis of gender differences and the maturity of the decision maker, although it should be noted that research results to date have not produced unanimity on this.
3. *Group influences* March (1994, p.45) suggested that the organization as a whole may provide the context 'in which riskiness is estimated and risk-taking propensities are enacted into the taking of risk.' Hence groups within the organization may reflect this in terms of their decisions, although there may be some differences in terms of the particular decision taken (e.g. R&D investments).

These examples illustrate the potential importance of this dimension of the Contingency Model although this will not be explored further in the present discussion.

Metrics

Accepting that risk management in the context of the supply chain concerns a balance between eliminating, reducing or resolving the inherent risks in a situation against the performance parameters then we could illustrate this tension as in Diagram 3.4. The suggestion is that without effective risk management in the supply chain the tendency will be for the supply chain to deteriorate with increasing risk and a simultaneous decline in performance. The earlier formulation suggested that measuring performance could be based on profit performance and the resulting risk inherent in the organization as:

Aggregate Business Performance = f (Profit)*(Risk) = f (Quality, Availability, Cost.....) * (Risks associated with Quality, Availability, Cost......)

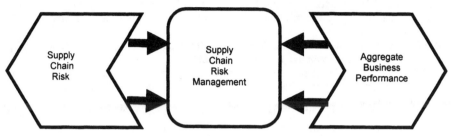

Diagram 3.4 Managing Supply Chain Risk and Performance

Conclusion

The chapter has explored the development of a Contingency Framework for Risk Management within the context of supply chains. We have recognized that such a Contingency Framework may provide a number of benefits in terms of mapping the research outputs in the field and seeking to clarify the key influencing or contingency variables that are likely to impact on the risks that prevail or are perceived to prevail in given decision situations. In a more pragmatic sense, the Contingency Framework may be less appealing since it provides less formulaic or prescriptive advice to practitioners than might emanate from a more generic formulation. However, the belief that there is a generic toolkit that decision makers may apply in almost every context has proved to be misleading in almost every area of the decision sciences. Equally, the situational approach provides little opportunity for the decision maker to apply any form of knowledge transferred and experience gained from other decisions taken previously.

The most significant contribution of developing the proposed Contingency Framework is in the research field. It should prove possible to either locate the outcomes from research studies within this initial Framework, in a sense reinforcing the dimensions of the Framework or substantiating the individual parameters and contingency variables. It is recognized that there are likely to be gaps in the initial Framework and that an immediate task is to seek to fill these gaps whilst simultaneously seeking to integrate research in adjoining or complementary fields (e.g. human risk and decision behavior).

A further dimension of the Framework that deserves attention concerns the metrics. The current drive to develop metrics (e.g. Marketing Metrics – Ambler, 2003) is also reflected in the field of risk management. Decision makers are seeking some means of measuring the effectiveness of decisions taken to resolve risks and improve the performance of the business. This relates to the point made earlier that practitioners value more highly a Framework that provides practical guidance and means of measuring the quality and effectiveness of their decisions.

References

Ambler, T. (2000), *Marketing and the bottom line*, Prentice Hall, UK.

Appelbaum, S.H., Bregman, M. and Moroz, P. (1998), 'Fear as a Strategy: Effects and Impact within the Organization', *Journal of European Industrial Training*, Vol.23, No.3, pp.113-127.

Brindley, C.S. and Ritchie, R.L. (2001), 'The Information-risk Conundrum, *Marketing Intelligence and Planning*, Vol.19, No.1, pp.29-37.

Child, J. (1975), 'Managerial and Organizational Factors Associated with Company Performance', Part 2: A Contingency Analysis, *Journal of Management Studies*, Vol. 12, pp.12-27.

Dewar, R. and Werbel, (1979), 'Universalistic and Contingency Predictions of Employee Satisfaction and Conflict', *Administrative Science Quarterly*, Vol.24, pp.426-448.

Forlani, D. and Mullins J.W. (2000), 'Perceived risks and choices in entrepreneurs' new venture decisions', *Journal of Business Venturing*, Vol.15, No.4, pp.305–322.

Kleindorfer, P.R. and Wassenhove, L.K. (2003), 'Managing Risk in Global Supply Chains', Paper presented to *Wharton Insurance and Risk Management Department Seminar*, 27th February 2003, Wharton University.

Knight, F.H. (1921), *Risk, Uncertainty and Profit*, Houghton and Mifflin, Boston and New York.

Kogan, N. and Wallach, M.A. (1964), 'Risk Taking: A Study in Cognition and Personality', Holt Reinhart and Winston, New York.

MacCrimmon, K.R. and Wehrung D.A. (1986). *Taking Risks: The Management of Uncertainty*, Free Press, New York.

Makhija, M.V. and Stewart, A.C. (2002), 'The Effect of National Context on Perceptions of Risk: A Comparison of Planned Versus Free-Market Managers', *Journal of International Business Studies*, Vol.33, No.4, pp.737-756.

March, J.G. (1994), *A Primer on Decision Making*, The Free Press, New York.

Mentzer, J.T. (editor), De Witt, W., Keebler, J.S., Min, S., Nix, N.W., Smith, C.D. and Zacharia, Z.G. (2001), *Supply Chain Management*, Sage Publications Ltd., USA.

Min, S. (2001), 'Inter-corporate cooperation in Supply Chain Management', in Mentzer, J.T. (editor), *Supply Chain Management*, pp.391-410, Sage Publications Ltd, US.

Nix, W.N. (2001), 'The consequences of Supply Chain Management: Creating value, satisfaction and differential advantage', in Mentzer, J.T.(editor), *Supply Chain Management*, pp.61-76, Sage Publications Ltd, US.

Paulsson, U. and Norrman, A. (2003), 'Supply Chain Risk Management Articles – external characteristics and contents', Working Paper presented at International *Supply Chain Risk Management Conference*, Manchester Metropolitan University, 13-15 October 2003.

Ritchie, R.L. and Brindley, C.S. (2000), 'Disintermediation, Disintegration and Risks in the SME Global Supply Chain', *Management Decision*, Vol.38, No.8, pp.575-583.

Ritchie, R.L. and Marshall, D.V. (1993), *Business Risk Management*, Chapman Hall, London.

Rowe, W.D. (1977), *Anatomy of Risk*, Wiley, New York.

Slovic, P. (1972), 'Information processing, situation specificity and the generality of risk taking behavior', *Journal of Personality and Social Psychology*, Vol.11, pp.128-134.

Ward, A. and Smith, J. (2003), *Trust and Mistrust*, Wiley, UK.

Warren, F. (1992), *Introduction in: Royal Society Study Group, Risk Analysis, Perception and Management*, The Royal Society, London.

Chapter 4

Risk Management in Supplier Relationships and Networks

Jukka Hallikas and Dr. Veli-Matti Virolainen

Introduction

This chapter looks at issues surrounding the risks associated with supplier networks. Risk management and network sourcing have been the subject of separate vivid debate but have not been discussed together. The development and management of the supplier network is one of the most important functions of industrial companies.

For suppliers, network arrangements have recently been perceived as a strategic weapon in their quest to secure targeted customers and hence, gain access to the end markets on which their business depends. The importance of this to SMEs is even more relevant, as many customers reduce their supplier base and turn towards single sources of supply in pursuit of lean management philosophies.

Business relationships have changed during the last twenty years. Supplier relationships have become more important through increasing outsourcing and networking of companies. The traditional role of supplier relationship assessment has been to analyze supplier performance from the buying company's point of view taking the supplier's aspects into minor consideration. However, risks related to the collaboration are not merely dependent on the one company's goals and objectives, although in many relationships there is a dominant party, whose aspiration is to take the responsibility of managing the entire supplier network. The increasing sharing of responsibilities and the dynamic nature of relationships requires the assessment of relationships in a dyadic fashion.

In the first part of this chapter, we deal with network and risk management theory. A TCE model is developed in order to explain theoretically the most critical elements of a typical subcontracting decision, with special emphasis on technology-related factors, such as asset specificity, appropriability of knowledge, the role of complementary assets in the value chain and the nature of innovation. Next we look at the risks surrounding different kinds of relationships because we believe that the type of relationship has an effect on the perceived risks of different parties. Furthermore, we present some main risk categories in supplier networks and their role in sourcing strategy development. Finally, we illustrate a framework for risk management in supplier networks.

On Networks

Companies are no longer independent entities acting on their own in a business environment. To be successful in the market, companies have to interact with other companies and organizations. One successful type of interaction is networking. A supply network can be defined as a set of supply chains, describing the flow of goods and services from original sources to the end customer. It can also be defined as a specific type of relation linking a defined set of persons, objects or events (Harland, 1996). According to Håkansson and Johanson (1993) the components of networks are actors, resources and activities. There are strong interdependencies between all these three elements in the real business environment. One important aspect of a network is its structure. Nishiguchi (1994) has reported how Japanese companies have organized their suppliers into hierarchies: first-tier or primary suppliers provide systems rather than components. This reduces the number of first tier suppliers and also makes the buying company more dependent on the supplier.

Networking has had a strong influence on the strategy formulation of companies. Concentration on core competencies and businesses and outsourcing other activities has increased the strategic importance of capabilities and resources embedded on the outside of firm boundaries. This work of defining the factors that determine the internal and external boundaries of the firm is derived from transaction cost analysis (Williamson, 1979). Here, the term asset specificity is used to determine the specificity of a relationship. From the strategic management point of view Reve (1990) similarly emphasizes that the important aspect of making strategic decisions is on what companies make in-house and what they procure from outside. Reve (1990) suggests that companies should concentrate on core competencies and skills in order to respond to the changing environment. This stresses the need for considering the dynamic aspects of relationship development more profoundly. Companies have to make continuous strategic sourcing decisions based on the changes in external and internal business conditions and environments.

Gadde and Håkansson (2001) distinguish between high and low-involvement relationships. They argue that the low-involvement approach may lead to significant hidden costs and offers minimal opportunities to gain cost and revenue benefits. High-involvement relationships, in turn, can offer significant cost and revenue benefits. This may, however, increase the relationship-handling costs because of increased co-ordination, adaptation and interaction. Doz and Hamel (1998) have expressed the importance of strategic relationships and continuous relationship development. They argue that due to growth opportunities in global markets and wider skills required by new technologies, companies have to turn to strategic partnerships and alliances with other companies to be able to get access to resources and capabilities and to pursue new opportunities. Furthermore, the firm's ability to exploit external knowledge is an important capability of innovation and thus, a substantial source of corporate renewal.

The primary tools employed by the Japanese to implement supplier coordination and individual supplier development are cross exchange of staff between buyer and supplier and one-to-one supplier development. Maybe the most important vehicle to align suppliers with the policy set by the customer is supplier association (see Hines, 1996). Another important feature of network sourcing is the tiering of supply, with firms in the various supplier tiers operating a maximum buy strategy.

Furthermore, Pfohl and Buse (2000, p.391) suggest that attention could be paid to strategic networks and virtual enterprises, which are dynamic and non-hierarchical in nature. Virtual enterprises represent dynamic networks, whereas strategic networks can be seen as more stable in nature. The tiers in the network make coordination difficult, as the responsibilities must be shared between the first tier supplier and the multi-tier suppliers. Additionally, the logistics and other service providers between the buyer and the first tier supplier make the network structure more complex. In a virtual enterprise, companies no longer produce complete products in isolated facilities. Instead, they operate as nodes in a network of customers, suppliers, service providers and other specialized players. The main objective of a virtual enterprise is to allow a number of organizations to rapidly develop a common operating environment. The main reason for a virtual enterprise is customer focus. The variety of virtual enterprise structures is caused by different kinds of demand and business environments. Other motives for companies to enter a virtual enterprise are:

1. to maximize flexibility and adaptability to environmental changes
2. development of a pool of competencies and resources
3. reaching a critical size to be in accordance with market constraints
4. optimization of the global supply chain.

Virtual enterprise structures are highly dynamic. Their life cycle can be very short. Reactivity and flexibility are the major benefits of a virtual enterprise. The main objective of the virtual enterprise structure is to link different organizations to make them work together in a collaborative and reactive manner. It is essential to understand that virtual enterprise structures are information system-centered. The competencies that have to be developed are then an information system working with different organizations.

According to Martinez et al, (2001) there are a large variety of virtual enterprise organizations which can be classified into three groups: short term virtual enterprise, extended enterprise and consortium virtual enterprise. A virtual enterprise organization can evolve from one kind of structure to another along its life cycle. The creation of a short term virtual enterprise is usually based on a single market opportunity. It includes all the structures at the beginning of the virtual enterprise project life cycle. Extended enterprises span company boundaries and include complex relationships between a company, its partners, customers, suppliers and market. Another possible evolution of a long term collaboration in a virtual enterprise environment is a consortium. This is a partnership where the internal flexibility will stay high.

Generally speaking, through networking the firms aim at reducing financial and technological risks and improving their competitive advantage, through deeper specialization. The increasing challenges are due to e.g. shortening time to market and lead times, fast developing technologies and the globalization trend. Strategic networks and virtual enterprises are thus, emergent concepts in business.

On Risk Management – Some Points of Departure

Our awareness of business risks and risk management thinking is changing. The opening of new markets, rapid technical development and keen globalized competition are still often experienced as threats. Uncertainty seems to be a disturbing factor in organized life and continuous change feels like a threat to social life and economy. Of the factors having a strong effect on change in the business environment may be the formation of conglomerates, the networking of enterprises and increasing dependence on each other, the avoidance of storage, the introduction of JIT approaches, changing legislation, increasing international interchange among production and trade, the growing risk awareness of consumers and the fast development of the importance of services (Kuusela and Ollikainen, 1997).

According to Herz and Thomas (1983) one view of 'risks' that is common in the management literature is that a risk is thought of in terms of variability or uncertainty, however imprecise the two latter terms may be. On the other hand, in the insurance industry, the term 'risk' is an accurate item to be insured. In this category, the writers seek to differentiate the two categories of risk, i.e. 'pure' risk and 'speculative' risk. In the following we will use the concept related to business risks, introducing business risk categories due to different activities of the enterprise.

The first risk class consists of factors connected with the personnel, i.e. the risks that can hinder either directly or indirectly the enterprise from pursuing its goals e.g. wrong choice of personnel, low productivity of personnel, key person risk and lack of skilful employees.

The second source of risks is due to the increasing and changing legislation that an enterprise must take into account to be able to avoid unnecessary losses. According to Sadgrove (1996) the requirements on risk assessment are growing. Already the EU requires firms to carry out risk assessment in health and safety, as well as in product liability and finance. Closely tied with legislation risks are also liability risks and issues due to the claims reserve.

Initiatives to increase the requirements of risk management may also be due to: changes of customer attitudes (corporate customers often want to pass legal responsibilities to their suppliers and customers that are more litigious, are less likely to accept product failure); shareholders who are more aware of risks, thus seeking for information about the company's exposure to risks; the public, which expects higher standards of corporate behavior. Increasing use of information technology also creates new types of risks. The objects of data security can be listed as follows: confidentiality, integrity, availability and accountability. There are also risks related to financing activities. They can be divided to the following areas: solvency risk, credit risk and market risk. The market risk comprises risks due to investments in shares, interest rates, currencies and prices of commodities (Uusi-Rauva, 1998).

Transaction Cost-Based Framework for Network Risk Analysis

To analyze the risks associated with networking decisions in a more exact way it is necessary to introduce a transaction cost theory (TCE) based framework. The concept of transaction cost has been used in explaining the range of the activities (transactions) in which the company engages itself. TCE offers an analytical device which makes it possible to understand why a company insources, outsources or networks when acquiring the competencies (capabilities) needed for efficient supply chain organization (for more on these issues, see Kyläheiko, 1999). According to Coase (1937) when the marginal costs of using markets (i.e. transaction costs) are higher than the costs of using the company (i.e. management costs), a transaction should be organized within the company and vice versa. Williamson (1991) regards transaction costs as organizational failures due to environmental (uncertainty, asset specificity, small number of potential trading partners) and human (bounded rationality, opportunism, information asymmetry) determinants. Asset specificity refers to the ease with which an asset can be redeployed to alternative uses. The more dependent a company is on its buyer/supplier, the higher are the TC's and vice versa.

The original idea of Coase (1937) was that without transaction costs the market solution (i.e. outsourcing) should be preferred because it would make it easier to exploit the economies of scale and scope (i.e. the fruits of specialization) and to use more efficient high-powered incentives.

Later Teece (1984; 1988) has taken into account also some technology-related transaction cost determinants, which are relevant in our industrial context. To make sense of his ideas it is useful to interpret a firm as a Porterian value chain of adjacent transactions (activities). They can be put together through different governance systems, i.e. by using outsourcing, different sorts of networks or own manufacturing. The strategic problem is to find out the governance structure which economizes on the sum of transaction and management costs.

Teece (1986) has launched two other TC determinants related to the appropriability regime and the role of complementary competencies. The former refers to the factors that make it possible to profit from innovation. The most important factors are the very nature of technological knowledge (from tacit to fully codified) and the existence of legal mechanisms of protection (i.e. patents, trade marks, copyrights). The more tacit (or legally effectively protected) the new knowledge is, the lower the associated transaction costs, the better is the outsourcing or loose networking option and vice versa.

On the basis of the above discussion it is possible to introduce the conditions under which the network option should be preferred. Networking always includes elements typical of both the pro-market outsourcing and own manufacturing solution. Networks are useful when market and/or technological uncertainty is fairly high, knowledge is fairly generic or codified (e.g. science-based) and hence, hard to appropriate, there are economies of scale due to specialization and the markets for complementary competencies are not very competitive. Often, high-powered incentives are badly needed. Under these conditions it is very likely that the firms will network together.

Compared to the pure market solution, networks make it possible to co-ordinate interrelated competencies better and to reduce the risk of being trapped by the monopolistic holders of complementary competencies. In addition, networks give the partners more strategic decision-making power without a fear of opportunism. In relation to the own manufacturing option networks make it possible to share financial risks of sunken costs, to exploit economies of scale and scope, to utilize more high-powered incentives and to reduce complexity and uncertainty through common routines and competencies. Moreover, some of the traditional advantages of the vertical integration option can be obtained because of closer co-ordination and large common knowledge pool, which makes its easier to cross-learn and internalize external competencies (Kyläheiko et al, 1999).

In accordance with modern TCE literature (Teece, 1988; Williamson, 1991; Kyläheiko, 1995) the main sources of risks emerged in the network context can be appraised as follows:

1. *Asset specificity related 'hold up' risks*: Our hypothesis concerning these risks is that the higher the asset specificity and uncertainty and the greater the danger of opportunism, the higher the 'hold up' risks related to outsourcing/loose networks and the better options are insourcing/tight networks (e.g. joint venture) and vice versa (see Williamson, 1991).

2. *Competency markets-related 'inefficiency' risks*: Our hypothesis is that the more competitive the markets of complementary competencies, the more there are potential buyers/suppliers and the less are the transaction cost-related risks (Teece, 1988).

3. *Nature of knowledge-related 'spill over' or 'appropriability' risks*: Our hypothesis is that the more appropriable the new knowledge is, the smaller are the risks related to outsourcing/ loose network options and vice versa

4. *Time horizon-related 'timing' risks*: Our hypothesis is that the greater the differences between the planning horizons between the buyer (typically more myopic) and the suppliers (typically more patient), the higher are the risks of networking and vice versa.

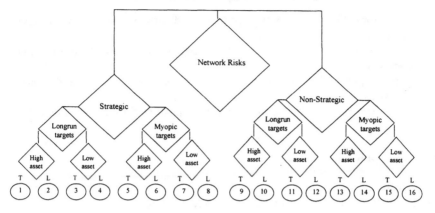

Figure 4.1   Transaction Cost-Based Risk Typology Concerning both the Buyers and Sellers (Huttunen et al, 2000)

In Figure 4.1 TCE-based risks concerning buyers (B) and suppliers (S) are presented, where Strategic = Strategic (firm-specific) complementary competencies generated by suppliers, Non strategic = Non-strategic (generic) complementary competencies generated by suppliers, High asset = High asset specificity of investment, Low asset = Low asset specificity of investment, L = loose appropriability and T = tight approppriability.

In the light of Figure 4.1 the following risks can be associated with the network environment:

1. Hold-up risks for the supplier and a bit stronger position for the buying company.
2. Hold-up and spill over risks for the supplier which means relative strong position for the buying company.
3. Excellent opportunities for the supplier. Low risk for both.
4. Spill-over risk for the supplier. Fairly strong position for both parties.
5. Hold-up and timing risks for the supplier. Fairly strong position for buying company.
6. Hold-up, spill over and timing risks for the supplier. Strong position for the buying company.
7. Good opportunities for both parties. Some timing risks for the supplier.
8. Spill-over and timing risk for the supplier. Fairly strong position for the buying company.
9. High hold-up risk for the supplier. Strong position for the buying company.
10. High risk for the supplier. Strong position for the buying company.
11. Some opportunities for the supplier. A bit stronger position for the buying company.
12. Small opportunities and competition risks for the supplier. Strong position for the buying company.

13. High competition risk for the supplier. Very strong position for the buying company.
14. Very high risks for the supplier. Extremely strong position for buying company.
15. Some opportunities for the supplier. Fairly strong position for the buying company.
16. Small opportunities for the supplier. Strong position for the buying company.

Risks in Supplier Networks

By networking, firms aim at reducing risks and improving their competitiveness in the continually changing business environment. In today's industry, increasing challenges are due to e.g. shortening turnaround times, fast developing technology and globalization. Risks brought about by networking are for example, risks that are related to the barriers of network formation and network change. These factors are mainly connected to the network resistance towards changes, new technologies, practices and members, as well as with problems and risks that may arise in network management or in setting up appropriate development activities. Also, increasing requirements of communication and cooperation activities add claims for e.g. information systems, openness, trust and production systems.

Sadgrove (1996) has introduced some problems due to supplying and suppliers. Bad planning and extended delivery chains may cause problems with keeping delivery promises. Also, markets where there are only a few suppliers cause problems e.g. a fire or a production problem by a major supplier may cause delays. The tendency to reduce the number of suppliers makes the supply chain more vulnerable to an interruption of supplies.

According to Sadgrove (1996) sourcing from abroad also carries a higher risk, as there can exist political and cultural risks as well as problems with distance. With single sourcing the firm no longer has competitive pricing, so there can be a risk for higher prices. Also, Just-In-Time activities may increase the risk when taken to their extreme.

Zanger (1997) has studied 863 companies with a minimum of 25 and a maximum of 250 employees. She suggests that the following risk areas may arise in the network of suppliers (Zanger, 1997, pp.13-14):

1. Network partners surrender their decision-making sovereignty in the field of activity in which the cooperation takes place.
2. The risk of conflicts over objectives arising can result if SMEs are made to place their own aims in second position to those of the network, in which case economically second-best behavior has to be consciously accepted.
3. Depending on the intensity of the links among the network partners, there is a risk of individual partners losing their flexibility.
4. In the case of individual network partners' opportunistic behavior, there is a risk of a loss of know-how advantages and misuse of information.

5. Strong differences between the partners' cooperation cultures have an adverse effect on the trustful atmosphere of partnership within network. They can lead to inner opposition to the cooperation from management and employees.

The specific risks of procurement activities are closely tied with the network of suppliers. Treleven and Schweikhart's (1988) risk/benefit categories introduce five categories: disruption of supply risk category, price risk category, stock and schedule category, technology category and quality category. Other risks, mentioned by Virolainen and Tuominen (1998) are availability risk, configuration risk and currency risks. Configuration risk includes the proper gross purchase and definition of quality.

In the model of Treleven and Schweikhart (1988) presented below the basic idea in the decision process is to evaluate all of these risk/benefit categories separately. All the risk/benefit categories are assessed in terms of probability and the degree of risk/benefit. Treleven and Schweikhart (1988) suggest that an interval rating scale (+10 to −10) would be used to measure the impact for each category and a weighting factor would determine the relative importance of each category.

$$I_T = P_{ds}*I_{ds} + P_{pe}*I_{pe} + P_{is}*I_{is} + P_{ta}*I_{ta} + P_q*I_q$$

Where

I_T = the total impact of the sourcing strategy
P_i = the probability impact i being realized
I_i = the impact of the factors in risk/benefit category i
P_i*I_i = the expected value of the impact of risk/benefit category i
ds = the disruption of supply risk/benefit category
pe = the price risk/benefit category
is = stock and schedule risk/benefit category
ta = technology risk/benefit category
q = quality risk/benefit category

Source: Treleven and Schweikhart (1988)

The objective of the conceptual risk/assessment model is to facilitate managers' sourcing strategy decision making. As it is essential to understand the contents of the above mentioned categories, we will elaborate each of the these briefly below:

Disruption of Supply Category

The disruption risk category is usually seen as one of the most commonly cited arguments against single sourcing. Whatever the cause: fire, strike, natural disaster, there is concern about what happens if the supply is disrupted. The degree of concern will vary, depending not only on the likelihood of it occurring, but also on the impact that it would have on the organization. In practice, the move toward a partnership type of relationship is often coupled with JIT programs. In these JIT environments, even temporary disruptions may be unacceptable.

There are different ways of how companies can handle these risks. One of the most appropriate means nowadays is partnership sourcing. Usually some kind of qualification period precedes the partnership relationship. This means that the buyer requires the supplier to have been doing business with it for some specific number of years before entering partnership sourcing (see Treleven and Schweikhart, 1988, p.97). Another and commonly used approach to the disruption of supply risk is to conduct an intensive examination of the supplier's business, including its capability and financial records. A contingency plan should in every case be developed, describing the steps to be taken in case a disruption in supply occurs. The contingency plan can have a variety of forms. Maybe the most common is that a company chooses to maintain a dual source of supply to offset the supply risks. In this case, a very large portion of the demand is typically supplied by one supplier with the other supplier, supplying just enough to keep the relationship going.

Price Escalation Risk

The price escalation risk category is the other most commonly cited risk associated with single (partnership) sourcing. This is the risk of the supplier escalating its prices once it becomes the buyer's only source of a particular product or service. In traditional buyer/supplier relationships the buyer pays several suppliers off against each other to obtain the best (lowest) price for a given input. The aim of the buyer is to squeeze out the lowest possible purchasing price (see Virolainen, 1998). The traditional opinion has been that in a case of single sourcing this threat is absent. However, partnership sourcing can result in a decrease of the supplier's prices. Partnership means that both parties make efforts to decrease the real costs. The basic question is always, which sourcing strategy results in greater exposure to price escalation risks? Nowadays, there exists a strong belief that partnership sourcing is a way to decrease the transaction costs associated with procurement.

Inventory and Schedule Category

This category includes the benefits associated with changes attributable to the sourcing strategy, in the way that inventories are managed and the way in which inputs flow into the organization. The impact of single sourcing (partnership) in these areas is often connected to the impact of a JIT-program. When the supplier base is trimmed in a move toward partnership sourcing, the ability to schedule the delivery of the purchased products and services increases. Typically, with a trusting, long term relationship that develops out of single sourcing situations comes a sharing of production schedule information.

From the standpoint of inventory management, improvements in the scheduling of deliveries allow the buyer to carry a smaller amount of each product in stock. Taken to the extreme, with schedules linked precisely together there should be no raw materials and component inventory at all (compared to the JIT approach).

Technology Access Category

Partnership sourcing, if it means single sourcing as well, provides both risks and benefits to the buyer in terms of access to technology. On the risk side the company cannot select one supplier until the very last minute to meet all their demands for that particular product. This way the buying organization maintains access to a greater variety of potential sources of the latest technology and is thus, more likely to avoid locking-in on an 'old' technology. The potential benefit of partnership sourcing is that the buyer typically gains greater access to the technological knowledge of its partner, than it would in a multiple sourcing arrangement. With this kind of cooperative relationship the buyer is more likely to become involved in joint development efforts with its suppliers.

Partnership sourcing facilitates the buyer's access to more in-depth technological information from its suppliers, while multiple sourcing provides a broader coverage of potential sources of technological development (at the industry level), although perhaps not as in-depth. According to Treleven and Schweikhart (1988, p.103) a buyer can maintain access to the various potential sources of new technology within an industry, through multiple sourcing of product development and still derive the benefits from single sourcing of supply.

Quality Category

This is the area that companies usually recognize as the prime reason for moving toward a collaborative relationship with a supplier. Partnership sourcing results in improved quality in a variety of ways. Communication is easier, more frequent, more complete and more accurate. Time can be spent to ensure that the supplier completely understands the buyer's needs, including the uses of its products in the buyer's processes. This type of communication can lead to product and process design changes that are beneficial to both parties. From the quality standpoint, partnership sourcing would typically expose the buyer to less risk than multiple sourcing.

Risk of Supplier Opportunism

All transactions carry the risk of supplier opportunism (Smeltzer and Siferd, 1998, p.38). Reducing the number of transactions can reduce the risk of opportunism. Risks associated with procurement are threats to supply assurance, possibility of improper supplier selection, problems with environmental constraints, increased company liability and uncertainty of supply lead time. Substantial risks occur when purchasing is not included in the strategic planning process. Partnership as a part of proactive procurement is good risk management.

Risk-Based Assessment For Supplier Relationships

Relationship-Specific Investments

Relationship-specific investments are inevitable in any buyer-supplier relationship. Bensaou (1999) has segmented the relationships in terms of the degree of investment specificity. In the matrix presented in Figure 4.2 the vertical axis presents the buyer's investments, the horizontal axis presents respectively the supplier's specific investments to the relationship.

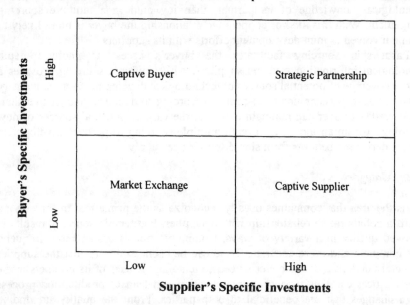

Figure 4.2 Types of Relationships (Bensaou, 1999)

When the buyer's and supplier's specific investments are both on a high level, the relationship can be called strategic partnership. This kind of relationship emphasizes high mutual commitment and long-term goals and objectives. Current and future resource and capability needs are planned on a complementary basis. According to Teece (1986) complementary capabilities emphasize the external capabilities needed to complete a firm's internal capabilities. In a partnership type of relationship it is usual that parties are involved in the early stages of the development processes. This means for example joint R&D activities, knowledge sharing and common development of business processes.

Although partnership relationships offer many advantages and success factors, there are certain risks inherent in the relationships. If both parties invest highly in the relationship they become mutually dependent on each other. The parties distinctly sell their dependency to each other. The trust that develops is, however, exposed to some biases. One risk is related to the inefficiency of the relationship. It follows that high investments in the relationship generally do not yield profit. Gadde and Håkansson (2001) have stated that high involvement relationships may provide substantial benefits but also substantial costs. Therefore, the point is to continuously monitor and assess the costs and benefits involved in the relationship. It is also important to adapt dynamically the degree of involvement to the changing conditions.

When the relationship-specific investments are in asymmetry as a result of the buyer's or the supplier's higher investment to the relationship there is a danger of a lock-in. If one party's involvement and thus, dependency is lower and it can switch to any other customer or supplier without high switching costs, it has a power advantage and possibility to behave opportunistically. The risk of timing in the relationship is associated with the asymmetric specific investments. If the supplier or the customer looks at issues surrounding the relationship from a different time span, the relationship is not likely to endure drastic changes in business conditions because one of the parties is not committed to the continuity. Furthermore, the risk of investment is not shared equally if one party has to take the whole responsibility and risk of investment. In asymmetric relationships, the investment risk management strategies may involve risk sharing and even a situation where the customer takes whole responsibility of supplier specific-investments and vice versa.

In market exchange relationships, both involved parties have made low relationship-specific investments and the switching costs and investment risks are thus, low. The transaction costs, quality and time are the main drivers of success and risk in market exchange relationships. If the specific investments are low, both parties have consistent comprehension about the timing of the relationship. The result will be that the expectations of the parties are regarded to be similar and the perceived risks of the relationship are fairly easily identified and controlled. The challenging task in a market exchange or 'arms-length' relationship is to increase the degree of involvement so that the organizations understand the risks, challenges and responsibilities in a new fashion.

Organizational Lock-in

There are many situations in business relationships, which can lead to an organizational lock-in. This means that the organization is so dependent on the other organization that it has only a limited ability to choose or decide. Heijden et al,. (2002) explain that a lock-in is a feature of a system that feeds back and is thus, hard to perceive and manage. The inherent characteristic of the dynamics of an organizational feedback system is the organization's inability to see the complex cause-and-effect relationships in a system over time. It follows that the focus stays on a diminishing amount of activities because the organizational system feeds back efficiently. However, at the same time the organization's ability to respond to the changes weakens since it concentrates on a too specific field of action. As a result, the company is at risk of a lock-in on the system.

It can be argued that the reason why many inter-organizational relationships fail is due to a customer or supplier lock-in. One important driver for a lock-in is related to relationship (asset) specific investments, which increase the dependency on the other organization. According to Bensaou (1999) asset-specific investments are difficult or expensive to transfer to another relationship or they will lose their value outside of the relationship.

Asymmetry in a relationship causes high level of uncertainty and risk. Even though organizational commitment and dependency are essential in partnership-type of relationships, it can be argued that if the balance of the relationship-specific investment is too high between the supplier and customer, the relationship is at risk of a lock-in. If the specific assets invested in the relationship are in balance and thus the dependency the between customer and the supplier is in symmetry, the risks inherent in the relationship are best understood and managed. In order to effectively reduce the risk of a lock-in, the companies should also be involved in other networks at the same time.

Relationship Dynamics

It is obvious that no business relationship is static by nature. Supplier relationships vary dynamically over time, emphasizing the needs and goals of the parties. The dynamic capability view offers one strategic explanation for the development of a firm's resource base. Teece et al,. (1997) define that dynamic capabilities as the firm's ability to integrate, build and reconfigure internal and external competencies to address rapidly changing environments. Moreover, they state that dynamic capabilities refer to the company's capacity to renew, augment and adapt its core competencies over time. Gadde and Håkansson (2001) state that companies need different types of relationships because suppliers make different types of capabilities and resources available to the buying company. It follows that the level of involvement must be continuously monitored and adapted to the changing conditions. They also argue that over-designed relationships are not only costly but tend to be risky as well because the specific investments may lose their value.

The parties involved in a relationship are investing in an uncertain future, where the needs and requirements are likely to change. The level of involvement is based on the best available information about the current and future conditions but there are situations where it is particularly risky to continue on the selected course of action. The inertia in decision making to change the direction will put the organization at risk of loosing its ability to respond to the changing needs. According to Bazerman (1998) one important bias in decision making is related to sunk costs, i.e. the time and expenses already invested. Sunk costs are the costs that are historical and should not be considered in any future course of action. Furthermore, the reference point for action should be in the current state and all alternative courses of action should be considered by evaluating the future costs and benefits associated with each alternative. In business relationships this means, as Gadde and Håkansson (2001) point out, that a company should be able to dynamically change its involvement according to changing conditions and potential benefits associated with the different relationships. It follows that both increasing and decreasing the level of involvement are thus, strategic options to be considered.

Approach For Risk Management In Supplier Networks

A typical risk management process of an enterprise consists of:

1. Risk identification
2. Risk assessment
3. Identification and implementation of means for risk reduction
4. Risk monitoring

Basically, the risk management process in the network environment can have the same phases. The most important differences between the risk management process of a single enterprise and that of a supply network are due to the interconnections of enterprises in the network and due to possibilities of partial sharing of the risk management process. In the following we will briefly discuss the risk management process from the network point of view. The framework presented below has been adapted from Hallikas et al (2002).

Risk Identification

Risk identification can be seen as a fundamental phase in risk management practice. It follows that by identifying risk, a decision-maker or a group of decision makers become conscious about events that may cause uncertainty. The main focus of risk identification is thus, to recognize future uncertainties to be able to manage these scenarios proactively. In the networked environment, risk identification becomes more difficult because of dependencies with other organizations. Interruptions, quality failures and delivery fluctuations are common strong signals of risks in production systems. However, not all risks are easy to identify. Feedback loops and chains of dependent events create additional challenges for risk identification.

A generic list of risk events can be used as a basis for risk identification. Following the branches of the risk tree, the events relevant to enterprises can be traced to the root causes. As the result of this phase, a list of categorized risk scenarios can be generated for closer examination. Table 1 shows an example output list of the identification phase in one examined case network. The example shows randomly selected risk scenarios in the 'risk in fulfilling customer deliveries' category.

Supply Chain Risk

Table 4.1 Output List from the Identification Phase

Subcategory	What may cause the risk in fulfilling customer deliveries
Internal processes	Problems in production planning.
	Project delivery performance fails.
	Bad usability and failures in enterprise resource planning system.
	Deficiency in inventory.
	Repeated interruptions due to long set-up times.
	Too long or uncertain production lead times.
	Too wide product range.
	Quality failures.
	Obsolescence of inventory.
Interorganizational Processes	Customer demands shorter delivery times.
	Forecast failures.
	Failures in information transmission.
	Product ramp-up/ramp-down problems.
	Failures in product specifications.
	Deficiency of critical material component.
	Uncertain or long delivery times of suppliers.

Information gathering, transmission and filtering are important features in the risk identification phase. When information is shared effectively, risks can be identified more easily. In the networked environment, where business relationships are largely based on partnerships between organizations, effective information sharing between organizations is the key factor to decrease external and internal uncertainty. The risk identification phase is important for the understanding of current and future customer needs and uncertainties. If future needs and goals are shared and understood effectively among the network partners, it is highly probable that risks can be managed in a better manner.

Risk Assessment

In addition to risk identification, there is a need to be able to protect oneself against identified risk factors and to choose suitable management actions according to the situation at both company and network level. Therefore, it is important to be able to assess and prioritize risks. Below we will demonstrate a simple method for risk assessment. The main purpose of the method is to recognize the most important single risk events in terms of the consequence and probability dimensions of risk. This helps in allocating risk management resources effectively. Risk prioritization is possible only when the risks have been assessed. Here two key components of risk, the probability and the consequences of a risk event, are assessed separately on a five-class scale. Linguistic assessment is simple and it does not require much knowledge of probabilistic risk assessment methods.

The main purpose of the assessment method is to gain understanding or cognition of the environment and to help the management to take the required course of action. As a preliminary assessment of risks, the approach identifies the need for further investigation of the risks instead of taking risk reduction activities.

When assessing the subjective probability of a risk event, the company's own experience and other companies' performance are also likely to give direction in the assessment. In addition, it is essential to pay attention to environmental factors. The operational environment, which includes customers, suppliers, partners and competitors, forms the basis for the assessment. Also, evaluation of the potential environment (potential customers, suppliers, competitors and partners) supports the risk assessment phase. The evaluation of trends and particular signals can also offer valuable information and scenarios for the risk assessment. The trends and their effects may differ significantly depending on the company's position in the network.

Prioritization of Risk Management Actions

When the identified risks have been assessed, it is useful to present them in the form of a risk diagram (see Figure 4.3). The risk diagram gives an overall view upon all risks and identifies the most important risks requiring the most attention. Furthermore, it indicates whether the risks can be reduced by decreasing their probability or by their consequences.

After the identification and assessment of risks, it is necessary to consider carefully the possible strategies for the modes of management action. The generally used strategies include:

1. Risk transfer
2. Risk taking
3. Risk elimination
4. Risk reduction
5. Further analysis of individual risks

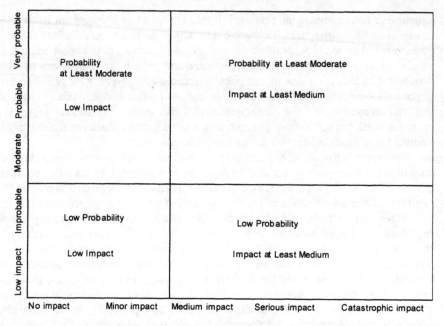

Figure 4.3 Risk Diagram

Risk Management Process in the Network Environment

In the network environment, risks can be managed especially by developing a common network strategy, best practice modes of action and contract policies. Risks can be analyzed jointly and common targets for development are likely to cause best results. The fundamental principle in network collaboration is to avoid interdependency with a single company. Effective information sharing among network partners can help in cost management and pricing, shorten lead-times, lower inventories and reduce failures caused by wrong or missing information.

In a network some risks may require companies' own control policies and others can be controlled best by joint effort. However, to be successful in the future, companies need to develop their external business processes and interorganizational information systems constantly. This requires common planning procedures, goals and deeper understanding of 'win-win' relationships in terms of sharing risks and opportunities. In this connection, the risk management process can be partially carried out together with the business partners. This is likely to mean that the risk management processes of individual companies are linked together. In the example in Figure 4.4, both companies have their individual risk management processes, which consist of the above mentioned phases. The companies operate in an environment where some risks and uncertainties are mutual.

Operational Environment

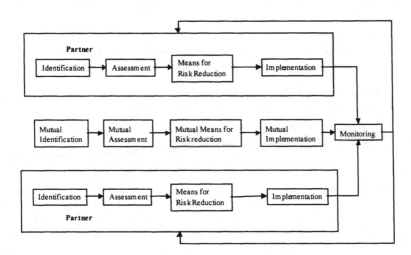

Figure 4.4 Risk Management Process in a Network Relationship

In a network relationship the companies are able to compare the identified risks independently and assess their common importance. Part of the companies' risks can be regarded as common but on the other hand, some risks in a single company have an effect on the other company's business. Collaborative risk identification and common consideration of risk control and management actions is a feature which distinguishes network risk management from traditional risk management approaches. Thus, a network relationship presupposes more advanced modes of action that help to monitor disturbances and uncertainties which arise from the whole network.

Risk analysis may take place in a risk management or strategy meeting, where common goals are evaluated. By the aid of a common audit it is possible to identify and reduce environmental uncertainty. Interorganizational risk analysis helps companies to compare and share knowledge on the causes and effects of risks and uncertainties. After identification, assessment and comparison, some of the identified risks and uncertainties may require common action or they may be involved in the company's own planning and decision making processes.

One important aspect of risk management is the timing of management actions. In principle, the company's or the network's risk management process should be continuous. Companies observe their operational environment and business processes and carry out decisions and planning procedures, which have an effect on risks. This may be difficult in practice and it is advantageous to restrict the process to certain situations. We have identified the following situations where risk analysis is at least worth considering:

1. At regular intervals (e. g. semi-annually) in company-wide risk audits.
2. At regular intervals (e. g. annually) in a network or a few companies-wide risk audits.
3. When a risk has occurred in the company or network.
4. Due to changes or increasing uncertainty in the business environment.
5. When a financial or possession arrangement takes place in the business environment.
6. At the beginning of large projects.
7. In connection with large investments or purchases.
8. In the selection and assessment of business partners.
9. Whenever requested by the business partner.

The activation of the risk management process is particularly associated with situations and events that are new and therefore, cause uncertainty. Such situations can be related to the establishment of a new network and changes in network relationships. Large purchases or projects and external signals, like customer or product specific investments and technology decisions also cause uncertainty. Identification of the company's internal signals may sometimes be a more convenient way to analyze uncertainty in the business environment. For example, disturbances in the company's internal business processes may be caused by weaknesses in interorganizational processes.

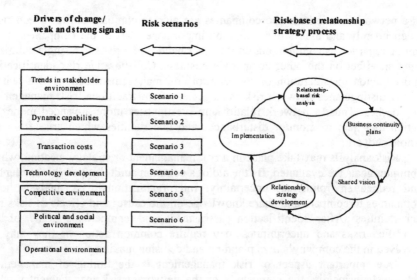

Figure 4.5 Generic Framework for Risk-Based Relationship Assessment

Figure 4.5 presents our view of a systemic relationship between the elements in a generic framework for risk-based supplier relationship assessment. As the relationship-based risk management process is a complex issue and it is difficult to produce a generic model for the process, we claim that it is necessary to understand the process in terms of drivers of change and weak and strong signals, different risk scenarios and the risk-based relationship strategy process. In the framework the first step is to identify the different environmental trends and signals which may cause changes and risk in relationships. These factors may be linked to such attributes as stakeholder environment, dynamic capabilities, transaction costs, technology development, competitive environment, political and social environment and the operational environment. These drivers formulate the understanding of the future plausible risk scenarios, which may have a certain effect on the suppler/customer relationships. Risk analysis is likely to reveal the most important relationship-based risk factors in terms of impact or possibility of risk scenarios. Organizational and interorganizational continuity plans will be developed for preventing and reducing the apparent risk scenarios. Scenario-based risk analysis and business continuity plans accompany the shared vision about the current and future conditions of a relationship. The aspiration of the process is to generate alternative, dynamic options for the network relationship strategy formulation and to test these options in terms of developed scenarios. The best strategic options will be chosen and implemented according to the associated organizational objectives, risks and benefits.

Implications

The emphasis on this chapter has been to illustrate the risk management in supplier relationships and networks. As research shows, network of ties among organizations are essential in order to manage risk in business relationships. The implications of social network researchers on strong and weak ties would provide important insights to the research subject. According to Levin and Cross (2002) strong ties are more likely to lead to the receipt of useful knowledge than weak ties because of inherent trust in the relationships. Further, trust in the relationships may also be involved in the weak ties, describing the relationships beyond the prior organizational relationships and providing access to non-redundant information. In terms of network relationships, both kinds of relationships need to be addressed in order to make organizations more effective in creating and transferring knowledge. The strength of weak ties seems to be essential in order to manage the risks of lock-in or hold-up. If organizations concentrate too narrowly on the existing relationships (strong ties) and are not able to take a broader view on the environment in which many trends, driving forces and scenarios arise, they are less likely to be able to respond effectively to the changing needs and requirements.

Due to the turbulent business environment, virtual enterprises have became emergent concepts in business. These represent dynamic networks. The tiers in the network make coordination difficult, as the responsibilities must be shared between the different level of suppliers. This kind of business model includes many business risks as well. Therefore, supply strategy and risk management related to supply management should be seen as an essential part of a company's business strategy.

References

Bazerman, M. (1998), *Judgement in Managerial Decision Making*, John Wiley & Sons, New York.

Bensaou, M. (1999), 'Portfolios of Buyer-supplier Relationships' *Sloan Management Review*, Summer, pp.35-44.

Coase, R. H. (1937), 'The Nature of the Firm' *Economica*, Vol.4, pp.386-405.

Cox, A. (1996), 'Relational Competence and Strategic Procurement Management: Towards an Entrepreneurial and Contractual Theory of The Firm' *European Journal of Purchasing and Supply Management*, Vol.2, No.1, pp.57-70.

Doz, Y, Hamel G. (1998), *Alliance Advantage: The Art of Creating Value Through Partnering* Harvard Business School Press.

Gadde, L-E. and Håkansson, H. (2001), *Supply Network Strategies*, John Wiley & Sons, Chichester.

Håkansson, H. and Johanson, J. (1993), 'The Network as a Governance Structure. Interfirm Cooperation beyond Markets and Hierarchies' in: Grabher, G. (ed.) *The Embedded Firm*, Routledge, London.

Hallikas, J., Karvonen, I, Pulkkinen, U., Virolainen, V-M. and Tuominen, M. (2002), 'Risk Management Processes in a Network Environment', *Proceedings of 12th International Working Seminar on Production Economics*, February 18th-22nd, 2002. Igls, Austria.

Harland, C.M. (1996), 'Supply Chain Management: Relationship, Chains and Networks', *British Journal of Management*, March, pp.63-80.

Heijden, K., Bradfield, R., Burt, G., Cairns, G., and Wright, G. (2002), *The Sixth Sense: Accelerating Organizational Learning with Scenarios*, John Wiley & Sons, Chichester.

Hertz, D. and Thomas, H. (1983), *Risk Analysis and its Applications* John Wiley & Sons, Chichester.

Hines, P. (1996), 'Network Sourcing in Japan', *The International Journal of Logistics Management*, Vol.7, pp.13-28.

Huttunen, A., Kyläheiko, K. and Virolainen, V-M. (2000), 'Identifying and Avoiding Risk in the Advanced Internet Technology Partnership', *Proceedings of the 5th International Symposium on Logistics*, Japan.

Kuusela, H. and Ollikainen, R. (1998), 'Riskit ja riskienhallinta-ajattelu' in: Kuusela, H. and Ollikainen, R. (eds.) (1998) *Riskit ja Riskienhallinta*. Tampere University Press. Tampere, pp.15-56.

Kyläheiko, K. (1995), 'Coping with Technologies: A Study on Economic Methodology and Strategic Management of Technology' Dissertation Thesis. Lappeenranta University of Technology.

Kyläheiko, K. (1999), 'Strategic Management of technology: An Economist's View' in: Ichimura, T., Tuominen, M. and Piippo, P. (eds.) *New Methods, Theories and Practices for Management of Technology*, (1999), Lappeenranta University of Technology, Studies in Industrial Engineering and Management, No.3. Lappeenranta.

Kyläheiko, K. and Miettinen, A. (1996), 'Technology Management and Entrepreneuship: Critical View', in Birley, S. and MacMillan, I. (eds.) *International Entrepreneurship*, Routledge, London, pp.39-58.

Levin, D.Z. and Cross, R. (2002), 'The Strength of Weak Ties You Can Trust: The Mediating Role of Trust in Effective Knowledge Transfer'. Best Papers *Proceedings of the Academy of Management*.

Martinez, M.T., Fouletier, P., Park, K.H., and Favler, J. (2001), 'Virtual Enterprise – Organization, Evolution, and Control' *International Journal of Production Economics*. Vol.74, pp.225-238.

Nishiguchi, T. (1994), *Strategic Industrial Sourcing*, Oxford University Press, Oxford.

Pfohl, H.C. and Buse, P. (2000), 'Inter-Organizational Logistics Systems in Flexible Production Networks. An Organizational Capabilities Perspective' *International Journal of Production & Logistics Management,* Vol.30, No.5, pp.388-401.

Reve, T. (1990), 'The Firm as a Nexus of Internal and External Contracts' in: Aoki, M, Gustafsson, B. Williamson, O. (eds.) *The Firm as a Nexus of Treaties.* Sage, London.

Sadgrove, K. (1997), *The Complete Guide to Business Risk Management,* Gower Publishing Limited, Aldershot.

Smeltzer, L.R. and Siferd, S.P. (1998), 'Proactive Supply Management: the Management of Risk'. *Journal of Purchasing and Materials Management,* Vol.34. No.1, pp.38-45.

Teece, D.J. (1984), 'Economic Analysis and Strategic Management' *California Management Review,* Vol.26, pp.87-110.

Teece, D.J. (1986), 'Profiting from Technological Innovation', *Research Policy,* Vol.18, pp.285-305.

Teece, D.J. (1988), 'Technological Change and the Nature of the Firm', in Dosi, G. et al, (eds.) *Technical Change and Economic Theory,* Pinter Publishers. London, pp.256-281.

Teece, D.J., Pisano, G. and Shuen, A. (1997), 'Dynamic Capabilities and Strategic Management'. *Strategic Management Journal,* Vol.18, No.7, pp.509-533.

Treleven, M. and Schweikhart, S.B. (1988), 'A Risk/Benefit Analysis of Sourcing Strategies: Single vs. Multiple Sourcing' *Journal of Operations Management,* Vol.4, pp.93-114.

Uusi-Rauva, E. (1998), 'Rahoituksen Riskit' in: Kuusela, H. and Ollikainen, R. (eds.) (1998), *Riskit ja Riskienhallinta.* Tampere University Press, Tampere. pp.201-222.

Virolainen, V-M. (1998), 'Motives, and Success Factors in Partnership Sourcing' Dissertation Thesis. Lappeenranta University of Technology.

Virolainen, V-M. and Tuominen, M. (1998), 'Hankintatoimeen Liittyvät Riskit Teollisuusyrityksessä' in: Kuusela, H. and Ollikainen, R. (eds.) (1998), *Riskit ja Riskienhallinta.* Tampere University Press, Tampere, pp.164-178.

Williamson, O.E. (1979), 'Transaction-Cost Economics: The Governance of Contractual Relations', *Journal of Law and Economics,* Vol.22, pp.232-261.

Williamson, O.E. (1991), 'Strategizing, Economizing, and Economic Organization', *Strategic Management Journal,* Vol.12, pp.75-94.

Zanger, C. (1997), 'Opportunities and Risk of Network Arrangements among Small and Large Firms within Supply Chain', *Proceedings of the 6th IPSERA conference,* Naples, Italy.

Chapter 5

Risk Focus Towards Customers

Dr. Clare Brindley

Introduction

The imperative to focus on the customer, the ultimate point in every supply chain, is driven by three developments. Firstly, radical changes in the nature of the marketplace for most products and services, including more intense competition and the globalisation of markets. Secondly, the increasing power of the customer, given the readily available and inexpensive access to information and direct communications, with almost unlimited suppliers in the market. As a consequence of this, the customer is seeking and is in a greater position to demand, increased value, including reduced prices, in the product and service package ultimately received. A number of supply chain developments and innovations have been driven by these demands from the customer in the marketplace. The concept of the value chain paralleling the supply chain is generally accepted in the literature. Members at every stage in the supply chain have responded to these developments. For example, the impetus to create supply chains, which are *lean* and *agile* is a typical response to improve efficiency and reduce costs, as are *single sourcing* agreements. As a consequence, supply chains face multiple varieties of structures, rapid changes, new innovations, new partnerships and hence, greater unpredictability and uncertainty about future changes. The increasing incidence of disintermediation within existing supply chains poses further threats, uncertainties and risks for all organizations irrespective of size or position within the supply chain. Describing or prescribing an 'appropriate' supply chain has become problematic, given both the contingency dimension (see Chapter 3) and state of flux inherent in most sectors. This leads to increased risk and a need for closer relationships because of the multiple relationships and multiple channels etc. that now operate within markets and hence the need for the formulation of a new model. The characteristics of this *Amorphous Supply Chain Model* are:

1. Inherent instability in the sense that none of the members may rely on the structures and relationships remaining stable for any length of time. This vulnerability of the supply chain to increasingly frequent and significant shocks is addressed by Christoper et al (2002).
2. Unpredictability, given that there are a wider set of factors potentially influencing the organization and its supply chain (e.g. impact of global communications and the consequent competition).

3. Dynamic and fundamental shifts in the basis of competition and hence competitive advantages (e.g. changes in manufacturing process technologies or in the financial transactions via the internet).

A key feature of the Model outlined is that the customer is part of the supply chain and hence can ameliorate risks as well as creating specific risk issues. The chapter discusses the challenges facing a customer centric supply chain and the risk management techniques that need to be utilised. It is proposed that ICT developments are responsible for the greater integration of the supply chain, the fusion of product and services marketing and the movement of the balance of power towards the consumer, the consequences of which are the need to develop a new approach to managing risk in the supply chain.

The Impact of ICTs on Supply Chains

The primary assumption underlying the development and application of information and communication technologies (ICT's) to the supply chain is that customers will have access to information that will reduce their risk in purchasing and hence, their cognitive dissonance. Thus, information and the manner in which it is utilised by the buyer to influence their behavior becomes increasingly important in determining market performance. Indeed, as Sheth and Sisodia (1997) argued technological advancements will allow consumers to control a far greater amount of the information and communication flow in the exchange process than ever before. As customers can gain access to a wider range of information, for example on products/services, they can check product features, compare prices, delivery times, warranties etc. thus reducing the risk usually associated with purchase decisions.

Conversely, it could be argued with the impact of ICT developments, risk could increase because of the lack of trust inherent in virtual relationships. The ICTs themselves are not necessarily capable of generating the necessary environment/capability to build trust and in many cases may be viewed as more of a deterrent, given the remoteness of the individual and the non-personal interactions. The adaptation of the service provision to generate a sense of personal interaction and gain consumer confidence and trust are important dimensions of the supply chain strategies. Organizations therefore need to develop strategies to build trust as a pre-requisite to successful relationships. Evidence would suggest that the initial focus needs to be directed towards the business to consumer link in preference to the business to business link, though the latter may increasingly become the more important as consumer confidence builds with conducting transactions using the new technologies. The importance of utilising and sustaining brand loyalty was identified as a key strategy in seeking to reassure existing and new customers to build trust and reduce transaction risk.

To attempt to answer how this emphasis of the customer dimension is impacting supply chains and risk, certain questions need to be addressed: how does the buyer determine the information to seek?; what factors encourage or constrain the search process?; how might information influence the decision to purchase? and can information and its consequent processing change the choice between competing services?

ICT driven supply chains are exemplified by the concept of disintermediation. The availability of ICT resources means that new links and relationships in the supply chain can occur. For example, an organization may utilise the web to directly promote and sell its products to potential customers at home and overseas. This could effectively exclude intermediaries such as sales and promotion agencies, currently supporting the sales of the organization to the marketplace. This same development may also enable the organization to offer its products and services to markets not previously entered or considered commercially viable in terms of the initial entry costs of establishing representation and agencies. Alternatively, the changes in technologies will enable the organization to source alternative support agencies in the market. Hence, rather than maintaining exclusive relationships with a single intermediary the organization may seek to negotiate with a number of intermediaries simultaneously, effectively enhancing competition and reducing dependency on specific partners. At the same time, the customer/consumer may be pulling the supply chain members to deliver products/services to them in a particular way.

For Graham and Hardaker (2000) the impact of the internet and its impact on competitive structures requires the development of new commercially viable supply chains. They argue that the supply chain can encompass suppliers, manufacturers, distributors and retailers. Through the internet they argue that a web based supply chain integrates suppliers, customers, intermediaries and marketspace in new ways. Correspondingly, Sarker et al (1995) argued that the internet would not make intermediaries in a marketing channel redundant. They concluded that rather than intermediaries being driven out by electronic commerce, cybermediaries will become common in electronic marketplaces (Sarker et al, 1995). However, Jeavons and Gabbott (2000, p.620) suggested that '[e]vidence in some sectors, especially service businesses, has indeed seen intermediaries disappear...' They go on to argue that as the environment becomes more turbulent, 'intermediaries can be cut out of channels or compete with channel partners in disintermediated situations' (Jeavons and Gabbott, 2000, p.621). Berthon et al (1999) too when assessing the impact of the internet on the structure of distribution channels, concluded that the traditional distribution channel will be replaced by distribution media and that there will be a rise in commodidization and in disintermediation. What does appear to be occurring is as Weber (2000, p.162) argues, the 'new medium of the internet is a marketing environment' and there is a need to cooperate with a broad network of market players. A network of players that, include a more powerful customer group. In virtual supply chains there is also the issue of who creates the customer? Is the customer self-generated in terms of their contact with the supplier i.e do they seek out the supplier rather than the supplier seeking them out? Market knowledge is now longer only in the hand s of the provider but also the potential purchaser.

Gilmour (1999) examined the use of technology as an appropriate means of integration within the supply chain. For Graham and Hardaker (2000, p.289) there may be 'formal and loose integration mechanisms' with the new source of value in the supply chain being information. Similarly, van Hoek (1998) described the increasing complexity of supply chains. He argued that ICT development will result in increased partnerships within the supply chain resulting in even greater complexity of the supply chain. In the virtual supply chain 'integration and control is not based on direct ownership but rather on connectivity in the flow of information' (van Hoek, 1998, p.509). The issue is then how does the customer access this information and what do the customers do when they access the information?

The *Amorphous Supply Chain Model* responds to De Kare-Silver's (1997) call for an innovative approach to managing supply chains. The chapter posits that the supply chain concept is now multi-disciplinary and encompasses themes of relationships, networks, channels and partnerships. It therefore agrees with van Hoek (1998, p.187) who argued that 'Supply Chain Management is characterized by control based on networking and integration of processes across functional, geographical and organizational interfaces.' The traditional marketing distribution channel it is argued is limiting and the supply chain in the era of the internet involves upstream and downstream relationships that are driven by information and the customer. Thus, the supply chain encompasses all the links as the goods or services move from production to consumption but unlike the concept of the marketing channel it is not seen as a linear movement. Moreover, the supply chain is seen as customer centric.

Supply-Chain Management, Relationship Marketing and Risk Management

Risk management is primarily concerned with removing the degree of ambiguity or uncertainty concerning the task environment and the decision specific variables. The decision-maker is also seeking to minimize the exposure to risks in terms of ensuring the 'correct' decision which simultaneously reduces the degree of risk exposure, minimizes the likelihood and scale of the potential negative consequences and maximizes the potential positive outcomes. Attention is increasingly been devoted to the strategies and actions that organizations may take to manage risks in this way. Mitchell (1995) classifies a series of actions relating to the purchasing function in terms of their scope for risk reduction whilst Croue (1997) suggests strategies linked to managing risks within the supply chain. Ritchie and Marshall (1993) suggest a strategic approach which emphasises the need for managers to gain greater *understanding* of their situation, ensure more effective *learning* by the organization and to generate the capacity to acquire and develop *experience* and expertise.

However, with the advent of ICTs and amorphosity in the supply chain the decision maker can be seen as a customer. There is then been inherently, a change to the decision maker being a customer. ICTs have through their interactivity elements involved the customer and this has led to customer empowerment. Information is no longer in the hands of a particular players in the supply chain and power has been dissipated or 'switched' away from the traditional organization to the customer.

The evolving field of relationship marketing, what Gronroos (1994, p.4) categorises as 'a paradigm shift', represents a further source of concepts, themes and initiatives that may contribute towards the management of risk. Relationship marketing is receiving considerable interest in the marketing literature [see Berry (1983), Gronroos (1994), Gummesson (1994), Kotler (1992) and Sheth (1995)]. Tynan (1997) provides a synopsis of Gronroos (1994, p.9) definition of relationship marketing which allows for the salient parameters of relationship marketing to be outlined, namely relationship development; identification of partners; involvement; the issue of mutual benefit; the nature of the exchange process; the keeping of promises; and the timescale of relationships. For Morgan and Hunt (1994) the emphasis of relationship marketing is categorized into four domains or partnerships,

> the buyer,
> the supplier,
> the lateral,
> the internal partnership.

This domain model has similarities to Payne's (1993) six markets model which identified six dimensions of relationship marketing as *supplier markets, influencer markets, referral markets, recruitment markets, internal markets* and *customer markets*. In essence the first five of these dimensions and the marketing activities associated with them have an impact on the final dimension of the customer market, what Tynan (1997, p.698) calls the 'focal relationship'. The elements and parameters linked to relationship marketing are readily transferred into the supply-chain management field. Whilst relationship marketing may be directed primarily towards the customer and the marketplace it is concerned with the other relationships within the supply-chain as these contribute significantly to the total added value received by the consumer. Conversely, the supply-chain management field may focus more attention on the efficiency and effectiveness of the total supply-chain though the ultimate measure of success is adding value to the final consumer.

The principles of supply-chain management and relationship marketing tackle both components of risk by reducing the degree of uncertainty and ambiguity through improved relationships and by ameliorating the likelihood and possible severity of the negative consequences from risky strategic decisions. Relationship marketing and supply-chain management also bind together the elements of quality, customer service and marketing the corporate image thus reducing organizational risk.

Customer Centricity

Supply Chain Management and relationship marketing, share a number of common features in terms of their objectives and the means used to achieve them. For example, the objective of reducing uncertainty, identifying potential risks and assessing the scale of these include Supply Chain Management and relationship marketing strategies designed to generate greater understanding of the needs of other partners involved in supplying and marketing to the final consumer. Risk management strategies are designed to elicit better quality information and improved understanding of the competitive environment to improve knowledge and understanding and hence resolve uncertainties and risks. In this respect, both Supply Chain Management and relationship marketing contribute to the determination of risks and to their management. A further dimension of complementarity involves the approaches to managing the risks identified with the objective of minimising the likelihood of their occurrence and the scale of the impact should they occur. Risk and crises management seek to formulate strategies to position the organization to best achieve these objectives. Such strategies may involve supply-chain partnerships, long-term financial security arrangements or developments in the product/market portfolio. These strategic developments would encompass strands of the supply-chain and relationship marketing strategies designed to develop effective relationships within the supplier markets, influencer markets and customer markets respectively.

The developments of collaborative arrangements, partnerships and other associations are all means of addressing the increased uncertainty and risks that emanate from the developments of ICTs and their impact on the supply chains, i.e. a form of risk management. In the complex patterns that are emerging within most supply chains it is probable that any one organization will simultaneously engage in multiple relationships often involving different forms and degrees of association and trust. Cox (1999, p.170) reinforces these conclusions following a review of the current orthodoxy in supply chain thinking compared to the thinking and practices required in the new environment, suggesting the need to 'develop close, collaborative, reciprocal and trusting (win-win), rather than arms-length and adversarial (win-lose), relationships with suppliers.'

The concept of the supply chain now incorporates the new dimensions of customer-centric, non-linear processes of adding value and multi-channel approaches to the customer. The supply chain can no longer be seen as a linear input-output model but one that may take on a variety of shapes. Butz and Goodstein (1996) predict that business is entering an era of service industry in which competitive advantage will focus on customer value-building and developing 'emotional bonds' with customers. It will become increasingly difficult to segregate market segments in terms of design, technology, service levels and pricing (e.g. delaying implementation of new products to lesser developed market segments or economies may cease to be a viable strategic alternative). Engel et al (1995) and Lapersonne et al (1995), cited in Anurit et al (1999), confirm that situational influences will not only change the behavior of consumers, sometimes involuntarily, but will equally compel business organizations to respond if they are to survive. Parkinson (1999), reviewing the *Agile Manufacturing Organization* suggests that manufacturing processes will become more consumer led and less manufacturer led and will be increasingly reliant on communications and the sharing of information amongst all partners in the supply chain including the customer. Goldman et al (1995) define this trend as the process of formulating *virtual partnerships* which will be a distinguishing feature of 'agile manufacturing.'

The role of trust within the marketing activities was reviewed by Ali and Birley (1998) in the context of entrepreneurs establishing new ventures. They identified four constructs for the term trust: enthusiasm, association, shared vision and forgiveness. These constructs are readily applicable to the organizations forging new supply chain relationships, developing new markets and tackling the demands of ICTs on products, services and processes. The strength of the relationship will depend on the shared vision of the partners involved in the supply chain; their enthusiasm to develop and sustain the relationship; the nature of the association and the sharing of information etc.; and the willingness to forgive minor transgressions from the letter or spirit of the arrangements. Indeed, Ali and Birley (1998) suggest that the strength of the relationship may be measured by the willingness of the partners to exercise forgiveness.

A New Model: The Amorphous Supply Chain

The literature illustrates the complementarity between the fields of risk management, relationship marketing and Supply Chain Management. Whilst relationship marketing may be directed primarily towards the customer and the marketplace (Berry, 1987; Gronroos, 1994; Gummesson, 1994) it is concerned with the other relationships within the supply-chain as these contribute significantly to the total added value received by the consumer. Conversely, the supply-chain management field may focus more attention on the efficiency and effectiveness of the total supply-chain (Bailey et al, 1998) though the ultimate measure of success is adding value to the final customer. In essence, the evolution of both these approaches identifies the need to address the supply-chain in its widest context to recognize the support that each may provide to the other in addressing risk management.

With the changes in the supply chain, illustrated by the concept of the *Amorphous Supply Chain*, it is important that such new models of business practices and processes, build upon the synergistic nature of the fields of risk, relationship and Supply Chain Management. Through this exploration, organizations will have the ability to cope more effectively with both the exogenous and endogenous sources of risk (Ritchie and Marshall, 1993) created by ICT driven developments and have the tools to develop more effective relationships with their business partners and customers.

Consideration of the supply chains within any sector requires consideration of the context within which the supply chain functions and the parameters that either limit or facilitate development and change. Diagram 5.1 illustrates the main dimensions of the contextual environment that supply chains operate within.

1. *Consumer Attitudes:* the attitudes and purchasing behavior of the customer/consumer are both potentially a determinant of and determined by

the other contextual variables influencing the *Amorphous Supply Chain*. Wider social, political and economic trends will influence consumer attitudes and consequently supply chains to differing degrees. The changes in a supply chain may pose consequences for particular groups of consumers interacting with the specific supply chain.

2. *Global competitive environment:* previously this may have had little or often no impact on any other than the larger organizations operating at the national or international level. Developments in ICT's, the reduction in barriers to international competition and encouragement of international trade by most governments has created opportunities and threats for most organizations irrespective of their size and nature of their local markets.

Diagram 5.1 Contextual Environment: Supply Chains

3. *Industry Structure:* significant structural changes have taken place at an increasingly rapid pace in most, if not all, industries in the last decade. The causal factors have included changes in the global competitive environment, technology developments, product/service innovation and changes in consumer attitudes and purchasing patterns. The terms dynamic, fluid and turbulent are often used to describe the nature of the changes occurring in the structure of industry, some facing more rapid and radical changes than others. Abecassis et al (2000, p.428) researching the relationships between firms as a result of IT developments in France and the US noted that 'a change in the technology realisation of one operation may affect the whole chain and even alter the position which the actor, who has promoted the innovation occupies in the market.' Hence changes in one stage or element in the process may have a significant influence throughout the chain and the commercial partnerships already in existence.

4. *Supply Chain Relations:* within the context of the developments in the global competitive environment and the changes in industry structure it is not

surprising to expect that such changes are reflected in the supply chain structures and the business relationships that they imply. The focus of the current research is seeking to explore such changes, especially those generated through changes in ICT's. A more detailed exposition of the nature of these changes and consideration of the implications for the supply chain strategies, structures, relationships and operations is developed in the remainder of this chapter.

5. *Organization:* it is evident that the organization needs to adapt to this changing context within which it operates. Recognising the major developments at the global and industry level and responding to these appropriately may well be important for all organizations wishing to survive in the long term. Even more critical is responding to the developments in the supply chain which may be generated, as this has a more direct impact on all organizations irrespective of size, sector or geographic location. Another facet of these changes is the implication for the risk exposure of the organization. The sources of risk, the level of exposure, the probability of occurrence, the scale of the consequences and the approaches to effective risk management will be subject to change under this new scenario. Developing appropriate strategies, managing new relationships with other businesses, changing the relationships with existing customers, whilst introducing new product and process innovations, demands new structures, information databases, managerial skills and competencies. The case studies employed in the empirical research for this thesis are designed to explore in a qualitative sense these issues and the manner in which they are being addressed.

The change in these contextual factors suggested a closer examination of the developments of the supply chain characteristics. It is evident that consumers in both product and service markets are being influenced by changes not only in the structure of the supply chain but equally the changing relationships within this structure. They may, for example, receive new added value offerings from members of the chain with whom they already interface (e.g. financial services) or from members who have previously been more distant in the chain (e.g. offering supply of electricity as well as the supply of appliances). These developments to the supply chain may be encapsulated through the presentation of two conceptual models, the *linear supply chain* and the *amorphous supply chain*.

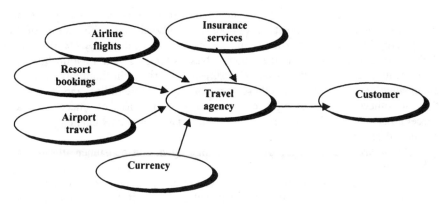

Diagram 5.2 Linear Supply Chain Model: Travel

The previous developments in the contextual factors resulted in the supply chain model being oriented in a manner, which is linear in terms of the value added contribution that the member of the chain provides at each successive stage. In the example shown in Diagram 5.2 the customer of the tourism product consumes the added value from a number of contributors who channel their contributions through the conduit to the consumer, in this case the travel agent. A typical feature of this model is that the consumer is generally purchasing a composite product/service and has limited choice over the elements within this or who contributes these. Changes in the context within which this supply chain functions, especially the developments of ICT's, provide the consumer with radically different sets of choices about the composition of the service and the respective contributors.

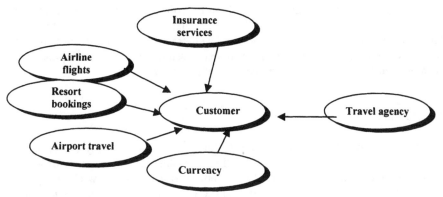

Diagram 5.3 Amorphous Supply Chain: Travel

Diagram 5.3 indicates that the consumer may make individual choices about each of the elements or indeed may still choose to select the travel agent to provide the majority of the service or opt to negotiate certain elements directly with the individual supplier.   This set of options not only changes the nature of the relationship between the consumer and the members of the supply chain but also their relationships one with the other.   New strategies and relationships and agreements need to be established to ensure their survival in the evolving supply chain situation. In some sectors these changes may be more radical and more rapid than in others. These changes engender a greater sense of uncertainty and perceptions of risks. The management of such risks poses new challenges for the business organization.

The nature and influence of these change agents on consumer attitudes and behavior will therefore be contingent on the supply chain model and relationships extant at that time within the market segment in question, exemplified by the *Amorphous Supply Chain Model*.   The selection of ICT developments as a significant change in contextual factors, *arguably* the most important currently, is designed to evaluate the emerging contingency variables and the responses in consumer attitudes in differing market segments. In short, the same developments in ICTs will produce differing influences on consumer attitudes contingent on the nature of the intervening supply chain, its structures, relationships, operations and its interface with the specific market segment.

The cluster of contextual variables relating to the development of technology provides the central focus of the research with a particular emphasis on the ICT developments.   Attention is directed towards these variables and the potential strategic implications they may have for the organization and the manner in which these are subsequently addressed.   Two particular dimensions of the strategic implication/response relationship are explored. The extent to which change agents are modifying the established risk profiles and frameworks within which the business operates and similarly the impact on the established relationships with other organizations in the supply chain. The evolving fields of risk management and relationship marketing are explored both in terms of how these may contribute to the strategic issues highlighted and the ways that they are being used at present. The outcomes to this process of strategic development and responsiveness may be addressed in terms of changes in customer/consumer attitudes and purchasing behavior and in relation to the performance of the organization.

Conclusions

It has been argued that the distinctive features of modern supply chains is that their structure, the inherent processes and relationships are increasingly driven by the customer/consumer.   The customer-centric *Model* poses new challenges for the organization in relation to defining potential customers and new market segments.   The capability to categorize customers into groups according to common traits or consumer behavior or purchasing patterns may prove increasingly difficult. New approaches to marketing communications utilising the ICT capabilities may be necessary to ensure effectiveness. A further dimension of the more customer-centric approach is the potential to directly involve the customer in the product development and design. For example, the customer may be involved in the detailed specification of the Bentley car they are purchasing prior to production, enabling decisions on engine, body style, colour etc. via a structured internet enquiry facility which would also provide price and delivery details.

The importance of trust has arguably been the foundation of the evolving fields of risk and relationship management (e.g. Morgan and Hunt, 1994). It has been argued that trust through the impact of ICT developments and the manner in which organizations need to develop strategies to build trust as a pre-requisite to successful relationships. The evidence suggests that the initial focus needs to be directed towards the business to consumer link in preference to the business to business link, though the latter may increasingly become the more important as consumer confidence builds with conducting transactions using the new technologies. For example, the importance of utilising and sustaining brand loyalty maybe a key strategy in seeking to reassure existing and new customers and to build trust. ICTs themselves are not necessarily capable of generating the necessary environment/capability to build trust and in many cases may be viewed as more of a deterrent, given the remoteness of the individual and the non-personal interactions. The adaptation of the service provision to generate a sense of personal interaction and gain consumer confidence and trust are important dimensions of the product/service and marketing communications strategies. The key facet is the need to develop new forms of relationships with supply chain partners and the final consumers. The nature of these new relationships or partnering arrangements are at a formative stage for many companies but more developed for others. The integration of a number of disciplines provides a more integrated and robust set of policy suggestions for organizations.

References

Abercassis, C., Caby, L. and Jaeger, C. (2000), 'IT and coordination modes: the case of the garment industry in France and US', *Journal of Marketing Management*, Vol.16, pp.425-447.

Ali, H. and Birley, S. (1998), 'The role of trust in the marketing activities of entrepreneurs establishing new ventures', *Journal of Marketing Management*, Vol.14, pp.749-763.

Anurit, J., Newman, K. and Chansarkar, B. (1999), 'Consumer behavior of luxury automobile: a comparative study between Thai and UK customers' perspectives', *Discussion Paper Series: Marketing* No.1 April 1999 Middlesex University Business School.

Bailey, P. Farmer, D., Jessop, D. and Jones, D. (1998), *Purchasing Principles and Management* 8th edition, Financial Times/Pitman Publishing, London.

Berry, L. (1983), 'Relationship Marketing', in (eds.) Berry, L.L., Shostack, G.L. and Upsay,G., *Emerging Perspectives on Services Marketing*, AMA, Chicago pp.25-28.

Berthon,P., Lane, N., Pitt, L. and Watson, R.T. (1998), 'The world wide web as an industrial marketing communication tool; models for the identification and assessment of opportunities', *Journal of Marketing Management*, Vol.14, No.7, pp.691-704.

Butz, E.H. and Goodstein, D.L. (1996), 'Measuring customer value: gaining the strategic advantage', *Organizational Dynamics*, Vol.24, No.3, p.63.

Christopher, M., McKinnon, A., Sharp, J., Wilding, R., Peck, H., Chapman, P., Jüttner, U. and Bolumole, Y. (2002), *Supply Chain Vulnerability*, Cranfield University.

Cox, A. (1999), 'Power, value and Supply Chain Management', *Supply Chain Management* Vol.4, No.4, pp.167-175.

Croue, C. (1997), 'Marketing international de l'achat contexte et mise en oeuvre: Le cas de la societe Wiggit Ltd', *Decisions Marketing* No.11, Mai-Aout, pp.51-60.

De Kare-Silver, M. (1999), *e-Shock 2000*, Palgrave, Basingstoke.

Engel, J.F, Blackwell, R.D. and Miniard, P. (1990), *Consumer Behavior* 8th Edition, Dryden Press, London.

Gilmour, P. (1999), 'A strategic audit framework to improve supply chain performance', *Journal of Business and Industrial Marketing*, Vol.14, No.5/6, pp.355-363.

Goldman, S. Nagel, R. and Preiss, K. (1995), *Agile competitors and virtual organizations* Van Nostrand Reinhold, New York, NY.

Graham, G. and Hardaker, G. (2000), 'Supply-chain management across the internet', *International Journal of Physical Distribution and Logistics Management*, Vol.30, No.3/4, pp.286-295.

Gronroos, C. (1994), 'From marketing mix to relationship marketing: towards a paradigm shift in marketing', *Management Decision*, Vol.32, No.2, pp.4-20.

Gummeson, E. (1994), 'Is relationship marketing operational?', *Proceedings of 23rd EMAC Conference*, Maastricht.

Jeavons, C. and Gabbott, M. (2000), 'Trust, brand equity and brand reality in internet business relationships: an interdisciplinary approach', *Journal of Marketing Management*, Vol.16, No.6, pp.619-634.

Kotler, P. (1992), 'Marketing's new paradigm: what's really happening out there?', *Planning Review*, Vol.20, No.5, pp.50-52.

Lapersonne, E., Laurent, G. and Le Goff, J. (1995), 'Consideration sets of size one: an empirical investigation of automobile purchases', *International Journal of Research in Marketing*, Vol.12, pp.55-66.

Mitchell, V.W. (1995), 'Organizational risk perception and reduction: a literature review', *British Journal of Management*, Vol.6, pp.115-133.

Morgan, R.M. and Hunt, S.D. (1994), 'The commitment-trust theory of relationship marketing', *Journal of Marketing*, Vol.58 July pp.20-38.

Parkinson, S. (1999), 'Agile Manufacturing' *Work Study*, Vol.48, No.4, pp.134-137.

Payne, A. (1993), *The Essence of Services Marketing*, Prentice-Hall International, Hemel Hempstead, U.K.

Ritchie R.L. and Marshall D.V. (1993), *Business Risk Management*, Chapman and Hall, London.

Sarker, M., Butler, B. and Steinfeld, C. (1995), 'Intermediaries and cybermediaries: a continuing role for mediating players in the electronic marketplace', *Journal of Computer-Mediated Communication*, Vol.1, No.3.

Sheth, J.N. (1995), 'Searching for a definition of relationship marketing', *3rd International Colloqium in Relationship Marketing*, Monash University, Melbourne, Australia, Proceedings, pp.105-111.

Tynan, C. (1997), 'A review of the marriage analogy in relationship marketing', *Journal of Marketing Management*, Vol.13, No.7, pp.695-703.

van Hoek, R.I. (1998), 'Logistics and virtual integration, postponement, outsourcing and the flow of information', *International Journal of Physical Distribution and Logistics Management*, Vol.28, No.7, pp.508-523.

Chapter 6

Supply Chain Risk Management

Ulf Paulsson

Background

The chain of transport and storage activities from first supplier to end customer has during the years changed character and gradually developed from a step-wise chain via a logistical chain into a supply chain (Cooper et al, 1997). This development has had many consequences. The one that is studied here is the *new and changed risks interest in the supply chain*. The number and character of the risks and the total risk exposure, change as the chain changes. Since the supply chain is made up of a number of links, where each link normally is an independent company, company risks change as well.

Company risks of different kinds have been more and more in focus during the last decade both in the media (Simons, 1999) and as a research topic. In some countries new legislation has been put forward making it compulsory to include risk assessment information in annual reports. The tragic events of 11th September have further stressed the vulnerability of our modern society and of its flows of material and information (Greenberg, 2002). An often heard opinion is that organizations as well as society as a whole in the future need access to more knowledge and will need to become more proactive to be able to handle those risks (Rasmussen and Svedung, 2000).

Risk is defined by The Royal Society 'as the probability that a particular adverse event occurs during a stated period of time, or results from a particular challenge' (The Royal Society, 1992, p.2) – in other words the probability that an event with negative consequences will occur. To be able to handle risks, risk management is needed. The same source defines *risk management* as 'the process whereby decisions are made to accept a known or assessed risk and/or the implementation of actions to reduce the consequences or probability of occurrence' (The Royal Society, 1992, p.5). Formulated in another way: 'Risk management means taking deliberate action to shift the odds in your favour' (Borge, 2001).

A number of trends during the last decade have affected the supply chain risk situation. One is that the supply chain should be lean, another that it should be agile as well (Christopher and Towill, 2000; Mason-Jones et al, 2000). A third trend is outsourcing resulting in more links in the chain. Single sourcing is still another trend and of course there is the issue of globalisation. All these trends lead to increased vulnerability (Juettner et al, 2002; Kajüter, 2003). For instance: By making the chain more lean through eliminating buffer stocks this will surely increase productivity but it will also, if nothing else is done, have less possibilities to handle disturbances. The existence of *a new risk situation in supply chains* is now becoming realized by more and more researchers and practitioners (Juttner et al, 2003; Kajüter, 2003).

Supply Chain Risk Management – A New Research Area

Supply Chain Management has been an established research area for at least ten years now and Risk Management for much longer than that. The development of the supply chain described in the previous section has made it necessary to get inspiration for new ways of handling the vulnerability in the chain and Risk Management has become an important area of inspiration. A new research area called Supply Chain Risk Management has developed.

Figure 6.1   Supply Chain Risk Management as the Intersection of Supply Chain Management and Risk Management

Today there exists no generally agreed definition of *supply chain risk management*. One definition suggested by Norrman and Lindroth (2002, p.7) is: 'Supply chain risk management is to collaboratively with partners in a supply chain apply risk management process tools to deal with risks and uncertainties caused by, or impacting on, logistics related activities or resources.' This definition which deals with collaborative situations will here be complemented with situations when a single company/actor in the chain is engaged in risk management issues on its own. This will lead to the following definition – a definition that will by used as a guide in this chapter:

> *Supply chain risk management is to, collaboratively with partners in a supply chain or on your own, apply risk management process tools to deal with risks and uncertainties caused by, or impacting on, logistics related activities or resources in the supply chain.*

The literature about supply chain risk management consists of scientific articles, conference papers and some books, reports and dissertations. The prime source for the presentation of new, quality-controlled knowledge is scientific journals and the study has therefore been delimited to articles in such journals.

Objectives

To be able to 'catch and describe' the present knowledge within the area of supply chain risk management as it is presented in scientific journals, relevant articles need to be identified and structured both by their external characteristics and by their contents. Consequently, the objectives of this chapter are, within the research area of supply chain risk management, to:

1. Identify existing scientific journal articles
2. Structure those articles by their external characteristics and
3. Structure them by their contents

Delimitations

Only published scientific journal articles are considered because they have passed the quality control executed by the journals' editorial board. Only articles written in English have been considered.

Method

Search for articles The search for articles has been conducted in several different ways.

1. Through searches in databases
   The searches were carried out in July and August, 2003.
   a. Articles have been searched for in *ELIN@Lund*[1]. The alternative 'All fields' has been chosen which means that the concept/s should exist in the 'Title, Journal title, ISSN, Author, Key words or Abstract.' No time restrictions (all years were used). Search in 'all' collections i.e. e-Journals, Ebsco Databases, IEE/IEEE Proceedings, e-Print archives, ABI/Inform Database and IEE/IEEE Standards were conducted. The searches have been undertaken using the following key words:
   Supply chain risk management *(1 hit)**
   and on the following combinations of key words:

Notes

[1] Elin@Lund is the electronic library information navigator of Lund University in Sweden. In April 2003 ELIN had, via agreements with a very large number of publishers and other information providers, access to about 10 million records.

Supply Chain Management + Risk management *(20 hits)**
Supply chain + Risk management *(55 hits)**
Supply chains + Risk management *(28 hits)**
Supply chain + Risk *(260 hits)*
Supply chains + Risk *(156 hits)*
Logistics + Risk *(336 hits)*
Supply chain + Risks *(116 hits)*
Supply chains + Risks *(67 hits)*
Logistics + Risks *(123 hits)*
Business continuity management + Supply chain *(No hits)*
Business continuity management + Logistics *(No hits)*
Business continuity planning + Supply chain *(1 hit)**
Business continuity planning + Logistics *(No hits)*

A search directly in the database *ABI/Inform*, which seemed to be the most relevant database was also conducted, on the combination of the two concepts 'Supply chain' AND 'Risk management' *(42 hits)*.

A search in *ScienceDirect* (Elsevier database for research journals) on the combination of the two concepts: 'Supply chain' AND 'Risk management' *(31 hits)*.

A search in *Scirus* (Elsevier database for scientific information only) on the alternative 'journal articles only', 'Exact phrases'. The search was conducted on the combination of the two concepts: 'Supply chain' AND 'Risk management' *(143 hits)*.

In the beginning of September 2003 a 'My Elin' on the five search profiles marked with an * in search 'a' above was created. It means that information about new references in the updated databases that match the search profiles are sent automatically by e-mail.

These different searches in databases, had in October 2003, resulted in more than 1200 hits. Many of them were duplicates.

2. Through searches in journals
    The contents of each of five central journals within the areas of Supply Chain Management, Logistics and Purchasing was searched for the period 1990 from (or if the journals starting year was later, the starting year) – up to August 2003. The chosen journals were:
    European Journal of Purchasing and Supply Management (1994 onwards).
    Journal of Business Logistics (1990 onwards).
    International Journal of Logistics (1998 onwards).
    International Journal of Physical Distribution and Logistics Management (1990 onwards).
    Supply Chain Management: An International Journal (1996 onwards).

3. Through the ISCRIM network
    Articles have also been found through the ISCRIM (International Supply

Chain Risk Management) network. Partly through their workshops, partly through their newsletter, which is distributed four times a year and partly through personal contacts within the network.

All the search activities had in October 2003 resulted in around 400 unique articles.

Selection of articles   Step 1: Trade journals were excluded and only 'hits' with a specified author mentioned were considered.   Step 2: A look at the title and if it seemed as if the article could deal with some aspect of 'supply chain risk management' the abstract was read. If the abstract also seemed relevant, the full text version was if possible printed out. After this step 141 articles were still found to be relevant. 131 of them were printed out in a full-text version. Ten have yet to be printed out as a full text copy.   Step 3: All the 131 full-text articles were assessed on two aspects:

1. it must *fit in on the chosen definition* of Supply Chain Risk Management (presented earlier), which meant that logistics related activities or resources had to be included in the article.
2. the issue of Supply Chain Risk Management had to be *central or rather central in the article* and not just a marginal issue.

The articles that did not fulfill those two conditions were excluded.

Step 4: Only the earliest publication was considered when the same article was published in more than one journal.   This left 80 unique articles and these were all reviewed.

Missed articles   The search for articles has mainly been based on searches in databases and since many databases have a limit of how far back in time they go this means that a number of older articles may have been excluded. Searches in databases have been based on particular concepts and combinations of concepts that should be present in the title or abstract or be used as a keyword. It means that if the article author had chosen to use some other concept, like 'cost' instead of 'risk', that article will be excluded, although its contents might well fit the required parameters. Finally, searches have been conducted in a number of important databases but far from all databases that might include relevant articles about supply chain risk management have been accessed.

Dimensions for structuring   The articles will be structured both by their external characteristics and by their contents. The *external characteristics* that will be looked at are: printing year, journal, author and author nationality.

To be able to characterize the *contents* of the articles within the area of Supply Chain Risk Management we need to look closer at the three dimensions: Supply Chain, Risk and Management. Robert Lindroth and Andreas Norrman present in another chapter (Chapter 2) in this book 'A Framework for Assessing and Positioning Supply Chain Risk Issues' in the form of a model covering those three dimensions. This model is presented below in Figure 6.2 and will here be used for structuring the contents of the articles.

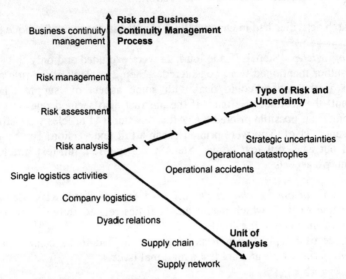

Figure 6.2   A Framework for Assessing and Positioning Supply Chain Risk Issues (see Chapter 2)

For each dimension in the Model a number of *dimension elements* are given. For instance the dimension Type of Risk and Uncertainty has the following three elements: Operational accidents, operational catastrophes, and strategic uncertainties.

To the three dimensions in the Model a fourth dimension will be added and that is the interest *direction* in the chain. Are we looking primarily upstream or primarily downstream? Or if we look at the supply chain from the perspective of a single firm in the chain: are we looking at the supply side, internal or the demand side? Here consequently the elements are: upstream, downstream, supply side, internal and demand side.

Article External Characteristics

Printing Year

The oldest article is from 1983 and the second oldest from 1987, there Is then a jump to 1995. The period 1995-2003 is then illustrated in Figure 6.3 below.

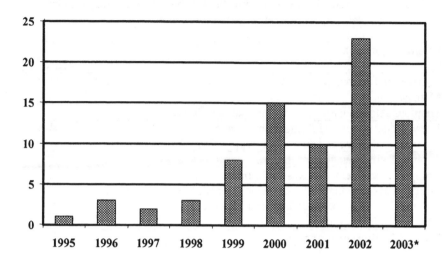

Figure 6.3   The number of Published Scientific Articles within Supply Chain Risk Management 1995-2003 (*Part of 2003 only)

The research area of Supply Chain Risk Management appears to be a fairly new area. The number of articles is clearly increasing during the period, indicating a research field under expansion. However, we must remember that the total number of produced journal articles in the world tends to rise each year.

Scientific Journal

The 80 articles were published in 53 different journals. Forty-two of the journals had just one article, eleven had two or more. The International Journal of Physical Distribution and Logistics Management had the most published articles, with eight articles. Four of them were written by the same author (Göran Svensson).

Table 6.1   Scientific Journals and the number of Published Articles within Supply Chain Risk Management

Scientific journal:	Number of articles:
International Journal of Physical Distribution & Logistics Management	8
Supply Chain Management: An International Journal	5
International Journal of Production Economics, Journal of Business Logistics, and Journal of Supply Chain Management	4
Supply Chain Management Review	3
Computers & Operations Research, International Journal of Logistics Management, Management Science, Manufacturing & Service Operations Management and PRACTIX	2
42 other different journals	1
Total: 53 different journals	**80**

Author and Country

The 80 reviewed articles were written by 133 different authors. One person was engaged in the writing of seven articles, one five articles, seven persons two articles and finally 124 persons one article.

Table 6.2 The number of Article Contributions for different Authors

Author:	Number of article contributions:
Göran Svensson	7
George Zsidisin	5
Vipul Agrawal, Clare Brindley, Lisa Ellram, Eric Johnson, Hau Lee, Bob Ritchie and Andy Tsay	2
124 other authors	1
Total: 133 authors	**150 article contributions**

On average an article had $150/80 = 1.88$ authors. 28 articles had one author, 38 had two, 10 had three and 4 finally had four authors. No article had more than four authors.

The articles were written mainly by persons living (i.e. working at a university or at a company) in the United States or in the United Kingdom but contributions came from 19 different countries.

Table 6.3 The number of Article Contributions for different Author Countries

Country:	Number of article contributions:
United States	72
United Kingdom	23
Sweden	9
China and Finland	7
Canada	6
Germany and Taiwan	4
Belgium, Netherlands and South Korea	3
Australia	2
7 other countries	1
Total: 19 countries	**150 article contributions**

Article Contents Characteristics

The contents of the 80 journals are structured by help of the model presented in Figure 6.2. The Model included three dimensions: Unit of analysis, Type of risk and uncertainty and risk and Business continuity management process (here called management process). A fourth dimension – 'Direction' – was added. Each dimension includes a number of characterizing elements. Each article has been categorized in the four dimensions by help of these dimension elements. For most articles only one element for each dimension has been chosen for the classification but for some articles two or more elements were used.

Unit of Analysis

Unit of analysis is described by help of the five elements: Single logistics activities, Company logistics, Dyadic relations, Supply chain and Supply network. Supply chain means that at least three links in the chain are studied with an integrating approach. Supply network is regarded as a supply chain with high complexity.

Table 6.4   Number and Percentage of Unit of Analysis Elements for the 80 Articles

Unit of analysis element	Number of articles	Percentage of the articles
Single logistics activities	0	0
Company logistics	1	1.3%
Dyadic relations	33	41.3%
Supply chain	49	61.3%
Supply network	8	10.0%
Total classification number:	**91**	

On average each article is classified by the help of 1.14 (91/80) elements. No articles deal with *single logistics activities* and only one with *company logistics*. This is not surprising as the area of the study is supply chain risk management. The most frequent element is *supply chain,* which fits well with the earlier stated definition of supply chain risk management, as does the element *supply network*. More surprising is that more than 40 per cent of the articles are classed as *dyadic relations*.

Type of Risk

Type of risk is described by help of the three elements: Operational accidents, Operational catastrophes and Strategic uncertainties.

Table 6.5 Number and Percentage of Type of Risk Elements for the 80 Articles

Type of risk element	Number of articles	Percentage of the articles
Operational accidents	30	37.5%
Operational catastrophes	32	40.0%
Strategic uncertainties	54	67.5%
Total classification number:	**116**	

Strategic uncertainties are the most frequent element followed by operational catastrophes and operational accidents. On average 1.45 element is chosen for each article.

Management Process

Risk and business continuity management process is described by help of the four elements: Risk identification/Risk analysis, Risk assessment, Risk management and Business continuity management.

Table 6.6 Number and Percentage of Management Process Elements for the 80 Articles

Management process element	Number of articles	Percentage of the articles
Risk identification/risk analysis	10	12.5%
Risk assessment	14	17.5%
Risk management	77	96.3%
Business continuity management	6	7.5%
Total classification number:	107	

The element *risk management* is here by far the most frequent element – only three out of 80 articles are not classified as risk management articles. One explanation is that risk management covers very many different kinds of risk activities, another that the purpose of many of the articles is to develop new models/new theories that will make the management process more efficient and effective.

Direction

The chain interest direction in each article is described by the help of five elements: Upstream, Downstream, Supply side, Internal and Demand side. The last three elements are used when the supply chain issues are studied from the point of view of an individual company in the chain, the two first elements are used when focus is on the supply chain as an entity and not on any specific link.

Table 6.7 Number and Percentage of Direction Elements for the 80 Articles

Direction element	Number of articles	Percentage of the articles
Uppstream	9	11.3%
Downstream	16	20.0%
Supply side	50	62.5%
Internal	8	10.0%
Demand side	39	48.85%
Total classification number:	122	

Supply side and *demand side* are the two most frequently used elements here. This means that most articles look at the supply chain from the perspective of an individual company. Since supply side dominates it might mean that the problems are experienced to be bigger at the supply side than at the demand side and/or that there are greater possibilities to handle these sort of problems.

Final Comments

Risk Sources and the Articles

Based on the reviewed articles five different *risk sources* have been identified. They are presented below in Figure 6.4 where they also are linked to the three different types of risk elements presented earlier. Each risk source will now be discussed and exemplified by suitable articles from the review.

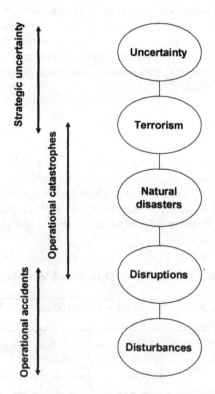

Figure 6.4   A Model of different Risk Sources and their Links to the three Types of Risk Elements

Uncertainty exists within a number of areas. A great number of the articles deal with the issue of how to handle *supply* side uncertainty. A classic here is the article by Kraljic from 1983, where the author presents a four-box-model that can be used to manage supply risks. Articles about supply uncertainty often focus on dyadic relations (like Svensson 2000; Zsidisin 2001) and are using methods like risk-pooling (Tagaras, 1999) and contracting (Eppen, 1997; Agrell, 2003). They are also in many cases applying mathematical models (Agrawal, 2000; Arcelus, 2002).

Uncertainty in *demand* is also dealt with in a number of articles (Cohen, 2000; Christopher, 2000). These articles are also often, like the supply articles, focusing on dyadic relations and applying mathematical models (Applequist, 2000; Kevin, 1999). There are also articles dealing with *both* uncertainty on the supply and demand side (Ritchie and Brindley, 2000; Johnson, 2001; Harland et al, 2003). Some articles are mentioning the *weather* as a source of uncertainty (Luc, 1997) and there are also articles stressing the importance of *political uncertainty* (Umali-Deininger, 2001 and Tsai, 2002).

Terrorism is a 'new' source of risk, at least when it comes to articles within supply chain risk management. None of the reviewed articles published before September 11, 2001 were explicitly dealing with terrorism. After that date there has been several articles about terrorism and its threat to the supply chain flows (Sheffi, 2001; Lee, 2003).

Flooding, *earth-quakes* and *hurricanes* are examples of traditional *natural disasters*. A new kind of natural disaster, at least in the reviewed articles, is the spread of *international illnesses* among humans and animals like SARS and BSE (Martha, 2002). Therefore, quality control and the ability to track and trace are of great importance, especially in the food chain (Ropkins, 2000; Fearne, 2001; Schroeder, 2002).

Disruptions and how to handle them are treated in a number of articles. Serious disruptions can lead to bankruptcies (Warren, 2000; Rice, 2003) and even catastrophes (Burrage, 1995).

Disturbances are also examined in a number of articles. Everything from minor everyday disturbances (Boronico, 1997; Owens, 2002) to the year 2000 problem (Jones, 1999).

Supply Chain Risk Management: A Complex and Expanding Area

The article review has pointed out that the area of supply chain risk management is a complex area covering many different kinds of problems and solutions. The area could be described as an area with many sub-areas but sub-areas that have one thing in common and that is that they are managing flow-related risks in the supply chain.

In the beginning of this chapter a number of trends were mentioned that tend to make the supply chain more vulnerable. The article review has added other vulnerability causes like natural disasters, terrorist threats, rapid consumer demand changes, shorter product lives and in many other aspects a more complex and vulnerable society than before. This means that for both internal and external reasons, supply chains and the individual links in those chains today tend to be more exposed to risks and indeed newer kind of risks. It is therefore reasonable to believe that in the future there will be an increasing interest in supply chain risk management issues, both as a practical application and as a research area.

Reviewed Articles

Abernathy, F.H. et al, (2000), 'Retailing and supply chains in the information age,' *Technology in Society*, Vol.22, No.1.

Agrawal, V. and Seshadri, S. (2000a), 'Impact of Uncertainty and Risk Aversion on Price and Order Quantity in the Newsvendor Problem,' *Manufacturing and Service Operations Management*, Vol.2, No.4.

Agrawal, V. and Seshadri, S. (2000b), 'Risk intermediation in supply chains,' *IIE Transactions*, (September).

Agrell, P.J., Lindroth, R. and Norrman, A. (2003), 'Risk, information and incentives in telecom supply chains,' *International Journal of Production Economics*, In Press.

Applequist, G.E., Pekny, J.F. and Reklaitis, G.V. (2000), 'Risk and uncertainty in managing chemical manufacturing supply chains,' *Computers and Chemical Engineering*, Vol.24, No.9-10.

Arcelus, F.J., Pakkala, T.P.M. and Srinivasan, G. (2002), 'A purchasing framework for B2B pricing decisons and risk-sharing in supply chains,' *Decision Sciences*, Vol.33, No.4.

Boronico, J.S. and Bland, D.J. (1996), 'Customer service: the distribution of seasonal food products under risk,' *International Journal of Physical Distribution and Logistics Management*, Vol.26, No.1.

Bowersox, D.J., Stank, T.P., and Daugherty, P.J. (1999), 'Lean launch: managing product introduction risk through response-based logistics,' *Journal of Product Innovation Management*, Vol.16, No.6.

Burrage, K. (1995), 'Risk management in safety critical areas,' *International Journal of Pressure Vessels and Piping*, Vol.61, No.2-3.

Christopher, M. (2000), 'The agile supply chain,' *Industrial Marketing Management*, Vol.29, No.1.

Cohen, M.A. et al, (2000), 'Saturn's supply-chain innovation: High value in after-sales service,' *Sloan Management Review*, Vol.41, No.4.

Eppen, G.D. and Ananth. V.I. (1997), 'Backup Agreements in Fahion Buying – The Value of Upstream Flexibility,' *Management Science*, Vol.43, No.11.

Fearne, A., Hornibrook, S. and Dedman, S. (2001), 'The management of perceived risk in the food supply chain: a comparative study of retailer-led beef quality assurance schemes in Germany and Italy,' *The International Food and Agribusiness Management Review* , Vol.4, No.1.

Fisher, M. and Ananth, R. (1996), 'Reducing the cost of demand uncertainty through accurate response to early sales,' *Operations Research*, Vol.44, No.1.

Gerard, J.L. and Brian, H. (2001), 'Perceived Environmental Uncertainty: The Extension of Miller's Scale to the Natural Environment,' *Journal of Management Studies*, Vol.38, No.2.

Hall, R. (1999), 'Rearranging Risks and Rewards in a Supply Chain,' *Journal of General Management*, Vol.24, No.3.

Hallikas, J., Virolainen, V.M. and Tuominen, M. (2002), 'Risk analysis and assessment in network environments: A dyadic case study,' *International Journal of Production*

Economics , Vol.78, No.1.

Harland, C., Brenchley, R. and Walker, H. (2003), 'Risk in supply networks,' *Journal of Purchasing and Supply Management*, Vol.9, No.2.

Helbing, D. (2003), 'Modelling supply networks and business cycles as unstable transport phenomena,' *New Journal of Physics*, Vol.5, No.1.

Hollister, K., Killmer, A. (2002), 'A risk/cost framework for logistics policy evaluation: Hazardous waste management,' *The Journal of Business and Economic Studies*, Vol.8, No.1.

Huang, G.Q., Mak, K.L. and Humphreys, P.K. (2003), 'A new model of the customer-supplier partnership in new product development,' *Journal of Materials Processing Technology*, Vol.138, No.1-3.

Iakovou, E.T. (2001), 'An interactive multiobjective model for the strategic maritime transportation of petroleum products: risk analysis and routing,' *Safety Science*, Vol.39, No.1-2.

Johnson, M.E. (2001), 'Learning from toys: Lessons in managing supply chain risk from the toy industry,' *California Management Review*, Vol.43, No.3.

Johnson, M.E. and Anderson E. (2000), 'Postponement strategies for channel derivatives,' *International Journal of Logistics Management*, Vol.11, No.1, pp.19-35.

Jones, C. (1999), 'Possible damages from the year 2000 problem,' *Logistics Information Management*, Vol.12, No.3.

Korpela, J. et al. (2002), 'An analytic approach to production capacity allocation and supply chain design,' *International Journal of Production Economics*, Vol.78, No.2.

Kraljic, P. (1983), 'Purchasing Must Become Supply Management,' *Harvard Business Review*, Vol.61, No.5.

Le Heron, R. (2003), 'Creating food futures: reflections on food governance issues in New Zealand's agri-food sector,' *Journal of Rural Studies*, Vol.19, No.1.

Lee, H.L. and Wolfe, M. (2003), 'Supply chain security without tears,' *Supply Chain Management Review*, 2003 (January/February).

Li, C-L. and Kouvelis, P. (1999), 'Flexible and Risk-Sharing Supply Contracts Under Price Uncertainty,' *Management Science*, Vol.45, No.10, pp.1378-1398.

Lieb, R.C. and Randall, H.L. (1996), 'A comparison of the use of third-party logistics services by large American manufacturers, 1991.' *Journal of Business Logistics*, Vol.17, No.1.

Luc, L. and Carruth, J.S. (1997), 'Simulation of woodyard inventory variations using a stochastic model,' *Forest Products Journal*, Vol.47, No.3.

Martha, J. and Subbakrishna S. (2002), 'Targeting a just-in-case supply chain for the inevitable next disaster,' *Supply Chain Management Review*, 2002 (September/October 2002).

Owens, S.F. and Levary R.R. (2002), 'Evaluating the impact of electronic data interchange on the ingredient supply chain of a food processing company,' *Supply Chain Management: An International Journal*, Vol.7, No.4.

Pagh, J.D. (1998), 'Supply Chain Postponement and Speculation Strategies: How to Choose the Right Strategy,' *Journal of Business Logistics*, Vol.19, No.2.

Palaneeswaran, E. et al. (2003), 'Curing congenital construction industry disorders through relationally integrated supply chains,' *Building and Environment*, Vol.38, No.4.

Peres, F. and Grenouilleau, J. (2002), 'Initial spare parts supply of an orbital system,' *Aircraft Engineering and Aerospace Technology: An International Journal*, Vol.74, No.3.

Ramcharran, H. (2001), 'Inter-firm linkages and profitability in the automobile industry: The implications for Supply Chain Management,' *Journal of Supply Chain*

Management, Vol.37, No.1.

Rice, J. and Caniato, F (2003), 'Building a secure and resilient supply network,' *Supply Chain Management review*, (September/October 2003).

Ritchie, R. and Brindley, C. (2000), 'Disintermediation, disintegration and risk in the SME global supply chain,' *Management Decision*, Vol.38, No.8, pp.575-583.

Ritchie, R. and Brindley, C. (2002), 'Reassessing the management of the global supply chain,' *Integrated Manufacturing Systems*, Vol.13, No.2.

Ropkins, K. and Beck, A.J. (2000), 'HACCP in the home: a framework for improving awareness of hygiene and safe food handling with respect to chemical risk,' *Trends in Food Science and Technology*, Vol.11, No.3.

Sabath, R. (1998), 'Volatile demand calls for quick response: The integrated supply chain,' *International Journal of Physical Distribution and Logistics Management*, Vol.28, No.9.

Savage, M. (2002), 'Business continuity planning,' *Work Study*, Vol.51, No.5.

Schroeder M.J.A. and McEachern, M.G. (2002), 'ISO 9001 as an audit frame for integrated quality management in meat supply chains: the example of Scottish beef,' *Managerial Auditing Journal*, Vol.17, No.1.

Schwarz, L.B. and Weng, Z.K. (2000), 'The design of a jit supply chain: The effect of leadtime uncertainty on safety stock,' *Journal of Business Logistics*, Vol.21, No.2.

Seo, Y., Jung, S. and Hahm, J. (2002), 'Optimal reorder decision utilizing centralized stock information in a two-echelon distribution system,' *Computers and Operations Research*, Vol.29, No.2.

Sharratt, P.N. and Choong, P.M. (2002), 'A life-cycle framework to analyse business risk in process industry projects,' *Journal of Cleaner Production*, Vol.10, No.5.

Sheffi, Y. (2001), 'Supply Chain Management under the threat of international terrorism,' *International Journal of Logistics Management*, Vol.12, No.2.

Sislian, E. and Satir, A. (2000), 'Strategic sourcing: A framework and a case study,' *Journal of Supply Chain Management*, Vol.36, No.3.

Smeltzer, L.R. and Siferd, S.P. (1998), 'Proactive supply management: The management of risk,' *International Journal of Purchasing and Materials Management*, Vol.34, No.1.

Snir, E.M. (2001), 'Liability as a catalyst for product stewardship,' *Production and Operations Management*, Vol.10, No.2.

Svensson, G. (2000), 'A conceptual framework for the analysis of vulnerability in supply chains,' *International Journal of Physical Distribution and Logistics Management*, Vol.30, No.9, pp.731-749.

Svensson, G. (2002a), 'A conceptual framework of vulnerability in firms' inbound and outbound logistics flows,' *International Journal of Physical Distribution and Logistics Management*, Vol.32, No.2.

Svensson, G. (2002b), 'A typology of vulnerability scenarios towards suppliers and customers in supply chains based upon perceived time and relationship dependencies,' *International Journal of Physical Distribution and Logistics Management*, Vol.32, No.3.

Svensson, G. (2002c), 'Dyadic Vulnerability in Companies' Inbound and Outbound Logistics Flows,' *International Journal of Logistics*, Vol.5, No.1.

Svensson, G. (2002d), 'Vulnerability scenarios in marketing channels,' *Supply Chain Management: An International Journal*, Vol.7, No.5.

Svensson, G. (2003a), 'Sub-contractor and customer sourcing and the occurrence of disturbances in firms' inbound and outbound logistics flows,' *Supply Chain Management: An International Journal*, Vol.8, No.1.

Svensson, G. (2003b), 'The principle of balance between companies' inventories and disturbances in logistics flows: Empirical illustration and conceptualisation,'

International Journal of Physical Distribution and Logistics Management, Vol.33, No.9.

Tagaras, G. (1999), 'Pooling in multi-location periodic inventory distribution systems,' *Omega*, Vol.27, No.1.

Tah, J.H.M. and Carr, V. (2001), 'Towards a framework for project risk knowledge management in the construction supply chain,' *Advances in Engineering Software*, Vol.32, No.10-11.

Thonemann, U.W. and Bradley, J.R. (2002), 'The effect of product variety on supply-chain performance,' *European Journal of Operational Research*, Vol.143, No.3.

Thuong, L.T. and Ho, C. (1987), 'Coping with international freight rate volatility,' *Journal of Purchasing and Materials Management*, Vol.23, No.3.

Tsai, M.C. and Su, Y.S. (2002), 'Political risk assessment on air logistics hub developments in Taiwan,' *Journal of Air Transport Management*, Vol.8, No.6.

Tsay, A.A. (2002), 'Risk sensitivity in distribution channel partnerships: implications for manufacturer return policies,' *Journal of Retailing*, Vol.78, No.2.

Tsay, A.A. and Lovejoy, W.S. (1999), 'Quantity Flexibility Contracts and Supply Chain Performance,' *Manufacturing and Service Operations Management*, Vol.1, No.2.

Tserng, H.P. and Lin, P.H. (2002), 'An accelerated subcontracting and procuring model for construction projects,' *Automation in Construction*, Vol.11, No.1.

Umali-Deininger, D.L. and Deininger, K.W. (2001), 'Towards greater food security for India's poor: balancing government intervention and private competition,' *Agricultural Economics*, Vol.25, No.2-3.

Van der Vorst, J. and Beulens Adrie, J.M. (2002), 'Identifying sources of uncertainty to generate supply chain redesign strategies,' *International Journal of Physical Distribution and Logistics Management*, Vol.32, No.6.

Van Landeghem, H. and Vanmaele, H. (2002), 'Robust planning: a new paradigm for demand chain planning,' *Journal of Operations Management*, Vol.20, No.6.

Vidal, C.J. and Goetschalckx, M. (2000), 'Modelling the effect of uncertainties on global logistics systems,' *Journal of Business Logistics*, Vol.21, No.1.

Wang, Charles X. (2002), 'A general framework of supply chain contract models,' *Supply Chain Management: An International Journal*, Vol.7, No.5.

Warren, M. and Hutchinson, W. (2000), 'Cyber attacks against Supply Chain Management systems: a short note,' *International Journal of Physical Distribution and Logistics Management*, Vol.30, No.7-8.

Weng, K.Z. (1999), 'Risk-pooling over demand uncertainty in the presence of product modularity,' *International Journal of Production Economics*, Vol.62, No.1-2.

Xu, K. and Evers, P.T. (2003), 'Managing single echelon inventories through demand aggregation and the feasibility of a correlation matrix,' *Computers and Operations Research*, Vol.30, No.2.

Zsidisin, G.A. (2001), 'Measuring Supply Risk: An Example from Europe,' *PRACTIX – Best Practices in Purchasing and Supply Chain Management*, (June).

Zsidisin, G.A. (2003), 'Managerial perceptions of supply risk,' *Journal of Supply Chain Management*, Vol.39, No.1.

Zsidisin, G.A. and Ellram, L.M. (1999), 'Supply Risk Assessment Analysis,' *PRACTIX – Best Practices in Purchasing and Supply Chain Management*, (June).

Zsidisin, G.A. and Ellram, L.M. (2003), 'An agency theory investigation of supply risk management,' *Journal of Supply Chain Management*, Vol.39, No.3.

Zsidisin, G.A., Panelli, A. and Upton, R. (2000), 'Purchasing organization involvement in risk assessments, contingency plans, and risk management: an exploratory study,' *Supply Chain Management: An International Journal*, Vol.5, No.4.

References

Borge, D. (2001), *The Book of Risk*, John Wiley and Sons Inc, New York.

Christopher, M. and Towill, D. (2000), 'Supply chain migration from lean and functional to agile and customised'. *Supply Chain Management: An International Journal*, Vol.5, No.4, pp.206-213.

Cooper M., Lambert, D. and Pagh, J. (1997), 'Supply Chain Management: More Than a New Name for Logistics'. *The International Journal of Logistics Management*, Vol.8, No.1, pp.1-14.

Greenberg, J. (2002), 'September 11, 2001 – A CEO's Story'. *Harvard Business Review*, October 2002, pp.59-64.

Juettner, U., Peck, H. and Christopher, M. (2002), 'Supply chain risk management: Outlining an agenda for future research'. *LRN 2002. Conference proceedings*. Editors: Griffiths, Hewitt and Ireland, pp.443-450. The Institute of Logistics and Transport.

Kajüter, P. (2003), 'Risk Management in Supply Chains' in: Seuring, S., Müller, M., Goldbach, M., Schneidewind, U. (eds.) *'Strategy and Organization in Supply Chains'*, Physica, Heidelberg, pp.321-336.

Mason-Jones, R., Naylor, B. and Towill, D. (2000), 'Engineering the agile supply chain', *International Journal of Agile Management Systems*, Vol.2/1, pp.54-61.

Norrman, A. and Lindroth, R. (2002), 'Supply Chain Risk Management: Purchasers' vs. Planners' Views on Sharing Capacity Investment Risks in the Telecom Industry', Paper presented at *the 11th International IPSERA conference*, Enschede, Netherlands, 2002.

Rasmussen, J. and Svedung, I. (2000), *Proactive Risk Management in a Dynamic Society*. Räddningsverket. Karlstad. ISBN 91-7253-084-7.

Simons, R. (1999) 'How risky is your company?', *Harvard Business Review*, May-June 1999, pp.85-94.

The Royal Society, (1992), Risk: Analysis, Perception and Management, *The Royal Society*, London.

PART II
TECHNIQUES AND APPLICATIONS

Chapter 7

Examining Risk and Supply Chain Collaborative Working in the UK Construction Industry

Dr. Simon A. Burtonshaw-Gunn

Introduction

The aim of this chapter is to provide an understanding of the importance of the construction industry in the UK and understand how a closer working relationship between primary supply chain members can provide cost savings together with other benefits for both client and contractor organizations alike. Although Supply Chain Management has grown in use and importance in other industries, notably those of retail and automotive, it is a relatively new concept for the construction industry, despite its many years of experience in sub-contracting specialist services. Whilst the relationship between the main contractor and the client organization is the principal focus of a partnering arrangement, it is also recognized that as a consequence of successful supplier relationships at this level, the role and importance of the full supply chain will also increase. In line with the theme of this book, the chapter also reports on the risks associated with a supply chain approach to construction by examining the internal and external factors acting upon the industry.

The construction industry has, like other parts of the UK business economy, witnessed previous major developments aimed to improve profitability and performance. Typically such initiatives have included sales and marketing in the 1980s followed by human resources and organizational design in the early 1990s brought about through downsizing, delaying and re-engineering. Since the mid 1990s, mainly as a direct result of the publication of the Latham Report (1994), the construction industry has seen an increasing interest in better Supply Chain Management and in particular, in the subject of 'Partnering'. It is widely stated that the principle of partnering first emerged in the construction industry some twenty years ago, predominantly in the United States of America where it was said to have been championed by the US Army Corps of Engineers. Since then it has gained momentum in New Zealand, Australia and the United Kingdom. In respect to the UK, the Latham Report 'Constructing the Team' (1994) has undoubtedly acted as a catalyst for a move towards adopting Supply Chain Management in the construction industry and in the use of 'partnering' between the client and the main contractor.

There is an almost uniform view that the aim of partnering is to eliminate or at least reduce adversarial relationships and replace them with a long-term relationship based on mutual trust and benefit, not just in the form of more harmonious working but also in reducing traditional project risks. The concept of partnering is based on the premise that important but complementary opportunities exist between two companies but also there are powerful barriers which obscure these opportunities and often preclude their realization. However, if the right people are brought together with an effective organization process, the risks to partnering can be managed, barriers removed and the positive opportunities can be identified, prioritized and pursued.

The chapter presents an overview of the UK construction industry, the use of Supply Chain Management in the industry and then examines the risks associated with collaborative partnering relationships in the industry before ending with a number of conclusions.

An Analysis of the UK Construction Industry

The construction activity involves assembling materials and components, designed and produced by a multitude of suppliers, working in a diversity of disciplines and technologies, in order to create the 'built environment.' Such activities can include the planning, regulation, design, manufacture, construction, maintenance and eventual decommissioning of buildings and other structures. Their scale, complexity and intricacy varies enormously, ranging from work undertaken by 'jobbing builders' to multi-billion pound schemes such as single or multiple major civil projects, for example, power station construction and one-off projects exemplified by the Channel Tunnel and the Millennium Dome in London.

From a 'value chain' viewpoint new construction can be regarded as a means of production or provision of services (a factory or office block); an addition to or improvement of the infrastructure of the economy (railway or roads); a social investment (hospitals); or provision to meet a direct need in the case of housing. As such, it plays a vital role in facilitating the competitive delivery of goods and services by the rest of the economy. In addition, the house-building industry also stimulates other services (estate agents, solicitors) and supports other industries (carpets, curtains, furniture etc). Furthermore, the construction industry is not only of major national importance but also features as an international industry. Even in 'developing countries' construction represents a significant input to Gross Domestic Product (GDP). Examining the UK construction industry from an international perspective shows it to be a major constituent of the UK's GDP, at approximately eight per cent although, this is smaller than many of its European competitors which contribute more than ten per cent to GDP. Looking even further afield, construction in Japan provides input to its GDP at 18 per cent. The British construction industry is the fourth largest in Europe and represents over ten per cent of the total European Union (EU) construction activity. It is exceeded by

Germany (30 per cent), France (16 per cent) and Italy (16 per cent). In addition UK construction companies are also responsible for a significant amount of work undertaken overseas, usually on behalf of British consultants and contractors. The latter typically represents between ten to 15 per cent of the annual turnover of the major British contractors.

Since the early 1990s the industry has reduced and deskilled its workforce, largely abandoned apprentice and other training schemes and continued its conflict-ridden competitive tendering culture, together with adversarial working relationships throughout its supply chain. Whilst other industries were leading the way with closer Supply Chain Management, the construction sector typically continued to pressure its suppliers into lower prices and delayed payments to them so that it could benefit from a level of investment interest. However, this practice placed additional risks on the supply chain with smaller businesses ceasing to operate or doing so at the expense of reduced quality. This industry norm so concerned the UK Government ten years ago, that it appointed Sir Michael Latham to carry out yet another government-funded review of the procurement and contractual arrangements in the industry. His report 'Constructing the Team' (Latham, 1994) recommended change for the industry and gave a number of specific recommendations including a change in culture aimed to move away from the traditional adversarial client/supplier relationship, which it noted had prevailed in the industry for a substantial number of years. Whilst this approach had previously been recognized and promoted by other industry initiatives, for example the DTI/CBI 1992 report, (Morris and Imrie, 1993), examining the Japanese style of sub-contracting also proposed that better Supply Chain Management would be a mechanism for '*moving from an adversarial form of contracting to higher trust obligational relationships.*' (Morris and Imrie, 1993, p.53). In particular the 1994 report 'Constructing the Team' (Latham, 1994) saw partnering as the development of a strategic long term commercial arrangement between a client, contractors and suppliers and went further by proposing that this was one of the techniques most likely to improve cost efficiency and customer relationships within the construction industry and reduce the risk of poor performance.

Building upon the 1994 Latham report a Construction Industry Task Force was established under the chairmanship of the British Airports Authority (BAA) Chief Executive, Sir John Egan, which resulted in the publication of the report 'Rethinking Construction' (Egan, 1998). This Report identified a number of areas that the industry needed to address and also made the following comment on partnering, stating that it:

> Envisages a very different role for the construction supply chain. In our view, the supply chain is critical to driving innovation and to sustaining incremental and sustained improvement in performance. Partnering is, however, far from being an easy option for constructors and suppliers. There is already some evidence that it is more demanding than conventional tendering, requiring recognition of interdependence between clients and constructors, open relationships, effective measurement of performance and an ongoing commitment to improvement (Construction Round Table, 1998, p.24).

From the examination of the various construction sectors within the industry, construction work is shown to be a temporary activity, carried out at the clients premises and is viewed as an enabling activity to allow the client organization to conduct its business; be this retail, manufacturing or service related. However, because of these reasons it does have a number of inherent problems such as low and discontinuous demand, low productivity when compared to other industries, low profitability and a fragmented industrial structure. Despite such fragmentation it has been subject to a wide range of developments over the last few years which have emerged from both the industry representative bodies, clients and the UK Government and have included:

1. Major industry reviews, reports and recommendations to identify and promote a more efficient and effective *modus operandi*, for example the reports of Latham ('Constructing the Team', 1994) and Egan ('Rethinking Construction', 1998).

2. Initiatives to improve construction performance, such as the UK Government Department of the Environment, Transport and the Regions (DETR) Construction Best Practice Program.

3. Tools to address client/supplier relationships and fragmentation, such as partnering and framework agreements, which are becoming increasingly used by companies in place of traditional competitive based procurement.

4. An increasing interest in tools and techniques for improving efficiency and quality learned from other industries, including benchmarking, value management, teamworking, Just-In-Time, concurrent engineering and Total Quality Management.

5. A number of developments in the standard forms of contract aimed to support collaborative working such as the New Engineering Contract, 1995 and more recently PPC2000 published by the Association of Consultant Architects, which is widely regarded by many industry experts as being the first standard form of project partnering contract.

Many of these initiatives, which have quasi-government backing have attempted to promote productivity increases in the industry through better quality products which satisfy the customer; the use of continuous improvement to make major and cumulative improvements and to foster better relationships in both government and industry.

However, it has to be stressed that because of the range of activities undertaken by this industry from the small self-employed builder to the multi-million civil/construction companies, the applicability of the above initiatives is also equally varied. Furthermore, as the industry is unregulated it is free to accept or reject the adoption of such advisory or recommendatory reviews and initiatives. Notwithstanding the above comment as more large spending, high profile clients seek better, improved services, better value for money and a greater degree of cost certainty, there is some desire from construction industry clients and contractors to embrace the 1994 Latham and the 1998 Egan recommendations.

Within the public sector Government departments/organizations have had encouraging experiences in partnering, yet neither the last government nor the present administration define 'partnership' in quite the same way as the construction industry. For the Government, partnership is almost entirely about getting the private sector to employ its resources and assets to take on as much risk as possible, including the risk of cancellation or postponement, often for little financial reward. As more projects are undertaken using a partnering approach it is suggested that this will encourage discussion and result in the development of a universally agreed definition.

Supply Chain Management in the UK Construction Industry

It has been suggested that for many construction organizations adopting a strategic Supply Chain Management approach would offer an opportunity for it to reduce the overall cost of construction and add greater value, while maintaining high quality levels. Research undertaken in the USA has cited many examples of cost savings from both the use of one-off project partnering arrangements and from the use of long-term strategic partnering agreements. In addition to reducing costs and potential client/supplier conflict there is also the view from the Construction Industry Board (1997) that partnering can also improve service quality, deliver better designs, help to make construction safer, meet earlier completion deadlines and provide everyone involved with increased profits. Whilst a partnering arrangement can give cost savings which are shared between all parties, together with the benefit from non-adversarial contracting and a continuity of workload, cognizance has to be taken of the legal and contractual implications for UK clients of forming partnership arrangements within the supply chain including EU Competitive law, UK law and the selection of an appropriate form of contract to support the partnering philosophy.

Undertaking research (Burtonshaw-Gunn, 2001) to understand if the construction industry is benefiting from their experience of partnering relationships has been difficult to establish with a degree of confidence. This is largely because of the differing levels of experience and progress on the 'partnering journey' when the practical experience is compared with the theoretical view cited in appropriate construction literature. This comment is made not to criticize those companies involved in partnering but to note that many have some way to go on the use of performance measurement, continuous improvement and target setting. Whilst there is some anecdotal evidence to suggest that a number of companies are supporting the concept of continuous improvement the degree to which this evident is difficult to quantify in practice. From the study undertaken and reported by Burtonshaw-Gunn and Ritchie (2003) the following specific items are considered to be key to commencing and building a successful partnering relationship:

1. The client must select the 'best in class' contractors with which to partner. Whilst traditionally a client will often investigate a contractor's past performance, (quality standards, health and safety records, past project

performance, resources and financial status) it should now also consider the cultural fit between the two organizations. Whilst experience in undertaking projects on a partnering basis might be considered important, such claims often need to be treated with some caution because of the difficulty in determining the level of commitment to partnering as against the use of the partnering concept being used as a 'marketing tool' by some construction companies. Similarly, the contractor needs to work with and understand the client, as selection must be a two-way process if mutually beneficial results are to be obtained.

2.   The main contractor organization must select its supply chains, which can then be developed with tangible benefits of the client/main contractor relationship and the overall project.

3.   The management style from all parties must be of a non-adversarial nature to create and promote an open forum for communication. This should be supported by the most senior management in both client and constructor organizations, often in the role of partnering 'champions' who together with the project sponsors are able to communicate at a high level to resolve disputes as they arise, without recourse to the contract or legislation. To support this further, the use of professionally facilitated workshops at the commencement and during the partnering relationship is widely regarded as being paramount to the process. This view is also endorsed by developments in newer forms of contract specifically applicable to construction partnering projects.

4.   Team selection and team building are very much key factors to the success of partnering as it is about relationship management and personnel behaviors. The involvement and participation of the project end-users, the contractors and suppliers is to be encouraged in the development of the partnering team.

5.   The client organization should encourage and recognize the importance of early supply chain involvement in the conceptual stages of a project, in order to be well placed to obtain benefits from alternative design, buildability, maintenance and alternative product selection.

6.   The use of any incentive mechanism often in the form of shared savings must be seen to be fair and equal. All parties in the partnering agreement can benefit via cost savings and increased quality but only with an acceptance of mutually agreed objectives, including the need for the constructor and supply chain members to make a fair and reasonable level of profit.

7.   Finally risk allocation must be proportionate to the value of the work being undertaken and the size of the participants organization.

8.   Whilst some advocates of partnering would suggest that a contract to bind the relationship together is not needed given a new way of working, it is suggested that this is a step too far for the vast majority of relationships, including those considered mature. More appropriately, the right form of contract needs to be chosen so that a mechanism is in place if ultimately the agreed problem resolution process fails.

9.   In the event of a dispute, alternative methods of dispute resolution should be exhausted before reverting to a contractual claim. This approach will allow

some recovery of the relationship particularly if the parties are expecting to work together over a period of time or across a number of repeat or series projects.

It is expected that because of the high spending, high profile, client interest in the use of partnering agreements and latterly increasingly in a Prime Contracting approach, where one contractor acts as the single point of contact for the entire supply chain, the construction industry is likely to witness a significant change over the next few years. This prediction is based on a post-2000 market understanding of a desire by major public and private sector clients to establish long-term, strategic partnering arrangements with construction companies, providing benefits in cost savings, reduced time and effort in their assessment of competitive tenders and gaining a closer relationship with their service providers. Such an evolution from Partnering to Prime Contracting can be regarded as a natural development for those companies with the necessary understanding and experience. However, for those companies without the benefit of such experience, an attempted move to Prime Contracting is likely to present a notable degree of challenge.

The Risks Associated with Partnering in the UK Construction Industry

The Construction Industry Board working group publication of 1997 entitled 'Partnering in the Team' clearly supports the recommendations proposed by Sir Michael Latham (Constructing the Team, 1994) in stressing that partnering should be applied throughout the supply chain. This relationship is represented in Figure 7.1 together with four areas of risk acting upon such a relationship and is used as the basis for examining the risks within supply chain collaborative working in the UK construction industry.

Environmental

Construction, by its nature as a systems integrator and as a stimulus for other parts of the economy, can be regarded as a basic economic multiplier. From a macroeconomic perspective the industry requires the three classic 'factors of inputs' of land, labour and capital, all of which can be affected by various government policies. From a political perspective the UK is neither a communist or a state controlled economy, nor is it at the other end of the continuum in being a free economy, following a *laisez-faire* policy of zero state intervention. The UK operates as a compromize mixed economy with a certain amount of government intervention at the National Government level this can be seen in the form of taxes, health and safety legislation, construction management legislation and general employment law. At the local government level additional risks to a construction project are exemplified by the control of planning approval and development schemes, adherence to local requirements and adherence to other statutory body regulations, particularly if the construction project can affect the surrounding environment. Additionally, over the last few decades it is noted that general economic Government policy also consequentially, affects the construction industry as in the creation of enterprise initiatives to combat declines of certain industries, often in particular geographic regions to encourage new business investment at these locations. This intervention is reflected by the construction industry in serving the market needs for new build, infrastructure, maintenance and housing projects in the high demand areas, with a corresponding reduction of all of these project types in those areas of low industrial or commercial activity. Indeed, there can be a significant variation in construction trends across the regions of Great Britain, with no simple 'North-South division'.

The construction industry's problems of discontinuity of demand for work are unique when compared to other UK industries, adding to the risk of poor performance from either a quality or financial viewpoint. Without a continuous demand it is difficult for companies to make long-term plans and forecasts, hence there is a reluctance to invest in plant, machinery and personnel training. In addition, faced with trying to win work from clients still applying the traditional competitive tendering process of 'lowest costs wins', the industry is forced to offer low prices and thus, consequently self-limit its income and its ability to make such investments.

Parkinson (1996, P.1) suggested that for many construction organizations the subject of strategic Supply Chain Management would be the key area where it could *'reduce the overall cost of construction and add greater value while maintaining high quality levels'*. Research has cited many examples from the USA which have resulted in cost savings from both the use of one-off project partnering and from long-term strategic partnering arrangements (for example, see Bennett and Jayes, 1995). In addition to reducing costs and conflict there is evidence that partnering can also improve service quality, deliver better designs, make construction safer, meet earlier completion deadlines and provide the contracted parties involved with increased profits.

Competition

The operation of the construction industry like many businesses can be viewed against a competitive strategy model developed by Michael Porter (1980) which, identifies five key driving forces on a business. These being:

1. Potential Entrants – the threat of new entrants
2. Industry Competitors – rivalry among existing firms
3. Substitutes – the threat of substitute products or services
4. Buyers – the bargaining power of buyers
5. Suppliers – the bargaining power of suppliers

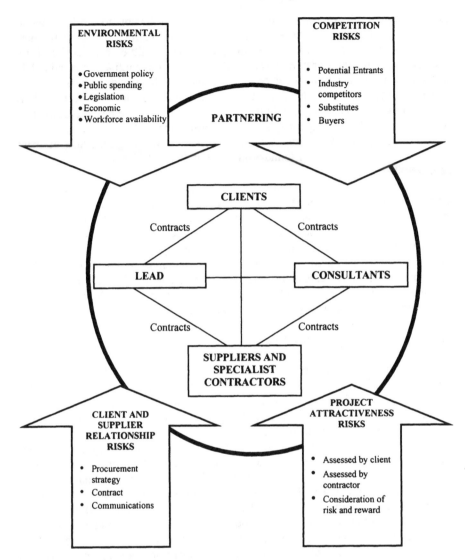

Figure 7.1 Risks in Construction Industry Collaborative Working

In looking at the first two of these key business drivers – Potential Entrants and Industry Competitors – it is recognized that the UK construction industry is, in the main, confined to competition from established UK companies. This is particularly so in the sectors of non-residential building and infrastructure because the construction industry operates differently to other industrial or economic sectors. Construction companies require not only manpower resources, plant and equipment but also health and safety procedures and various insurances to be in place, together with an established track record even to be able to bid for work in this sector. Consequently, these requirements impose significant barriers to entry to the UK construction market resulting in none, or little, competition from international companies or new entrants but only that from confined to existing UK companies or those international companies with a UK subsidiary operation. In looking at the third element, the threat of substitute products or services, it is logical to assume that there is little threat of substitution of site based construction activities although, the future may see an increase in the prefabrication of buildings or other factory-based building techniques. Even given a greater use of these techniques some site work of foundations, assembly and finishing will still need to be undertaken.

The final two forces covering the bargaining power of buyers and those of suppliers can be grouped together. This is because both forces are influenced by the same factors of the concentration of construction companies, the number of capital projects being undertaken within the UK market and the perceived importance and willingness to undertake work for a particular client. These two forces and that of competition have had an effect on client/contractor relationships over a period of many years and driven mostly by the level of supply and demand. The move to collaborative working reduces the tension of this balance together with a reduction of the risks involved in adversarial relationships.

Risks from Client and Supplier Relationship

The traditional *modus operandi* of a competition with other construction companies is driven in the main by the client's desire to achieve the lowest-cost bid which it equates with value for money, not only in the private sector but also in the public sector through the UK government inspired Compulsory Competitive Tendering process. As a result, and with very few exceptions, relationships have been adversarial with contractors concerned resorting to financial claims for any changes in the agreed scope of work and associated payment, this process which lengthens timescales and increases costs has a direct impact of the behavior of both parties. Where the client will only award work to the lowest price contractor, the contractor responds to this approach by submitting an uneconomically low price, which results in time and effort being spent by the contractor in finding reasons for which additional money will be sought. In essence it has become many contractor's traditional strategy to submit low prices in competition knowing that it will be supplemented by post-contract extras, variations and financial claims when delay and disruption opportunities present themselves. It is reported that within the construction industry *'less than 80 per cent of the projects are finished on time or budget'* (Carlisle, 1998, p.1). Furthermore, the traditional procurement systems and the contractual and legal framework by which participants are bound together are often criticized as being confrontational and adversarial. For these reasons the risk of trouble-free projects is very rare as legally binding contractual requirements necessitate both parties to advise and agree changes with respect to the scope of the work being undertaken or an extension to the original contract program. Both sides are thus forced into such communications adding to the adversarial nature of the relationship with increased risks of claims from the contractor and counter-claims from the client. Critchlow (1998) comments further on this relationship that:

> many employers let contracts by 'Dutch auction', and many contractors, desperate for turnover, bid at cost, and often less than that, to secure them. They then sought to recover their margins by building claims into the contracting process, and by withholding payment to subcontractors as a form of secondary financing. (Critchlow, 1998, p.1).

According to one report on the construction industry *'it has been estimated that in a typical year over a thousand writs may be issued, claims of £500 million – of which 80 per cent are settled out of court.'* (Carlisle, 1998, p.1). To many organizations involved in construction projects this will not be too surprising as it is widely recognized that the industry has an amount of fame for its adversarial attitudes. Indeed, the amount of time and money spent on litigation provides employment opportunities for a significant number of professionals, including claims consultants, quantity surveyors and construction lawyers involved more in project cost recovery rather than the actual construction process. Such recognition of the construction industry's adversarial attitudes has a long history and a number of UK governments have commissioned investigations into the industry, notably the reports of Sir Ernest Simon (1944), Sir Harold Emmerson (1962), Sir Harold Banwell (1964) and Sir Michael Latham (1994) which all tell a similar tale. With such traditional industry relationships between client and contractor over a period of many years a set of assumptions have developed that have become strong barriers to implementing partnering relationships in this industry. These barriers not only include the attitudes of the contractor/client relationship but also often concern the priorities and goals of the client, which in the past have been substantially different from those of the contractor. Also, increasing the risk of misunderstood requirements and expectations has been the client's appointment of a number of consultants on a project to design and supervise its construction. Often these will include architects, civil and structural engineers, mechanical, electrical and services engineers and quantity surveyors on a single project, with one of these consultants appointed to undertake the role of managing and coordinating the work of the others and the contract as a whole. With so many specialist groups often involved in a project, clients have long expressed concern that they have limited communication of progress and little, or no, control over the costs of construction, nor of the time taken to complete the project. Such comments arise from a long held reluctance to involve the client in the decision making process with a preference to keep any technical problems concealed from the client until the final payment demand is presented.

It is widely acknowledged that the traditional relationship between the industry and its clients is also based on a premise that the client does not understand the process and it (the industry) is best placed to interpret what the client wants. Clearly these attitudes significantly increases the risk of misunderstanding the client's requirements, often resulting in addition changes and re-work on completion attracting both time and cost penalties. In addition to poor communications, clients often feel that they are the victims of poor design, inadequate supervision, insufficient choice of materials and contract methods. These are all sources which inhibit effective working between consultants, contractors and the client and often are reasons for claims for additional costs and to justify time overruns. In recent years there has been a change in client requirements prompted by many becoming increasingly vocal about their dissatisfaction of this 'traditional' approach. To counter such problems a number of major clients, including the UK government, have demanded a change in the construction industry's behavior with a shift in emphasis from a 'production oriented' to a 'client oriented' outlook by the industry's members. Hence, the move towards partnering and collaborative working has been supported by many client organizations. This requires not only commitment to a specific partnership but also a deeper commitment to the general philosophy of partnering. Clearly the construction industry cannot partner without client support and the strongest criticism from the industry of its clients is their desire to '*run with the hare and hunt with the hounds.*' Some clients see this behavior as a risk reducing strategy of not being dependent on any one supplier, together with the ability to always obtain work at the lowest price. Curiously this approach is also typical of a number of clients who even have partnerships with many contractors and whilst being able to change them frequently, greatly increases the risk of undermining any commitment to a joint partnership. Indeed, many contractors find that that have been made a 'partner' only to discover themselves asked to competitively tender for the next project. This is more damaging than would first appear as partnering contractors have discovered that '*while they are constrained in their tender to use particular subcontractors, supplies and methods of working, open-book accounting and benefit sharing, they are competing against non-partners who are free to cherry-pick, to quote unrealistic costs, and, in short, to revert to the old industry type*' (Tulip, 1997, p.26). On this basis it is not surprising that the disparity in tender value prompts the client to question the price to be paid for partnering, particular if final procurement decisions are taken remotely from the direct project team by those with a traditional approach of obtaining only the lowest price which it equates as satisfying a value for money requirement.

In recognising the lessons from other industries and the unique nature of the construction industry in respect to relationship development, the Construction Industry Board's (CIB) publication 'Partnering in the Team' (1997) offers a word of caution. It advises that:

> Partnering empowers people and encourages them to work together but without rigorous management (measurement, benchmarking, goals) this can lead to 'cosy' relationships (even fraud), reduced exposure to raw market forces and overlong carrying of non-performers. (Construction Industry Board, 1997, p.5).

The concern of 'cosy' relationships is also highlighted in the Latham Report (1994, p.62) and covers not only the relationship between the contractor and the client but also that between the main contractor and its sub-contractors and supply chain. A similar message is given in 'Partnering for Profit' (1997, p.26) which while noting that partnering should not be adversarial, adds that the relationship should always remain aware of each other and the motto should be '*Close, but not cosy.*' Whilst Sir Michael Latham's report (1994) welcomes supply chain partnering, it also recommends that such relationships have the principal objective of improving performance and reducing costs to clients, stating in particular that the construction process exists to solely satisfy the client. Unlike other industries and parts of the British economy, particularly in the retail sector, there is a wide acknowledgement that contractors and other construction industry suppliers have not previously embraced the importance of 'the customer'. In looking at the risks of the client/supplier relationship the CIB report suggests that the risk of failure in partnering and collaborative working comes from people and the organizational relationships, adding that '*cynicism and lack of commitment by a few (particularly at senior level) will destroy the efforts of many*' (Construction Industry Report, 1997, p.5).

Risk of Project Attractiveness

As the concept of partnering is based on a relationship between the construction industry and its clients it is suggested that this is only really applicable to those projects which directly interface with the client or with an identifiable and assessable end-user. Indeed both the infrastructure or non-residential building sector (comprising industrial and commercial building) and public non-housing construction are best suitable to this practice by meeting this relationship requirement. This suggestion is made because it is these industry sectors that offer the scope of work in terms of complexity, physical size, financial scale and appropriate lengthy construction timescales which allow the concept of partnering to successfully develop. Additionally, projects in these sectors allow the working relationship to be developed between the client and/or end user of the construction project and the construction prime contractor and other supply chain members. On this premise the development of such a supplier/client relationship is not possible in other construction sectors such as 'housing' for example.

However, all projects even within this sub-sector may not be suitable for a partnering approach and each party will need to assess the attractiveness of the project with regard to both value and the level of risk. From the client viewpoint a suitable project for closer collaborative working may be one of a high value project and high risk this will need to be considered against the contractor's interest which is likely to be the prospect of a high value project together with a high attractiveness of the account which it may regarded as being core to its business. The Construction Industry Board (1997, p.4) provides the following matrices of client and supplier risk/value considerations, these are shown below:

Supply Chain Risk

High Risk	High Risk, Low Value - Ensures supplies - Cost insensitivity - Frequent review	High Risk, High Value - Ensure supplies - Apply close value management - Continuous review
Low Risk	Low Risk, Low Value - Automatic - Delegate - Low attention	Low Risk, High Value - Seek opportunities - Take risks - Wheel and deal
	Low Value	**High Value**

Figure 7.2 Client's Assessment of Supplier Risk

Attractiveness of account High	Development - Nurture client - Expand business - Seek new opportunities	Core - Cosset customer - Defend vigorously - High level of service - High responsiveness
Attractiveness of account Low	Nuisance - Give low attention - Lose without pain	Exploitable - Drive premium price - Seek short term advantage - Risk losing customer
	Low Value	**High Value**

Figure 7.3 Supplier's Assessment of Supplier Risk

Attractiveness of account High	Development - Potential match – work closely with supplier to expand business	Core - Good match – potential for partnering or strategic alliancing
Attractiveness of account Low	Nuisance - Very high risk – seek competition, raise attention	Exploitable - Great caution – seek competition, raise mutual dependency
	Low Value	**High Value**

Figure 7.4 Client's Responses for High Risk, High Value Areas

With respect to Figure 7.4 above, the Construction Industry Board naturally concludes that 'partnering' is most appropriate if both parties are positioned in the top right-hand box.

Whilst it is widely accepted that the UK Government, construction clients and the construction industry itself has been concerned that present procurement processes are both costly and time consuming, the comments on risk transfer already made may not just be confined to partnering. Indeed, examining the long-term future for the Public Private Partnership program confirms that the UK Government is expecting to transfer a greater proportion of project and financial risk onto contractors. However, should this change in favour of the client too highly then some contractors may even consider refusing to take on what they may then perceive as 'unreasonable' risk demands.

There is a widely shared view reported by Tulip (1997) that Governments are not necessarily the worst clients, just the biggest and the when looking at the requirements for successful partnering adds that:

> no matter how many signatures of contractors, subcontractors, suppliers, engineers, architects and surveyors are on the project charter, the really important one, the one that has to guarantee total commitment to the project and the partnership, is that of the client. (Tulip, 1997, p.26).

In other words this means that the construction industry even if attracted to a project cannot partner or attempt to work in any other form of collaboration unless the client wants to, put simply 'it takes two to tango!'

Major construction industry research, notably that reported by *inter alia* Bennett and Jayes (1995), the Construction Industry Board (1997), and the Department of the Environment (1998) – suggests that there are a number of risks in launching a partnering program which will need to be addressed. The Government's Construction Round Table headed by Sir John Egan also recognizes this in its report 'Rethinking Construction' by its observation that:

> Partnering is, however, far from being an easy option for constructors and suppliers. There is already some evidence that it is more demanding than conventional tendering, requiring recognition of interdependence between clients and constructors, open relationships, effective measurement of performance and an ongoing commitment to improvement (Egan, 1998, p.24).

Typically the risks which inhibit the growth of partnering often fall into three areas: corporate culture; the traditional client-contractor role; and the time required to develop the relationship.

Risk 1: corporate culture. With respect to corporate culture many managers educated in traditional business relations can find partnering relationships threatening to their company and their personal *modus operandi*. With attitudes influenced by their company's corporate culture some are uncomfortable with partnering because of an unwillingness to relinquish control and a reluctance to share company information, which they often consider to be of a confidential nature and of no business to other organizations including other supply chain partners.

Risk 2: the traditional industry relationship between client and contractor has led to a set of assumptions that, over time, have become strong barriers to implementing partnering relationships in the construction industry. These can result in adversarial attitudes resulting from traditional master/servant, client/contractor relationships and often concern the priorities and goals of the contractor which in the past have been substantially different from those of the client.

   Risk 3: The time and effort required in a partnership relationship may be significant to initially find the right partner and then to develop the partnering agreement. Both clients and suppliers must assess the attractiveness of the relationship, how both parties may have to function and understand how they may have to change under a partnering agreement to make the relationship and the project successful. Taking time to develop a mutual partnering arrangement is regarded as fundamental to the success of the partnership.

Conclusion

This chapter has described recent advances in supply chain partnering arrangement witnessed in the UK construction industry together with the identified risks covering four main areas: these being competition, environmental actors, relationship risks and perceptions of project attractiveness. Systematic risk management begins with recognising the risks in order that their potential can be quantified and mitigation activities taken to reduce their impact. Clearly of prime concern in this industry is the strength and trust within the relationship necessary for a partnering arrangement to succeed and provide a successful project resulting in benefits for the client, contractor and the supply chain partners. The Construction Industry Board agrees with Bennett and Jayes (1995) that the three essential features of partnering are 'the establishment of agreed and understood mutual objectives; a methodology for quick and co-operative problem resolution; and a culture of continuous, measured improvement' (Construction Industry Board, 1997, p.3).

   Embracing all aspects of these three features will clearly contribute to the relationship building from the outset, assist in the promotion of a long-term relationship based upon trust and hence, minimize cost and time over-runs through better, less formal, and more pro-active communications. Whilst partnering as a concept may then be regarded as a success, the contribution of risk management clearly plays a significant role.

   It is noted that there is a range of experience and progress made on the 'partnering journey' when the practical experience is examined. Whilst this is not to criticise such progress and the benefits that the partnering approach has made for the industry. It is noted that it does not appear to be an easy option, requiring both time and an on-going senior level commitment to the relationship from all parties. Despite this fact, many clients and contractors believe that there are benefits which partnering can offer them in both cost and time savings and in better, more productive working through the establishment of less adversarial behavior practices. There is also a recognition within these successful relationships that each party has often needed to change their behaviors to one another on completion of the selection process and award of a contract to undertake a project.

More recently, there has been a growing interest in the promotion of construction companies in the role of 'Prime Contractor' bringing in more Supply Chain Management techniques largely as a result of a number of major construction clients moving towards awarding multiple, long-term, projects to a smaller number of construction organizations. Collaborative working represents a change from the traditional *modus operandi* for the UK construction industry and although becoming more common place through partnering, there are many construction organizations and clients alike who have yet to experience the full benefits of working in this way. For those companies already embracing the partnering approach the development into Prime Contracting is regarded as a natural progression in developing more sophisticated client/contractor and supply chain relationships. Conversely, for others without such experience it is likely to present a significant challenge as client knowledge and expectations increase and the identified risks or barriers to this approach will remain significant hurdles to overcome.

As a final conclusion, if collaborative working in the construction industry is to flourish it will require constant attention by senior, strategic champions within both client and contractor organizations to maintain the momentum and manage the risks in the four areas shown in Figure 7.1 in order to gain maximum benefit.

References

Association of Consultant Architects, (2000), 'PPC 2000 ACA Standard Form of Contract for Project Partnering'.
Banwell, Sir Harold (1964), 'Placing and Management of Building and Civil Engineering Work, HMSO'.
Bennett, J. and Jayes, S. with the Reading Construction Forum (1995), *Trusting the Team – The Best Practice Guide to Partnering in Construction,* Thomas Telford Publishing.
Burtonshaw-Gunn, S.A. (2001), 'Strategic Supply Chain Management: Critical Success Factors for Partnering Relationships within the UK Construction Industry', *PhD Thesis*, Manchester Metropolitan University, UK.
Burtonshaw-Gunn, S.A. and Ritchie, R.L. (2003), 'Partnering in the UK Construction Industry', *IPSERA conference paper*, Budapest April 2003.
Carlisle, J. (1998), 'Supply chain thinking in construction Partnership – The leadership challenge', *ISPERA Conference paper*, Budapest, April 2003.
Construction Industry Board (1997), 'Partnering in the Team', *Construction Industry Board Working Group 12,* Thomas Telford Publishing.
Construction Industry Development Agency (1993), 'Partnering – A Strategy for Excellence, A guide for the Building and Construction Industry', Commonwealth of Australia and Master Builders Inc.
Cousins, P. (1992), 'Choosing the right partner', *Purchasing and Supply Management*, March 1992, pp.21-23.
Critchlow, J. (1998), *Making Partnering Work in the Construction Industry,* Chandos Publishing (Oxford) Limited.
Department of the Environment, Transport and Regions (DETR), (1998), 'Rethinking Construction: The Report of the Construction Task Force to the Deputy Prime

Minister, John Prescott, on the scope for improving the quality and efficiency of UK construction July 1998.

Department of the Environment, Transport and Regions (DETR), (2000), 'State of the Construction Industry Report', April 2000.

Department of Trade and Industry/Confederation of British Industry (1992), 'Making Partnership Sourcing Happen', DTI/CBI.

Egan, Sir J. (1998), 'Rethinking Construction Rethinking Construction' The report of the Construction Task Force to the Deputy Prime Minister, John Prescott, on the scope for improving the quality and efficiency of UK construction, July 1998.

Emmerson, Sir H. (1962), *Survey of Problems before the Construction Industries*, HMSO, London.

Hendrick, T. and Ellram, L. (1993), *'Strategic Supplier Partnering: An International Study'*, Center for Advanced Purchasing Studies.

Huxham, C. (1996), 'Advantage or inertia? Making collaboration work' *The New Management Reader, International Thomson Publishing*. Paton, R., Clark, G., Jones, G., Lewis, J. and Quintas, P. (Eds).

Lamming, R. (1993), 'Beyond Partnership: Strategies for Innovation and Lean Supply', Prentice Hall, London.

Latham, Sir M. (1994), 'Construction the Team: Joint Review of Procurement and Contractual Arrangements in the United Kingdom Construction Industry Final Report', HMSO, London.

Morris, J. and Imrie, R. (1993), 'Japanese style subcontracting – its impact on European Industries', *Long Range Planning*, Vol.26, No.4, pp.53-58.

Parkinson, L. (1996), 'The contribution of Supply Chain Management and Partnership Sourcing to the UK Construction Industry', AMEC Construction Limited.

Partnership Sourcing (1998), 'Partnering for Profit', Department of Trade and Industry and Confederation of British Industry Profile Pursuit Limited.

Porter, M.E. (1980), *Competitive Strategy – Techniques for analyzing Industries and Competitors,* Free press New York.

Simon, Sir E. (1944), 'The Placing and Management of Building Contracts', HMSO, London.

Toone, D. (1997), 'Achieving Continuous improvement through the use of strategic partnering', CIBSE National Conference 1997.

Tulip, S. (1997), 'The Commitments'. *Supply Management*, 13 November 1997, pp.24-27.

Chapter 8

Early Supplier Involvement as a Tool for Reducing Supply Risk

Dr. George A. Zsidisin and Michael E. Smith

Introduction

Numerous approaches have been considered as ways to reduce supply risk. For example, there has been extensive research on the implementation of buffers such as inventory management (Lee et al, 1997; Starr and Miller, 1962) and the use of multiple supply sources (Anupindi and Akella, 1993; Newman, 1989; Tullous and Utecht, 1992) in response to supply risk (Christopher, 2002). These buffers are expensive and often serve only as a temporary solution for reducing the effects that supply risk manifestation has on purchasing firms. Another method that purchasing organizations can use to manage supply risk is focusing organizational resources on reducing the probability that risk events occur. In this Chapter, we will present a case study that illustrates how Early Supplier Involvement (ESI) can be used to reduce the probability and effect of an adverse supply incident for new products.

This Chapter will begin with an introduction to ESI, to include its benefits and drawbacks. Next, ESI will be discussed with regard to how it facilitates supply risk management. Managerial implications and conclusions are then presented.

Early Supplier Involvement

ESI is a form of collaboration in which purchasing firms involve suppliers at an early stage in the product development cycle, often during the need recognition and description phases of the acquisition process (Leenders et al, 2002). ESI is a relative concept since the extent of supplier contribution in product development projects may vary considerably. One conceptualization of the range of relationships (Bidault et al, 1998) holds that, at the lowest level, a supplier may simply provide information about equipment and capabilities so that a client's design team can integrate this information into the product design efforts. Above this baseline, a supplier may provide the buying organization's design team with suggestions for cost and/or quality improvements. Involvement becomes more significant as the supplier takes an active part in development processes by, for example, executing detailed drawings based on rough sketches provided by the buying organization. The highest levels of ESI are reached when the supplier takes full responsibility for a part or sub-assembly, from concept to manufacturing. Table 8.1 provides an overview of various levels of integration as ESI evolves.

Table 8.1 Five Levels of ESI Involvement (adapted from Bidault et al, 1998)

Degree of Involvement	Description
Level 1	Supplier provided input into your product/design by sharing information about its equipment and capabilities
Level 2	Supplier provided feedback on your design including suggestions for cost and quality improvements
Level 3	Supplier participates significantly in the design of a part/component by executing detailed drawings based on your group's rough sketches
Level 4	Supplier took full responsibility from concept to manufacture for the design of an entire part/component
Level 5	Supplier took full responsibility from concept to manufacture for the design of a system/subassembly incorporating one or more parts with it also designed

Five activities that have been identified as part of ESI initiatives are: 1) establishing trust and a business case 2) selecting the right suppliers for the job 3) moving the competition up front 4) setting target costs early and 5) locking in those target costs (Minahan, 1997). In addition, in order for the purchasing firm to have a successful ESI program, certain conditions need to be met. These conditions include: 1) identifying specific processes and tasks that need to be carried out, aimed at the integration of product development and sourcing processes 2) forming an organization that supports the execution of such tasks and 3) staffing the organization with people that have the right commercial, technical, and social skills (Wynstra et al, 2001). Purchasing organizations engage in ESI programs to achieve various benefits. A description of several of these benefits is provided below and includes the management of supply risk, as well as a brief discussion of potential drawbacks associated with ESI.

Benefits of ESI

There are numerous benefits that organizations can enjoy by involving suppliers early in product development activities. The short-term goals of ESI are development efficiency and effectiveness. Efficiency can lead to the reduction of development costs and the reduction of development lead-time. Meanwhile, the effectiveness of ESI may lead to the reduction of product cost and the increase of product value. A long-term objective for achieving greater efficiency and effectiveness involves getting access to the technological knowledge of suppliers (Wynstra et al, 2001). These benefits result in the reduction of risk associated with product development cycle times, quality problems, technological issues, excessive cost and moral hazard and adverse selection.

Suppliers can play a substantial role in process development and improvement to facilitate achieving higher quality, promoting close coordination to reach cost objectives, and reducing new product time-to-market (McGinnis and Vallopra, 1999). Supplier involvement can contribute to process development/improvement in the areas of quality, cost and new product time-to-market. These contributions are greater if process is a source of competitive advantage and if purchasing and supply management (PSM) is involved (McGinnis and Vallopra, 1999).

Drawbacks of ESI

ESI does not always result in positive results. Mounting empirical evidence suggests that simply adopting the supplier involvement techniques cited in the literature will not necessarily increase a project's technical success or compress development time (Hartley et al, 1997). Risks of project failure with the joint development approach of ESI can be caused by breakdowns in understanding. These breakdowns may occur when mixing incompatible cultures or in the absence of a common structure and objectives to bind the two parties together (Rigby, 1996). Risks that need to be overcome include: 1) lack of mutual trust 2) linking with the wrong partner for your strategic direction and 3) ineffective internal processes leading to higher costs (Rigby, 1996).

ESI alone does not necessarily lead to decreased costs, development lead-time (Laseter and Ramdas, 2002) or higher quality of the final product (Hartley et al, 1997). In some cases, ESI implementation has resulted in higher product and development costs and even worse product performance (Birou and Fawcett, 1994; Wynstra et al, 2001). One common source of such problems occurs when suppliers are selected that are not sufficiently capable of product development collaboration (Wynstra et al, 2001). Another source of problems arises when manufacturers do not have a clearly defined product development process or strategy in place. Problems with the manufacturer may also arise due to resistance at the departmental level, which are most directly involved in and affected by ESI, specifically PSM and engineering/product development (Wynstra et al, 2001).

Improper sequencing and the incorrect level of supplier involvement may be another source of problems in ESI. Laseter and Ramdas (2002) used cluster analysis to categorize sourced products. They derived four clusters representing the interaction between the nature of a given supplier's contribution with respect to the customer's perception of the final product (either critical to that perception or invisible) and the complexity of the interface between the supplier's contribution and the final product (either complex or simple). When the supplier's contribution is critical to customer perception of the product, and the interface is complex, it is expected that a full implementation of ESI (see Table 8.1) would be appropriate. However, by contrast, when the supplier's contribution is invisible to the customer and the interface is simple, it is expected that supplier involvement would come later in the product development process and that the involvement would be at a less intense level.

ESI and Supply Risk Management

The rest of the Chapter provides a description of the research method used in this study and then details how ESI at an aerospace supplier helps that company manage supply risk. We close with a discussion of the management implications of ESI's role in supply risk management and concluding comments.

Research Method

The research process consisted of conducting a case study within the purchasing organization of an aerospace supplier. This organization was selected due to its extensive participation in ESI activities with suppliers and that it is a key participant in an industry, where the risk associated with supplier firms can have significant detrimental effects on the organization.

The case study firm was pre-screened through an initial face-to-face interview, then through subsequent e-mail and telephone conversations. A case study research protocol was created prior to data collection and based on prior research discussed in the literature review. The case study was conducted at the firm's production facility. Information gathering techniques such as obtaining historical data and documentation and conducting structured interviews with various professional purchasing personnel and other key informants, were implemented during the case study execution.

Since the goal of the research was to investigate how ESI reduces supply risk, the purchasing function was the unit of analysis. Purchasing professional participants were asked numerous questions about their ESI initiatives and how those initiatives affect supply risk. A copy of the research protocol questions is available upon request.

Research Findings

The research findings will first provide some organizational background information. This is followed by a description of the ESI process at the case study firm and an introduction into the supply risk factors perceived by the case study respondents.

Organization Background: The organization in this study is a major supplier of critical components in the aerospace industry, providing vital technology for civilian and military aircraft. The industry is cost and reliability driven and requires extensive investments in research and development. Their products represent significant cost and safety contributions to the aircraft where they are installed and require extensive sustained product development efforts that often take 3-4 years to implement and require investments of $500-600 million before returns are realized.

Further, supplier-provided components represent approximately 65-80 per cent of the cost of goods sold.

A newly hired purchasing executive introduced the ESI initiative in 1999. Since that time, ESI has become viewed as a critical activity due to an estimated 80 per cent of their products' costs being locked in during the design phase. ESI is seen as a way for the subject company to meet the goal of significant cost reductions required for new products. Organizational contribution from ESI includes, obtaining leverage with the supply base, improving design capabilities, instituting internal documentation of best practices for organizational learning and managing supply risk.

The Early Supplier Involvement Process: ESI is based and supported in Supply Chain Management (SCM) and operates as a support function to the various business units. Internal documents obtained as part of this study, present ESI as a process that engages potential suppliers in the concept design stage of product development to ensure that customers' functional requirements are met at the lowest possible cost across the entire life cycle. This process involves a 16-step process as shown in Figure 8.1. The ESI process begins with establishing critical customer needs, which allows personnel to identify projects appropriate for ESI. Generally, the earlier in the 'product design cycle that ESI is implemented, the greater the potential benefits of its implementation.

This firm has found that target costing is critical to their success in implementing ESI. Using customer requirements as a starting point, target costs are established by drawing on the knowledge of internal experts in both product and production-process technology. Having aggressive but realistic cost target goals allows them to achieve cost savings without damaging supplier relationships. However, such costing is dependent upon suppliers receiving adequate data and having technical expertise. The long life cycle and long lead-time of their products means this aerospace supplier has found it challenging to generate reliable, accurate, component-level 'should' costs.

Following the establishment of component-level target costs, a formal planning process is initiated to create milestones for meeting overall customer demand, cost targets and timelines for the ESI project. Then, the operating business units provide input regarding high level design alternatives and create a list of potential suppliers for initial engagement in the ESI process. These suppliers are evaluated through a supplier selection process within the ESI initiative. Engineers, direct buyers, commodity specialists and strategic sourcing personnel, participate in the selection of potential suppliers in a process based upon knowledge of the industry and past supplier performance.

With a slate of potential suppliers identified, the ESI team then turns its attention to producing packages of information that will be presented to these organizations. These packages explain program objectives and requirements, as well as communicate technical information about program requirements. Potential suppliers are also asked to prepare rough pricing estimates that will be submitted at a supplier workshop. At the time of the workshop, these rough pricing estimates are compared with the previously determined target costs.

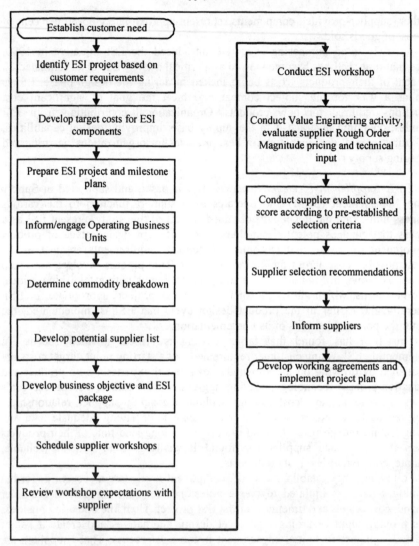

Figure 8.1 Early Supply Involvement Process Model

Once supplier workshops have been scheduled, the project leader contacts potential suppliers to review expectations for the workshop. At the workshop, these suppliers receive an overview of the ESI process, what is expected of them and how the process contributes to success for both firms. The suppliers are expected to provide a presentation about their core competencies, capabilities and progress in product development and evidence of successful performance as a supplier for other organizations. In addition, there is an exchange of technical and rough pricing information. At the time of the workshop, there are typically six to eight potential suppliers involved for each purchase category considered viable for ESI. However, suppliers competing for the same business do not attend simultaneously. The completion of these workshops usually reduces the number of potential suppliers.

Value engineering activities with the remaining potential suppliers are aimed at ensuring that customer requirements and cost targets are met. The activities include clarifying specifications and requirements, as well as considering specification revisions where lower costs can be achieved while still meeting customer requirements. Design alternatives can also be considered at this stage, including Design for Assembly and Design for Manufacturability. At the conclusion of these activities, the supplier evaluation is completed. Although the majority of the selection scoring has been accomplished according to pre-established criteria during earlier steps of the process, ESI project team members now meet to tabulate the results and issue their recommendations to the operating business units for the final supplier selection decision.

Suppliers are then notified of the selection results. Particular attention is paid to briefing suppliers that were not selected by stating the reasons for the decision and in many cases, they are given information about other opportunities for doing business. The notification process is seen as a way of demonstrating fairness in dealing with suppliers and promoting continued efforts by suppliers to possibly meet future supply requirements. At the conclusion of the ESI cycle, ESI personnel assist the supplier management team with developing memoranda of understanding and working agreements with the selected suppliers and providing communication guidelines to support smooth collaboration between the suppliers, engineering and SCM functions.

While the flow of this process for a given project can be seen as linear, from a strategic perspective, the ESI process can be seen as cyclic. In a business world that requires continuous improvement and innovation, the completion of one project represents the opportunity to begin again. The value provided by ESI has been recognized throughout this case study firm, which has driven greater demand for this support process with initial product design and product redesign.

The ESI process applies to both new and redesigned products. However, the potential value of ESI activities is considerably higher if engaged at the earliest possible stage of concept development. Correspondingly, the benefits of ESI are considerably reduced if the implementation of ESI in a project is delayed well into the product design phase.

Another aspect to ESI success is that the value yielded through ESI activities is dependent upon a productive relationship with the suppliers that are selected. The case study participants have found that the effort required to select world-class suppliers is richly rewarded because such suppliers are better prepared to manage close business relationships and provide the expertise that true design collaboration requires. In return for what the supplier brings to the ESI process, this aerospace supplier believes that they must openly and honestly share information in order to nourish the relationship and promote success. As one official noted, 'trust is the key ... share all that you can with the suppliers.' Honesty must extend both to internal and external participants. Hidden agendas can scuttle projects that otherwise show great promise.

ESI is a tool that has proven to be very successful in reducing new product costs. Target costing has helped to ensure that design efforts retain their focus on cost reductions instead of falling prey to tendencies toward ever-more-elegant designs. Cost management activities are driven by a market that is demanding greater efficiencies and by competitors who are claiming and achieving lower costs. During the early stages of the ESI program, support from top-level executives was required to generate internal customers for the process. Now, with the success achieved in two key projects, many of the operation business units solicit the assistance of the ESI team early in the product development process and momentum has built to such an extent that it taxes ESI support capabilities.

ESI produces value because of the organizational learning obtained through the successful projects. As ESI teams learn how to design better products and processes, it is considered important to capture these lessons so that they can be considered for other projects. In this way, success is magnified for both firms and knowledge about successes represents a powerful marketing tool for additional ESI activities.

How ESI reduces supply risk: There are several factors that affect supply risk perceptions at this firm. Most of the characteristics discussed originate from the supplier organizations. The characteristics discussed by respondents that significantly influence supply risk perceptions include: 1) excessive cost 2) legal liabilities 3) quality problems 4) supplier capacity constraints 5) extended product development times and 6) the inability to handle product design changes.

Excessive cost was a major impetuous for the ESI initiative. Prior to the initiative, the perception of upper management was that they were being priced out of an increasingly competitive marketplace. This led to invoking target costing as a major component in their ESI process. Further, 'world class' suppliers often have cost reduction programs already in place. Such, however, is not the case with less competent suppliers. ESI provides a method for working with suppliers to both convince them of the importance of cost reduction programs and help these suppliers develop cost management programs. As the ESI initiative has matured, this firm has increasingly fashioned a cadre of suppliers and an approach to working together with suppliers to assure continued cost reductions in design and redesign efforts. As the result of developing effective relationships with suppliers, this firm has significantly reduced perceived risks associated with non-competitive pricing of critical supplies.

Legal liability issues represent a potentially significant risk for firms involved in developing and marketing advanced technology products. Case study participants noted that the precise form of the liability depends on which party or parties have the expertise. Effective sharing of expertise reduces risk associated with product failure in the marketplace and agreements that provide for the sharing of gains reduce the potential risk associated with intellectual property rights concerns. ESI is one tool that can be implemented to reduce the likelihood that legal liability issues arise.

Quality problems can be resolved by ensuring alignment between designs and capabilities early in the design cycle. Concurrent design between suppliers and the purchasing organization helps to ensure that design problems that might lead to extensive rework and yield problems can be worked out up-front. Further, by the use of scorecards that record data about supply-base execution, this aerospace supplier is able to continuously track the performance of current suppliers and use this information in determining which suppliers will be invited to participate in new ESI projects. The effective utilization of performance data in selecting suppliers during the ESI process helps prevent risk manifestation from quality problems.

Supplier capacity constraints represent a risk associated with the managerial decision making of a firm's suppliers. Suppliers are engaged during the pre-selection process of ESI projects in areas such as planning process, past growth, current status and investments. Such information about the planning and implementation of capacity expansion is seen as critical to managing the risk of supplier capacity constraints by selecting firms that will meet the future needs of their production process. Even during times of difficult economic conditions, world-class suppliers may see substantial growth and could have capacity problems. The information sharing that is part of effective ESI efforts represents a valuable means for determining the adequacy of the supplier's capacity planning, and providing the supplier with information to drive more successful planning with regard to the buying organization's future requirements.

Extended product development times represent a risk in that they can increase development costs and delay the delivery of the new product into the market. ESI facilitates risk management by ensuring that development information is shared between the two firms. Thus, delays are readily recognized and steps can be taken to manage the process to mitigate the risk, including sharing of resources and making materials and design changes.

The inability to handle *product design changes* on the part of suppliers can jeopardize the entire product line. The information exchange that occurs in ESI helps manage the potential failure of product design changes because awareness of budding problems allows them to develop alternative strategies.

Managerial Implications

There are several managerial implications that practitioners and academics alike can glean from these research findings. The use of ESI as a risk management tool has implications for: 1) forming strategic relationships between buyers and suppliers 2) avoiding adverse selection and moral hazard 3) transferring risk to suppliers and 4) developing supply chains.

Forming Strategic Relationships

ESI can initially be seen as a method for aligning supplier behaviors with that of the purchasing organization. At first, before the supplier selection decision, there is no close relationship specified between the firm studied in this research and its suppliers. The purpose of ESI at the pre-supplier selection phase is to determine which suppliers, will be best able to meet the specified outcomes in terms of quality, delivery, cost and time line goals. However, there are also other aspects of ESI that are more closely related with aligning the goals of suppliers with those of the purchasing firm. During the initial stages of ESI, before the actual supplier is selected, the case study firm is most interested in understanding the culture and philosophies of each of the supplier organizations. This is because it is important to see that there will be goal congruency between the two organizations and that the philosophies and organizational cultures provide for a sound match. In addition, after the supplier selection decision is made, it is expected that a close relationship that is characterized by the exchange of critical, timely and sensitive information will arise and that the relationship between the two firms will continue for a long period of time.

When organizations and their suppliers work together as part of ESI projects, it is natural that information exchange improves. With better exchange of information comes better knowledge of the situations surrounding the dynamics of a supply relationship and with that information comes the greater potential for detecting, averting, and managing supply risk.

Avoiding Adverse Selection and Moral Hazard

The risk of adverse selection and moral hazard (Eisenhardt, 1989) is also managed throughout the ESI process. By having suppliers involved at the earliest stages of the new product development cycle, the purchasing organization is better assured that they will select the most qualified supplier that is capable to bringing engineering expertise to an aircraft sub-assembly, with an outstanding reputation for quality and similar corporate philosophies. In addition, since the process is rather lengthy in the beginning, suppliers must demonstrate a significant level of commitment up-front for supplier selection. If they are selected, they will be almost assured of enjoying continued business on a large scale if consistent in meeting cost and quality demands. Moral hazard is reduced by having suppliers that either cannot meet requirements up-front or are not willing to put forth the required effort to meet demand requirements are eliminated from further consideration early within the process.

Transferring Risk to Suppliers

Some level of risk is transferred to supplier organizations in the target costing process. Suppliers are appraised early within the ESI process that it is imperative that they meet the target cost for the sub-assembly for which, they have been included in the new product. This has the effect of transferring some of the risk for meeting cost goals to the suppliers that are actually selected to provide a component.

Developing Supply Chains

Throughout the early supplier involvement process, when investigating which firm to select for a specific sub-class of items, initial insights are obtained into who is a 'world-class' supplier. From a supply chain perspective, this goes beyond the traditional thoughts of concurrent engineering that encompasses simultaneous product and process design and goes into 3DCE, as described by Fine (1998), which consists of developing a supply chain in conjunction with product and process design. Given that there are only a limited number of suppliers available within this industry for many components, this process leverages their selection and development to the maximum extent possible. By involving multiple suppliers from the initial stages of product conception and going through the supplier selection process to gather information about those suppliers' philosophies, technological and production capabilities, past experience and desired goals, the case study firm is able to reduce many of the supply risk factors that exist. This portion of the ESI process facilitates selecting either a world-class supplier or one that is attempting to attain that status.

Conclusion

ESI can help firms manage characteristics of supply risk such as problems with quality, technological capabilities, and lengthy product development cycle times. The ESI process illustrated in Figure 8.1 and described in this Chapter provides for such management by supporting the selection of the proper suppliers using an exhaustive selection process, followed by developing solid information exchanges with key suppliers.

There are a number of areas that an organization can look toward for evidence of risk reduction through ESI activities. In the immediate case, cost reductions were a primary motivator for implementing ESI in order to ensure future business competitiveness. This concern led the buying organization to expend substantial efforts in developing cost targets prior to involving suppliers. Savings relative to established cost baselines and the new target costs represented important metrics for tracking reductions in business risk as a result of ESI. Further, the extent to which suppliers of important components had refined cost-reduction processes in place represents another potential metric.

Other areas that may be important in evaluating the extent to which ESI helps to reduce supply risk may include many of the standard performance measures associated with both supplier evaluation and product design efforts. Organizations may wish to consider developing measures and means for assessment of suppliers relative to quality, management systems/structure, organizational culture, capacity constraints, planning (particularly relative to the future needs of the buying organization), financial health, business continuity and contingency planning.

Areas for which there is shared responsibility that may be assessed include, design lead times, design risk and the extent to which there is the ability to respond to design changes.

All of these measures were identified by the buying organization in the present case as areas within which improvements were noted in their management of supply risk, both in terms of reductions in the likelihood of adverse supply events and in the magnitude of potential adverse events. However, perhaps the most important implication of the implementation of ESI with respect to supply risk was in identifying potential sources of supply risk. This ability to discover, evaluate and mitigate new sources of risk is valuable to any firm. While the assessment of such novel findings can only be determined in retrospect, managers are likely to perceive them as critical contributions to business success in an era filled with events that are hard to anticipate.

The material provided in this Chapter provides an 'effective practice' example of how ESI can be used as one tool within a supply risk management strategy. Although cost reduction was the original impetus behind the implementation of ESI within the case company, ESI can also serve as a technique for reducing, transferring and/or avoiding supply risk.

References

Anupindi, R. and Akella, R. (1993), 'Diversification under supply uncertainty,' *Management Science,* Vol.39, No.8, pp.944-963.

Bidault, F. Despres, C. and Butler, C. (1998), 'New product development and early supplier involvement (ESI): The drivers of ESI adoption,' *International Journal of Technology Management,* Vol.15, No.1/2, pp.49-69.

Birou, L.M. and Fawcett, S.E. (1994), 'Supplier involvement in integrated product development: A comparison of US and European practices,' *International Journal of Physical Distribution and Logistics Management,* Vol.24, No.5, pp.4-14.

Christopher, M. (2002), *Supply Chain Vulnerability,* Cranfield University School of Management.

Eisenhardt, K.M. (1989), 'Agency theory: An assessment and review,' *Academy of Management Review,* Vol.14, No.1, pp.57-74.

Fine, Charles H. (1998), *Clockspeed: Winning Industry Control in the Age of Temporary Advantage.* Perseus, Reading, MA.

Hartley, J.L., Meredith, J.R., McCutcheon, D., and Kamath, R.R. (1997), 'Suppliers' contribution to product development: An exploratory survey,' *IEEE Transactions on Engineering Management,* Vol.44, No.3, pp.258-267.

Laseter, T.M. and Ramdas, K. (2002), 'Product types and supplier roles in product development: An exploratory analysis,' *IEEE Transactions on Engineering Management,* Vol.49, No.2, pp.107-118.

Lee, H., Padmanabhan, V., and Whang, S. (1997), 'Information distortion in a supply chain: the bullwhip effect,' *Management Science,* Vol.43, No.4, pp.546-558.

Leenders, M.R., Fearon, H.E., Flynn, A.E., and Johnson, P.F. (2002), *Purchasing and Supply Management,* 12th edition, McGraw-Hill Irwin, New York, NY.

McGinnis, M.A. and Vallopra, R.M. (1999), 'Purchasing and supplier involvement in process improvement: A source of competitive advantage,' *Journal of Supply Chain Management*, Vol.35, No.4, pp. 42-50.

Minahan, T.(1997), 'Allied Signal soars by' *Purchasing*, pp.38-47 (September 18, 1997).

Newman, R.G. (1989), 'Single sourcing: short-term savings versus long-term problems,' *Journal of Purchasing and Materials Management*, Vol.25, No.3, pp.20-25.

Rigby, B. (1996), 'Continuous acquisition and life-cycle support: The risks and benefits of early supplier involvement in the development process,' *Logistics Information Management*, Vol. 9, No.2, pp.22-26.

Starr, M. and Miller, D. (1962), *Inventory Control: Theory and Practice*, Prentice-Hall, Englewood Cliffs, NJ.

Tullous, R. and Utecht, R.L. (1992), 'Multiple or single sourcing?' *Journal of Business and Industrial Marketing*, Vol.7, No.3, pp.5-18.

Wynstra, F., VanWeele, A. and Weggemann, M. (2001), 'Managing supplier involvement in product development: Three critical issues,' *European Management Journal*, Vol.19, No.2, pp.157-167.

Chapter 9

A Risk Analysis Framework for Marine Transport of Packaged Dangerous Goods

Arben Mullai

Introduction

There has been a rapid proliferation in the development of new chemical compounds and their extensive use. Over 11 million chemical substances are known and some 60,000 to 70,000 chemicals are in regular use. Of those, approximately 3,000 account for 90 per cent of total commercial and other uses. On average, three new chemicals are licensed for commercial use each day. Only a fraction of chemicals in use have adequate toxicological data.

Large amounts of different types of dangerous substances, materials and articles (dangerous goods – DG) are present in communities around the world. They are also present in transit via highways, railways, waterways, air and pipelines. Dangerous goods/cargoes are carried by water in bulk (e.g. oil, oil products, liquefied gases and some chemicals) and *packaged form* (hereinafter *packaged dangerous goods* – PDG). Ships with large quantities of many different types of PDG penetrate estuaries, harbours and narrow channels to take them through or into large centers of population. Between 10-15 per cent of cargoes carried by water are PDG. Dangerous goods are also carried in 'limited quantities', for example in the form of passengers' personal effects, on board passenger (cruise) and ferry ships. The principal international rules for the carriage of PDG by sea are set in the International Maritime Dangerous Goods (IMDG) Code, which has been harmonized with the 'United Nations Recommendations on the Transport of Dangerous Goods' and other modal regulations.

A large proportion of accidents involving dangerous goods, in many cases with fatal consequences and severe damage to the environment, happen during transportation. The review of many accident case histories has shown that ships carrying PDG are, in many cases, involved in serious and very serious marine accidents in which many people have been killed, injured and suffered ill health. Many ships have been totally lost with dangerous cargoes on board in coastal and sensitive areas. On average, 230 ships with a gross registered tonnage of 1.1 million are lost worldwide every year. In addition, every year many PDG are lost overboard. Miles of beaches have been sealed for many days and thousands of people have been engaged in costly recovery or cleaning up operations.

The risk-related costs of dangerous goods are the costs attributable to the hazardous properties of such goods which alone can represent more than 13 per cent of the transport costs (UNEP, 1997). Legal settlements and environmental remediation costs together represent more than 80 per cent of the overall risk-related costs.

Enhancing safety and health and protecting the marine environment are the key goals in the strategic planning at different levels. The increasing amounts of dangerous goods carried by water and the risks they pose have raised public concerns, requiring greater emphasis on sound and proactive risk management.

Literature Review

The literature review of the past 10-15 years shows that a large number of studies have been conducted in chemical life cycle risks. However, the literature in the field of the risks of marine events involving PDG is generally limited, if not lacking in some aspects, for example, the human risks (Haastrup and Brockhoff, 1990). In many countries, in particular in Europe (see Goulielmos, 2001; Gade and Redondo, 1999) and North America (LaBelle and Anderson, 1996), the main concerns have been the risks of major accidents involving dangerous bulk cargoes (Stanners and Bourdeau, 1995), such as oil, oil products, LNG, LPG, and a few chemicals carried in bulk (Romer et al, 1995; Giziakis and Bardi-Giziaki, 2002), excluding others materials and substances. Numerous studies cover individual major and dramatic marine accidents such as Exxon Valdes (see Miraglia, 2002; Gilfillan et al, 1999), Braer (see Hall et al, 1996), Sea Empress (see Batten et al, 1998), or Erika.

Data availability, costs and time are often quoted as big barriers to conducting risk analyses. Detailed risk analyses are generally very time-consuming and resource intensive. In some examples covered by the OECD (2000) study, the costs of analysis in chemical risk management have ranged from US$180,000 to $8 million.

Risk assessment frameworks have increasingly been developed and applied in recent years in many areas, including human health and safety and marine environment protection. For the shipping industry these are primarily developed for the analysis of risks concerning shipping in general i.e. not necessarily related to hazards of dangerous goods (e.g. Sii et al, 2001; Fowler and Sorgard, 2000). Numerous frameworks have been specifically designed for the assessment of individual or aggregated risks (i.e. the risks of all dangerous cargoes without any distinction) associated with dangerous bulk cargoes such as oil and oil products (e.g. Reed et al, 1999; Onyekpe, 2002), LNG (e.g. Fay, 2003) and LPG and other chemicals carried and handled and stored in ports in large quantities (e.g. HSC, 1991; Goulielmos and Pardali, 1998; Saccommanno, 1993). Some frameworks serve a specific purpose in a specific country (e.g. HSC, 1991; Donk and de Rijke, 1995). However, no single methodology has the capability of serving all essential safety and environmental decision problems and needs within shipping (EC, 1999), including the risks of marine events involving PDG.

Recognising the limitations in knowledge and the increasing attention that issues of the risks of PDGs receive, together with the developing specifications of marine transportation of PDGs, it is important to have a specific risk analysis framework. Further, the continuous improvement, refinement and development of new and more advanced methods, techniques and tools in all fields, including marine transport of dangerous goods, continue to be important tasks. Therefore, the objective is to develop a framework for the analysis of the risks of marine events involving PDGs.

Methods and Data

This study is based on the combination of the literature review, empirical data and the author's prior research (Mullai and Paulsson, 2002) in the field of the marine risks. Many studies covering risk management practices, risk analysis/assessment frameworks and techniques employed in shipping and other sectors have been reviewed. In order to develop a framework to suit the marine transport system consideration needs to be given to structures, problems, risk elements, data quality, the operation of risk assessors and management needs.

This study intends to contribute in the improvement of the safety and the marine environment protection through improvements in the risk assessment methodology. A better methodology can contribute to a better understanding of the risks through more detailed and adequate information. A better understanding of risks may contribute to more informative and improved decision-making.

A Risk Analysis Framework for Marine Transport of Packaged Dangerous Goods (PDG)

A risk analysis framework for application in marine transport of PDG relies on the principles of risk analysis. In addition to many other sources quoted elsewhere in this report, further information on these principles was derived from a number of sources (e.g. Purdy, 1993; Royal Society, 1992; HSE, 1991; HSE, 1998; Nicolet-Monnier and Gheorghe, 1996; HSE, 2002; EPA, 1989). The framework consists of three main stages (Figure 9.1) and each stage consists of a number of steps. In order to facilitate the analysis, two analytical techniques, namely Fault Tree Analysis (FTA) and Event Tree Analysis (ETA), are adopted and integrated into the framework. Although presented in a sequential order, the process, like any other scientific research process, is usually cyclical and some of the steps are inseparable. The process begins with the problem identification and formulation extending through data collection, analysis process, conclusions and recommendations.

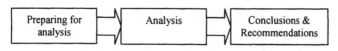

Figure 9.1 The Main Stages of Risk Analysis and Management

The main purpose of risk analysis is to inform the decision makers about the risks. Kaplan and Garrick (1981) suggest that three interrelated fundamental questions need to be answered: *'What has gone and can go wrong?'* *'What are the consequences?'* *'How likely is that to happen?'* This triple definition (Figure 9.2) has become widely accepted in the field of marine transport (e.g. ASC, 1998; Ruxton, 1996). The processes that facilitate the answers to these three fundamental questions constitute the core of risk analysis. The overall process comprises a number of over-lapping and integrated stages.

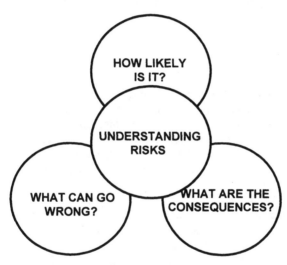

Figure 9.2 The 'Triple Definition'

The development of this framework and its practical application within the context of marine transport of packaged dangerous goods is presented within three distict stages:

Stage	Associated Group of Activities
1	Preparing for the analysis
2	Risk analysis
3	Conclusions and recommendations

Within each of these three stages there are a number of steps, each of which contains a number of activities. The description of this framework and its application will focus primarily on the major steps with brief descriptions of the important activities within each of these.

Stage 1: Preparing for the Analysis

This stage consists of a number of interrelated steps for conducting risk analysis and is generally cyclical. The order in which these are presented below may not necessarily reflect the sequence in practice.

Step	Associated Activities
1	Preliminary screening
2	Problem formulation
3	Selecting methods of analysis
4	Data collection

Step 1: Preliminary screening

Risk analysis may vary from simple screening to major analysis that require years of effort, substantial resources and large teams of experts. Resources spent to manage risks vary significantly across regions, countries, communities and industries. Detailed analyses inevitably require more resources (see Morgenstern and Landy, 1997; Hokkanen and Pelline, 1991). Generally, large volumes of high quality, risk-related data is expensive to obtain. It is important to remember that the costs of the risk study may outweigh its benefits.

In order to determine whether the risks posed by PDG are likely to be acceptable or unacceptable, it may initially be necessary to undertake a preliminary or screening level analysis eliminating in-depth analysis of low-risk elements (e.g. the type of marine events, ships, dangerous goods, vessel traffic, activities, and geographical locations). Screening, which is often conservative, makes use of data at hand, easily accessible and inexpensive, such as case histories. Key parameters for consideration are consequences and threats posed by PDG. The next stage may comprise a more detailed risk analysis. The depth and breadth of the analysis may vary on a scale from low to high, depending on a number of interrelated factors including the extent of risks, concerns, urgency, interests and risk management options to control risks, costs, the amount and quality of data available.

Who should conduct risk analysis? Decision makers have to ensure that any person carrying out the analysis is knowledgeable in risk analysis and familiar with the requirements of regulations governing the marine transport of dangerous goods and has practical understanding of these activities. Detailed risk analysis draws expertise from various fields and branches of science such as engineering, statistics, chemistry, marine biology, epidemiology, toxicology, economy and sociology. In some countries the role of experts has become formal, explicit and documented.

Identify interested parties. Risks and related decisions on the transport of dangerous goods affect a wide range of interests and stakeholders. Their views about risks, benefits and the acceptability of risks may vary from being similar or convergent to being very different. With their involvement come many benefits, including greater accessibility to a larger quantity of better quality, risk-related data, together with greater acceptance and better understanding of the goals. In order to avoid conflicts, the legislation in some countries (e.g. in Europe, USA, Canada) requires an active involvement of the effected interests. The list of interested parties in marine transport of PDG is endless: ship owners, cargo interests, shareholders, general public, governments and many other public and private shipping interests.

Step 2: Problem formulation

Identify risk generating activities. Marine transport of PDG and other related activities, such as packing, handling, stowage, loading and unloading of PDG, give rise to risks. The analysis may address the risks associated with individual activities, combinations thereof or the entire PDG life cycle, where marine transport of PDG has its share on the risk contribution.

Identify and formulate problems. The risk analysis may address these interrelated generic issues: human safety and health, marine environment pollution, property damage, economical aspects and others, for example, social concerns and security. The security of marine transport of PDG has become an issue of concern in recent years. These risk issues may be viewed in the context of other sources of risk in other industries, sectors, human activities or phenomena.

Set the objective(s). Problems can be tackled in different ways by different means. The generic objective of a risk study is to facilitate decision makers with information and tools, which would enable them to make informative decisions for managing risks. Some specific categories of objectives include improved:

1. Knowledge: e.g. enhance or consolidate understanding of the risks and provide recommendations for better management of risks;
2. Procedures: e.g. improve handling, packing, securing, and documentation of PDG;
3. Technology: e.g. improve or develop hardware, software, and IT;
4. Methodology: e.g. develop, adopt, improve or refine risk analysis methods, techniques and tools.

Define boundaries. Every study is at some point confined in time and space. The boundaries can be broadly categorized into physical or system boundaries and analytical boundaries. However, because of their interrelations a clear-cut distinction between them may not be possible. The breadth and depth of the analysis may vary widely. It may be impractical, if not impossible, to conduct a detailed study for all elements of the risk management system. Further, studying all elements of the system and their possible interconnections becomes a very difficult task. By defining boundaries analysts, inter alias, avoid overlooking some key elements and unnecessarily scrutinising some others. Some examples of boundaries are:

1. *physical*: types and amounts of dangerous goods; form in which dangerous goods are carried; transport activities; geographical locations;
2. *analytical*: the risk management encompasses risk analysis, evaluation and management – e.g. conduct risk analysis only;
3. *qualitative or quantitative* – e.g. employ a quasi-quantitative analysis approach;
4. *level* of analysis varies from high to low levels of resolution – e.g. focus on problems related to packing, handling, securing and carrying of PDG;
5. *types* of risks – risks are divided into human, marine environment and property risks – e.g. deal with individual or aggregated risks posed by PDG.

Step 3: Selecting methods of analysis

Select methods and techniques. Generally, risk analysis is a rigorous scientific process performed by means of standardized formats, which employs certain specific techniques and methods – e.g. Fault Tree Analysis (FTA), Event Tree Analysis (ETA), Hazard and Operability Analysis (HAZOP), Failure Modes and Effect Analysis (FMEA). Whilst, there is no single appropriate technique for a specific activity, there are techniques that are more suitable than others. The choice is affected by a number of interrelated and complex factors including the extent of risks, objectives, data, time and resources available, decision makers' requirements and relevant regulations (see EC, 1998).

Risk related data and data collection methods. The risk analysis, regardless of how simple, requires information to aid in the decision-making process. In many cases, a wide range and large amounts of data is collected from different sources by employing different data collection methods and techniques.

Step 4: Data collection

Data collection. Risks studies can employ a wide range of data collection methods and techniques, such as: interview, observation, field study, experiment and testing, simulation, survey, archival or documentary, literature review, and statistics. Grounding in the actual experiences means that the risk studies based on case histories are generally preferred (see DNV, 1995; Carol et al, 2001). The amount, variety and accessibility of data are some other reasons why historical data is so widely used.

With regard to the data available, risk studies can combine different approaches:

1. make use of sufficient data available for the system or phenomena in question,
2. in cases of insufficient data, available data is combined with information from previous studies from other places or applications of similar systems adjusted to the system under study and conditions of the local environment;
3. if limited data exists the analysis, or certain aspects of the analysis, can make use of simulations or theoretical models; and
4. expert judgments.

For the purpose of the study a sample size of N numbers of cases can be drawn from a 'population' of marine events. The sample may be designed based on certain criteria including: the form in which dangerous goods are carried, types/sizes of ships and dangerous goods, activities, locations and consequences. The data availability and accessibility, time and the resource availability are some of the factors that determine the sample size.

Sources of data. Marine transport risk-related data is held for different purpose by different organizations. Data sources vary from public access, limited access for example for 'members only', non-accessible to confidential and very confidential. Reasonably accurate and well-defined statistical databases are prerequisites for risk analysis and subsequently risk management. Good access to data and information is also critical for risk analysis. Given the sensitivity of the risk issues, in particular the risks posed by many PDGs, the limitation of data available may be an obstacle to develop a robust risk analysis. Before conducting a risk analysis it is important to identify relevant sources, evaluate and discuss with the decision makers about the availability, accessibility and costs of data.

There are numbers of databases designated for industrial accidents involving dangerous goods that have occurred at fixed installations and during transportation. However, despite of the extensive search, no single designated database available for marine events involving PDG has been found. Numerous private and public databases are specially designed for the marine events involving oil spills. Even the best source available does not provide all necessary risk-related data. Therefore, data may be acquired from different sources. In some cases, appendices of codes or guidelines for the risks/safety management contain compendium of data sources. Some relevant sources include: chemical industry; occupational health and safety authorities, enforcement agencies, class and insurance organizations, port authorities and maritime organizations. The following are some relevant accident and incident databases that have been identified:

Database	Country/Organisation
Major Accident Reporting System	European Union
Major Hazardous Incidents Database System	Safety and Reliability Directorate, UK
Failure and Accident Technical Information System	TNO, The Netherlands
CHEMAX database	Joint Research Centre, Ispra, European Commission
OECD database on industrial accidents	OECD's Expert Group on Chemical Accidents
Centre for Chemical Process Safety	Chemical process organizations
Accidental Release Information System	Environment Protection Agency, USA
Emergency Response Notification System	USA
Chemical Incident Reports Centre	U.S. Chemical Safety and Hazard Investigation Board
APELL disasters database	United Nations Environment Protection
Hazardous Material Incident Reporting System	USA
Institution of Chemical Engineers	Institution of Chemical Engineers
National Response Centre	USA
Laboratory of Maritime Accidents	International Maritime Organization
Marine Accident Reporting Scheme	Nautical Institute UK, IMO
Lloyd's List Casualty Watch	Lloyd's Maritime Information Services
International Underwriting Association	UK
Swedish Maritime Administration and Coast Guard	SMA and Coast Guard, Sweden
Casualty Reports	US Coast Guard
Hazardous Cargo Bulletin Log	Hazardous Cargo Bulletin, UK

Quality of data. Generally, data is not defined and recorded with specific risk analysis and management requirements in mind. Data accuracy and completeness are often related with the severity of events. Fatal and marine environment pollution events contain generally more reliable and complete data because they are easy to identify, hard to conceal and involve a wider coverage. Uncertainty surrounds the 'most reliable' sources and the reliability also varies. However, in any study, reasonable efforts should have been made to select, verify/triangulate, compliment and make use of data from the 'best' sources available.

Stage 2: Risk Analysis

The risk analysis stage comprises a number of interrelated steps which are summarized in the table below. The order in which these are presented may not necessarily reflect the sequence in practice.

Table 9.1 Risk Analysis Steps

Step	Associated Activities
1	System definition
2	Analytical process
3	Hazard identification
4	Exposure analysis
5	Consequence analysis
6	Exposure evaluation
7	Consequence evaluation
8	Risk characterisation and presentation
9	Sensitivity analysis

Based on the risk-related data and information and risk analysis techniques, the risk elements or attributes are analysed at this stage. The analysis can be performed based on the model provided in Figure 9.3. The model combines two elements:

1. The structure of the framework consists of the key steps of risk analysis – i.e. *hazard identification, exposure and consequence analysis, quantification/likelihood estimation,* and *risk characterisation and presentation;*
2. The structure of analysis techniques – Fault Tree (FTA) and Event Tree (ETA), which are adopted and combined into a single hybrid model with the FTA plotted sideways on the left and the ETA plotted sideways on the right in the model (see Figure 9.3). The top or initial event is plotted in the middle.

Thus, identification of the transport hazards and likelihood estimation thereof can be performed by means of FTA. Consequences analysis and likelihood estimation can be performed by means of ETA. The analysis attempts to provide answers to the fundamental questions – the triple definition. The structure of the model reflects the marine transport system of PDGs, risk elements and causes of marine events involving PDG.

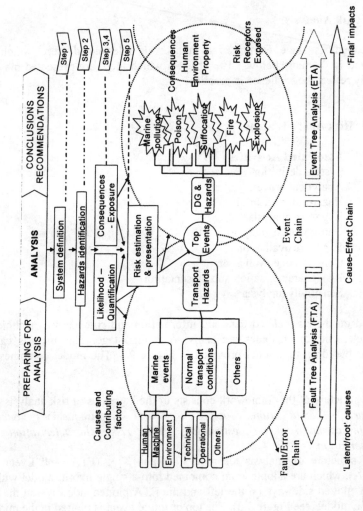

Figure 9.3 A Risk Analysis Framework

Step 1: System Definition

Define and describe the marine transport system of PDG including other essential risk-related elements. The system is separated into its constituent elements at different levels of resolution and described accordingly, as a detailed description would be prohibitively expensive (HSE, 1991). The risk assessors and decision-makers should agree the degree of detail and the potential need for additional data collection.

Elements	Description – examples of sub-elements or properties
1. Ships:	Ships carrying PDG and other ships interfering with PDG traffic: e.g., type, size, flags/nationality, age
2. Dangerous goods:	PDG and other dangerous goods/cargoes: e.g., classes 1-9, 'limited quantities'
3. Packaging/units:	Packagings and cargo transport units (CTU): e.g., type/form, material, packaging group
4. Vessel traffic:	PDG and other traffics, for example, passenger, oil and chemicals carried in bulk traffic: e.g., type, number, and size of ships; amount, number and size of shipments of PDG
5. Activities:	Cargo loading and unloading, packing, stowing, securing, and documentation, navigation, manoeuvring and other marine transport-related activities
6. Marine transport infrastructure:	Navigation systems, e.g., canals, waterways; terminal/ports, equipment and warehouses
7. Weather/sea conditions:	Winds, precipitations, humidity, temperature, state of the sea, currents, seawater properties, water depths, and other navigation situations
8. Marine environment:	Fauna and flora, marine resources, protected/designated sensitive areas and coastlines
9. Exposed population:	Ship's crew/personnel, passengers, stevedores/workers, inspectors/surveyors, pilots and local community
10 Properties and activities ashore:	Individual and common properties, business and other activities ashore.

Review the current state-of-the-art of the regulations governing marine transport of PDGs. The marine transport of PDGs, including technical, operational, safety and health and environmental protection aspects, is highly regulated. Complying with regulations provides the common level for safety and marine environment protection. Therefore, the current state-of-the-art of the regulations and safety technology should be reviewed. What comprises the regulatory system for the marine transport of PDGs? What is the current state-of-the art? What are other appropriate safeguards in place? These are some of the issues that should be addressed in this step. The review of the regulations will also provide the ground for dealing with some important issues for risk analysis and management.

Evaluate the state-of-the-art of the regulations. Identify and describe regulations related issues, some of which can be identified in the risk analysis process, including: Does marine transport of PDGs conform to good practices and established rules? How and to what extent have regulations contributed to the risks?

Step 2: Analytical Process

The analytical process begins with hazard identification. However, prior to this, it is important to understand the chain of events and determine the 'top events' from which the analysis process starts. This will further describe the model's elements. In order to have a better understanding of the analysis process, the model (Figure 9.3) could be used as a guide. The graphical representation of the model allows easy visualization of the process.

The risks of marine transport of PDGs are about the risks of events associated with the release or simply involvement with dangerous goods. It is important to understand these potential events initially. The review of many case histories has shown that marine events involving PDG are generated and propagated in the form of a chain of events. This is an open cause-effect chain in which effects of one or a combination of events may become causes for another subsequent event or a chain of events. For example, dangerous goods lost at sea can cause contamination of the seawater and sediments, which can cause contamination of fish. This, in turn, can cause poisoning of people consuming the contaminated fish. The chain 'starts' with 'latent or root' causes and 'ends' with 'final' consequences. In between, it is difficult to tell apart causes from effects. The time span between 'root' causes and 'final' consequences vary widely for individual events, which could vary from a few seconds or minutes (e.g. a massive explosion following an impact or fire) to several years (e.g. spill of dangerous substances from corroded containers that have been poorly maintained for a long time), and even decades (e.g. marine pollutants getting into the food chain). In many risk analyses a large number of events are often taken into consideration, sometimes, as many as a hundred or even thousands of events. Generally, the chain is long and dominated by large and complex combinations of events and conditions.

Define the top events. It is customary to define one or a set of events, known as 'top' or 'initiating' events (terms used in FTA and ETA respectively) from which the analysis starts. The definition of 'top events' varies across industries, which sometimes becomes a matter of choice. In shipping, 'marine events' such as grounding, collision, fire/explosion, machinery failure etc., as defined by the IMO and Lloyd's Register of Shipping, are generally taken as the top events. Given the vast range of DG and packaging, large numbers of events and conditions in marine transport of PDGs, the determination of top events becomes very difficult. Based on the review of case histories, the following are defined as the top events:

1. *Breach of package.* This category includes ruptures, punctures, or any other form of failures or damages that can lead to spillage or release of dangerous goods. Large amounts of different types of dangerous goods are carried by sea in various types of packagings in liquid, gas or liquefied gas forms and many are corrosive, flammable, explosive and toxic. For many of these substances, the release is the necessary, but not sufficient, condition for DG to come in contact and cause harm to humans, the environment and property.
2. *Other events.* This category includes other events that can lead to the release/involvement of dangerous goods or an unsafe situation that is the result of deviations from the intended functions of packaging or transportation, but which is not covered by the category of 'breach.' For example, the events involving materials, such as fires in cargoes of cotton or fishmeal, do not necessary involve any breach of package or release of dangerous goods.

The top events defined above are used as the common joint points for both FTA and ETA. In other words, both trees 'spring' from a single set of events. Further, the top events 'divide' the cause-effect chain into two areas, namely:

1. the 'cause or error' chain consisting of events and conditions (i.e. transport hazards and their causes and contributing factors) that can lead to top events, which can be analysed by the FTA, and
2. the 'effect' chain consisting of events and conditions (i.e. the release of dangerous substances and their subsequent consequences) following top events, which can be analysed by the ETA.

Step 3: Hazard Identification

Identify and describe hazards, including their cause and contributing factors, and the sequence of events that have or can lead to loss of containment and involvement of dangerous goods. The term 'hazard' may take different meanings in different contexts, but in this part it is used to denote the situations or conditions that have the potential to cause damage to DG containments. Many hazards are associated with the marine transport system of PDGs including physical, chemical, biological, climate and other hazards. The analysis should take a systems approach, in which the marine transport system should be considered as a very complex socio-technical-environment entity that is formed of human and man-made entities operating in a physical environment. If sufficient quantitative data is available, hazards and their cause and contributing factors that contribute most to the risks, which can be readily managed, should be identified. As mentioned earlier, for the purpose of hazard identification the Fault Tree Analysis (FTA) technique has been adopted.

As a principal rule, the analysis begins with the 'cause/error' chain. The analysis is accomplished by using a 'backward logic' (See EPA, 1992) asking questions like: 'Why?' 'How can this happen?' or 'What are the causes and contributing factors of this event or failure?' The purpose with this line of questioning is to identify and visually model those events and conditions that solely or in combinations lead to the top events together with their logical relationships. The structure is a graphical logic diagram showing how the packaging system can fail and dangerous substances can be released and/or involved. The model contains numbers of branches developed at various sequential/successive levels of resolution. The analysis proceeds from the upper to deeper levels. At each level the above-mentioned questions are asked at deeper levels until the underlying causes and contributors of events involving PDG are 'uncovered.'

Subdivide the system. FTA and ETA techniques are based on the 'division' of the system under the study. There are mainly three approaches for subdividing the system: hardware/equipment or technical, functional and hybrid approach. However, this division alone is not sufficient for the analysis of risks in the marine transport system of PDGs, as the system does not operate in isolation and things are complex and interrelated. The physical environment affects the system performance. The fault tree is structured on the marine transport system's components, events and conditions. The key elements of the fault tree structure and their levels of resolution are:

1. 'Marine Event': events as defined by the IMO and Lloyd's Register of Shipping, London, namely collision, contact, grounding, foundering, fire/explosion (excluding fire/explosion events due to dangerous goods), listing/capsizing, hull/water tightness, and machinery. Causes and contributing factors of marine events include human, technical, operational and environmental factors.
2. 'Non-marine events' or 'normal' transport conditions:
    The marine transport system of PDGs is subdivided into subsystems by structure/technical and function:
    *   Structure/technical: system's technical/equipment failures: e.g. ship, packaging, handling and securing equipment, including problems related to design, construction and materials.
    *   Functional/operational: system's functional failures: e.g. loading, discharging, packing, segregation, separation, securing, stowage, caring and documentation of PDG.
3. Environment – physical environment: weather/atmospheric and sea conditions.
4. Other: this category includes causes and contributing factors that are not attributed to any other category and, for want of sufficient reasons, cannot be classified, for example, deliberate acts.

FTA is mainly based on logical and sequential procedures (i.e. algorithm). However, given the large number of different types of events considered, data and information availability and system complexity, a 'genuine' logical analysis cannot be expected. Situations are complex and interrelated and perfect 'fitting' into the tree structure is not always possible. Marine events involving PDGs are often attributed to combinations of many different factors. A categorisation based purely on technical, procedural, environmental or human factors may not entirely be possible. In order to make use of all data available and provide a better understanding, other more 'relaxed' approaches to the analysis could be employed. In order to reflect interrelations among categories some cross-references could be made. For example, technical problems may be described in the context of human, operational or environmental factors.

Step 4: Exposure analysis

Identify and describe 1) exposure and 2) actual consequences of hazards of DG to the risk receptors. The exposure and consequence analysis concerns the identification of the nature and estimation of the extent of exposure and consequences caused by hazards of DG. The key steps consist of the identification of the list/inventory of PDGs and their hazards, risk receptors, distribution or dispersion and concentration of DG, dose-effect relationships, and consequences including many influencing factors and conditions.

Identify and describe the nature/categories and 2) estimate the size of the risk receptors exposed to hazards of DG. The exposed risk receptors (i.e. human, the environment, and property) are those potentially subjected to the effects of hazards of DG. One common form of characterising risk is the measurement of the actual consequences relative to the exposure to hazards of DG i.e. the ratio between consequences and exposures. This has become a legal requirement in many countries (e.g. EU, USA and other OECD countries). Therefore, the identification and measurement of the population exposed to hazards is an important input. The analysis may concern the past, present and anticipated exposures. The exposure analysis involves these main interrelated steps:

Identify and describe dangerous goods and their hazards that cause undesired outcomes (i.e. consequences) to the risks receptors. *Dangerous goods:* List PDGs for the time and location under the study including all classes of dangerous goods and packaging types; provide other information related to dangerous goods and their properties, for example, amounts (in kg or tonnes), the form in which they are carried (e.g. liquid, gas, solid or mixture), physical and chemical properties.

Dangerous goods hazards (DGH): the risks of marine transport of PDGs concern the risks of dangerous goods posed *by virtue of their inherent hazards only.* The nature and magnitude of consequences and exposures and the sequence of events following the release/involvement of DG depends very much on their hazards. The major hazards that could be taken into consideration in the risk analysis are: toxic/poison, fire, explosion, marine environmental pollution hazards.

Risk receptors: identify and describe the main categories of risk receptors exposed to the hazards of DG. The main categories of risk receptors include: a) human: individuals, groups, society; b) the marine environment: water, sediments, fauna and flora, land – shorelines and beaches, including also the air; c) property: individual, common, business property or assets such as ships, cargoes, equipment, facilities and other assets.

Identify and describe sequences of events following the release and/or involvement of dangerous goods that can lead to consequences for the risk receptors. Based on the release or emission modelling, the amount, duration and rate at which dangerous goods are released from the containment, are estimated. The amount released is an estimate based on historical data of direct monitoring or the use of computer models.

The carriage of PDGs is, somewhat, different compared to the carriage of bulk dangerous cargoes and other activities in the supply chain. They are carried on board ships at different levels of packaging. The ship is a 'large packaging' and 'environment' in itself consisting of numerous complex systems. ETA can be employed in modelling sequences of events and their consequences resulting, for example, from the rupture of containers with flammable and toxic liquids on board ships. However, ETA cannot provide sufficient information on the exposure and affects of marine pollutants, for example, dispersion and concentration of contaminants. Therefore, other models could be adopted from other environment or ecological assessment frameworks including these sources (e.g. NOVA, 20001; ACS, 1998; EPA, 1992).

Describe distribution/dispersion and concentration of released dangerous substances and/or hazards. Once released from their containments many different types of dangerous substances and/or hazards travel through the media of transportation (water, air and land) undergoing complex processes and changes. For example, many toxic substances are dispersed and concentrated into the environment released, for example, through air or water. While, non-soluble substances released into the water simply move away from the source by means of the water currents and waves.

Hazards ranges and amounts. Dangerous substances can move at different directions and reach different distances from the containment/ship at different levels of concentration or intensity. In order to estimate the nature and extent of consequences and the exposure of risk receptors to dangerous goods, it is important to consider: a) the distance from the sources substances/hazards can reach and expose risk receptors; b) the amount of substance/hazard present at different distances from the source i.e. the level of concentration (e.g. toxic substances and marine pollutants) and c) the intensity (e.g. fire radiation or blast/shock waves) relative to time, distance, and direction from the sources of release. The dispersion and concentration are affected by many different factors including the amount and types of dangerous substances involved and sea and weather conditions. The distribution/dispersion and concentration are estimated in various ways and by different means, such as real time monitoring, historical data, case scenarios and technical analysis. Such data are very limited for marine events involving PDG, as they are seldom reported. Some in depth case histories can provide information on the distribution and concentration modelling for some dangerous substances.

Identify and describe the ways and routes through which the dangerous substances and/or hazards come into contact and interact with the risk receptors. The risk receptors come into contact with DG/hazards in different ways including: a) human and other living organisms may come directly and/or indirectly in contact with DG/hazards: e.g. inhalation, skin absorption, ingestion, pressure wave contact, flying debris, radiant flux exposure, and other modes of contact; b) marine environment: e.g. dispersion and concentration of toxic substances into water, sediments, biota, and land; c) property: e.g. surface, pressure wave, and flying debris contact, radiant flux exposure and other modes of contact.

Describe and estimate dose-effect relationships. By virtue of their hazards dangerous goods can cause different types and degrees of harm to risk receptors when in contact. This depends on a particular damage mechanism (dose-effect relationship). The biological, physical and chemical effects to risk receptors can only occur after a certain level of exposure is exceeded. The relationship between the dose level and the resulting consequences is affected by various interrelated factors and conditions such as duration, frequency, and level of exposure, and physical conditions of people exposed.

Step 5: Consequence analysis

Identify and describe the nature of actual consequences of hazards of DG for the risk receptors. The main categories of the risk receptors and their nature of consequences include: a) *Human* – human health and safety – effects of DG such as death, injuries, acute or chronic illness and other health effects such as, for example, uptake and accumulation of pollution into the food chain, evacuation, confinement, economic losses, and psychological or emotional effects; b) *Ecosystems/marine environment*: contamination of the water, sea bottom, sediments and effects to the biota including aesthetic consequences. As the people perceive the environment values differently, highly perceived consequences may not necessarily be high from the ecosystem point of view; c) *Property*: damage and losses to individual, commercial or public properties; d) *Other*: undesirable outcomes such as business, communication, navigation system or other activities (e.g. fishing, marine cultivation or agriculture) interruptions, and other forms of effects. The above categories of consequences are often interrelated, for example, human health problems may arise from contamination of the marine environment. The above consequences can be expressed or measured in terms of monetary units i.e. the economical or financial consequences.

Quantify risk elements. Identification and quantification are inseparable procedures. However, for the purpose of presentation they are described under separated headings. Regarding the risks of marine events involving PDG, depending on the amount and quality of data available, the likelihood could be estimated for almost any element of the risks, including top events, transport hazards and their causes and contributing factors, hazards of DG and their consequences. Given the large number of risk elements and sequences of marine events involving PDG, the compound likelihood may consist of individual likelihood, for example, the likelihood of a specific consequence (e.g. fatality) of a specific hazard (e.g. explosion) for a specific risk receptor (e.g. ship's crew) in a specific time period (e.g. in one year).

There are various methods of estimating and expressing the likelihood including quantitative, semi-quantitative, and qualitative methods. Quantitative methods are usually based on extrapolation of historical data, in which the likelihood is expressed as numbers. Semi-quantitative methods employed both quantitative data and judgements, in which the likelihood is expressed, for example, 'less than', 'greater than' or within a range of a given or specified likelihood. Qualitative methods are mainly based on the perceptions, reliance or judgments on the degree of the compliance with guidelines or legal and technical criteria. Some qualitative expressions of the likelihood are: high, frequent, infrequent, probable, improbable, low, and negligible.

A comprehensive analysis should not rely on the estimation of the likelihood alone. Quantitative or statistical analysis can provide additional information and more precise results than qualitative (descriptive) analysis and the likelihood estimation alone. Quantification is broader and encompasses the likelihood estimation. The inference statistics could be employed to identify the existent and measure the directions and amounts of the relationships among variables representing various concepts of the marine transport system and risk elements. For example, measure the relations between fatalities/injuries due to hazards of DG and types of ships and dangerous goods. Quantification based on case histories may be extended to those levels of resolution and risk elements for which data is available. The quality of estimates vary widely, depending, inter alias, on the quality and amount of data, methods employed, judgements and assumptions.

With reference to the analysis of hazards, causes and contributing factors of damage/breach of packages by mean of Fault Tree Analysis (FTA), after the tree structure has been explored, the next step is quantification. If necessary and possible, the quantification of the elements of the structure is performed to provide answers to the question 'How often?' The FTA technique is mainly based on algorithm analysis, in which branches of the tree structure are quantified based on historical data. Because of the complexity of the system and events associated with it, interrelations with other systems and data available at hand, the analysis cannot always rely solely on sequential and logical organization. In order to simplify things, make use of all available data and enhance further understanding of the risk elements, other forms of quantitative analysis can be employed.

Step 6: Exposure Evaluation

Estimate the size/extent of the risk receptors exposed to hazards of DG, along with the magnitude, duration, and spatial extent of exposure. Exposed risk receptors are those receptors that are bound by the range of hazards of DG. Table 9.2 shows the main categories of risk receptors and some examples of the measurement units of exposure.

Table 9.2   Categories of the Risk Receptors and Examples of Measurement Units of Exposure

Nr	Category of the risk receptors	Examples of measurement units of exposure
1	Human: individuals, groups, society - Ship's crew/personnel - Passengers - Others - Shore personnel - Local community	-Total number of people (all categories) -Number of personnel on board of all ships and ships carrying PDG only -Number of passengers: all ships and cargo/passenger ships - passenger/crew-miles/hours -Number of shore personnel: all personnel and personnel involved in PDG activities - Number of people ashore: around ports, waterways and transport routes
2	Marine Environment -Biota: fauna and flora -Water -Sediments -Shore/coastlines	-Amounts/numbers e.g. numbers of protected or sensitive sea areas -Tonnes/volumes -Shorelines/inland waters: km and miles -Sea/inland waters area: km^2 and $mile^2$
3	-Property: ships, cargo and property ashore -Activity: transport, port and other activities	-Total tonnes, tonnes-miles and shipments-miles for a) all categories of cargoes/commodities and b) all and each class of PDG -Ships number, dwt or grt, ship miles or km for a) all types of ships b) ships carrying PDG only -Properties ashore: amount/number -Activities: hrs, days and weeks – e.g. transit time or working hrs in port
4	Financial	Monetary units – price/value/cost of any of the mentioned categories

The extent of exposure for each category could be measured in different ways (Table 9.2). The monetary unit may be assigned as the common unit of exposure for nearly all categories. Any of the above measurements can be related to the time unit of exposure, which is usually taken as one year. Some other forms of time units are lifetime (expressed in hours or years), working lifetime (expressed in hours or years), the total working hours per year, the total working hours with dangerous goods per year and so on. The number of people exposed can be estimated with computer models using information from census and maps. Demographic data for the ship's personnel, passengers, people working in ports and living in the vicinity of sea transport routes, waterways and around ports, is used to estimate the human exposure.

The marine environment and all properties and activities ashore bounded by the hazards of DG should be inventoried and possibly quantified. All protected, designated and sensitive marine environment sites with their specific physical, ecological, social and economic features should be identified. The exposure estimation may be difficult and resource consuming. The review of numerous marine accident databases shows that exposure data is inadequate, if not lacking, to support this analysis for marine events involving dangerous goods. Generally, databases contain data on accidents and their consequences and some elements of the system. However, exposure data could be collected from other databases or through other data collection methods and techniques.

Step 7: Consequence Evaluation

Estimate the extent/magnitude of actual consequences of hazards of DG to risk receptor including influencing factors. A single event release of DG may be associated with one or a combination of hazards, which can affect N or more numbers of different risks receptors with different degree or magnitude of severity. The human consequences, for example, may vary from undetectable or insignificant effects, serious but recoverable injuries, permanent severe health problems to death. Similarly, the aquatic community in a marine environment will be affected differently as it is comprized of a wide variety of organisms with quite variable physiology, and accordingly they have very different sensitivities and responses to different chemicals for different concentration levels.

Consequences are measured and expressed in quantitative, semi-quantitative, and qualitative terms. Table 9.3 provides some examples of parameters that can be used to measure the actual consequences of hazards of PDG for each specific risk receptor. Some of these parameters may serve as direct measurements, while others may simply serve as indicators, in particular in the absence of the former.

Table 9.3 Risk Receptors, Consequences and their Measurements

Nr	Specific risk receptors	Specific consequences	Measurement units: specific magnitude of consequences for specific risk receptor
1	Human -Ship's crew/personnel -Passengers -Others -Shore personnel -Local community	-Fatality -Injury -Other safety/health effects	-Number of fatalities -Number of injuries -Number of people with other safety or health effects
2	Marine Environment -Biota: fauna and flora -Water -Sediments -Shore/coastlines	-Pollution -Losses	-Shore length contaminated -Area contaminated -Amount/number of biota affected -Amount/number of PDG lost at sea -Ships affected: numbers, dwt/grt involved, e.g. sunken or grounded ships
3	-Property: ships, cargo and other property ashore -Activities: transport, ports and others	-Damage -Losses -Interruptions	-Ships affected: numbers, dwt/grt, e.g. constructed total loss -All cargo/package and PDG only: number/amount damaged or lost -Properties: number/amount of properties damaged, specific degree of structural damage -Interruptions or suspensions of activities: hrs, days or weeks
4	Financial	-Financial: losses, claims	-Monetary units: costs arising from the losses/damages to any of the above categories due to hazards of PDG only

The estimation based on the actual accident experiences is preferable. But, for many events with a very few or non-existent toxicity or environmental data, consequences are also estimated based on theoretical models or experts' judgements. Elements of consequences can be measured by non-metric and metric measurements and related to each other and other elements of the risks and system.

The compound consequence may consist of individual consequences of specific hazards outcomes (e.g. fire, explosion or toxic) of specific magnitudes (e.g. number of fatalities or injuries per event) for specific risk receptors (e.g. human, environment or property). Because of the incompatibility in consequence's measurements, the compound consequence for all risk receptors can be measured and expressed in qualitative form.

The use of death and injury as the only parameter for measuring consequences may not be entirely appropriate. The hazards of DG cause a wide variety of effects, for example, nuisance (odour), irritation, incapacitating or other irreversible effects. The use of effects dose as a measure of consequences may be considered as appropriate in some situations. However, for the lack of such data, the mortality and injury are often used as the human consequence measurements. Some measurement units used in estimating the exposure and predicting the consequences are concentration (e.g. parts per million – ppm) overpressure delivered (e.g. grams/cm^2). In such cases, the magnitude of consequences is measured as the difference between the changed value and the 'original' value. The marine environment contains different substances at various natural concentrations. One approach to measuring the magnitude of the contamination of the marine environment would be the measurement of the difference between the values of concentration after the introduction of pollutants into the sea and the natural concentration.

Step 8: Risk Characterisation and Presentation

Characterise/estimate risks by combining: a) the likelihood (frequency/probability) and consequences; b) the consequences and exposures to hazards of DG. Table 9.4 shows how the information is combined to characterise risks – similar terminologies often used interchangeably are risk estimation, risk calculation or risk measurement. The risks cannot always be estimated, calculated or measured by mathematical procedures, e.g., by multiplying or dividing numbers.

Two main approaches in common use for characterising risks are: 1) the likelihood (i.e. frequency and probability) is combined with consequences (C) (quantitative measurement: R=FxC); 2) the consequences are combined with exposure (E) (quantitative measurement: R=C/E). The ratio between the consequences and exposures (C/E) is in itself the probability of the consequences that may be experienced by exposed risk receptors.

The risks are characterized in quantitative and qualitative terms or a combination of both. In quantitative terms, for example, the human risks are expressed in some numbers of deaths and injuries over a lifetime or working lifetime in a population. Qualitative characterisations such as 'low', 'medium' and 'high', are used whenever risk quantification is neither feasible nor necessary. The quantitative risk characterization may be deterministic, for example, where a point estimate of exposure is compared to a point estimate of consequences, or probabilistic where the distribution of exposure data is compared to the distribution of consequences data and risk is reported as the per cent of people or species in the aquatic community expected to be affected.

Table 9.4 Examples of Risk Characterisation Approaches

Risks	=Likelihood*Consequences					=Consequences*Exposures
Risk	Likelihood	Consequences				Exposures
		Individual consequences by				Individual exposures
		Risk receptors	Hazards	Types of consequences /magnitude	Location & activity	Population bounded by hazards of DG
Individual risks	Individual likelihood	-Human -Marine environment -Property & activity	-Fire -Explosion -Toxic -Corrosion -Suffocation -Infection -Radiation -Marine pollutants -Others	-Fatality -Injury -Others-health -Pollution -Losses -Damages -Others	-Local -Regional -National -International -Ships -Waterways -Ports -En-route -At port	-Risk receptor -Location -Activity -Ship -Cargo/DG -Traffics -Events
Compound/ aggregated risk	Compound/ aggregated likelihood	Compound/aggregated consequence				Compound/ aggregated exposure

The likelihood, consequences and exposures, subsequently the risks themselves, can be related to any element of the system and risk (Table 9.4) such as risk receptors, types of hazards DG, locations, ships and activities. This allows the comparison of the adverse effects associated with different activities and components of the system. The compound (overall or aggregated) risk consists of individual or specific risks, which can be expressed: (1) $\Sigma Ri = \Sigma Fi*Ci$ and (2) $\Sigma Ri = \Sigma Ci*Ei$. The sign (*) does not necessarily imply mathematical procedures. Given the wide range of different incompatible measurement units used to express the likelihood, consequence and exposure, the compound or aggregated risk may not always be a simple arithmetical sum of the individual risks.

The way in which the risks are characterized and presented depend on many various factors such as the objective, the scope and depth of the study, interests and the legal requirements, if any. In some industries and countries risks are characterized and presented in accordance with the established guidelines. The American Institute of Chemical Engineers, for example, provides some commonly used risk measures and procedures for calculation of the human risks, including both societal and individual risks, for the chemical industry, which can be suited for application in risks analysis for marine transport of PDG.

Risk indices. Risk indices are single numbers or tabulations, including these forms: Fatal Accident Rate (FAR) – number of fatalities per exposure hours (Lees, 1980); Average Rate of Death (ARD) – average number of fatalities per unit of time from all possible incidents (Lees, 1980); Individual Hazard Index (IHI) is the FAR for a particular hazard (Helmers and Schaller, 1982); Mortality Index (MI) for hazards of toxic materials (Marshal, 1987).

Individual risk is defined as the risk to a person/individual in the vicinity of a hazard. Because of limited data available, risks are often estimated for irreversible injury and fatality. Individual risks are estimated for exposed individuals and groups of individuals at particular places or an average individual in an effected zone. Some individual risk measures are: Individual Risk Contour (IRC), Maximum Individual Risk (MIR), Average Individual Risk (AIR) (for exposed population), Average Individual Risk (AIR) (for total population), and Average Individual Risk (AIR) (exposed/working hours).

Societal risk is a measure of risks to a group of people that is often expressed in terms of the sum of the frequency distribution of multiple casualty events at a local, country or regional level (e.g. F-N curve). Estimation of the societal risks requires definition of population at risk and information like gender and age, likelihood of people being present to a given location such as port/terminal or shipping route.

Injury risk. Another form of expressing human risk is the usage of the injury risk measure, but this is less applicable. Because of the lack and high degree of uncertainty of injury data, many risk assessments in transport of dangerous goods have not taken into account injury risk measures. One approach of expressing the injury risk is to use the ratio of deaths to injuries.

Consequences per unit measure of the system components and activities (Table 9.4). For marine transport of PDG it is possible to relate the detriment, that is the numerical measure of consequences, to a variety of measures of activities or elements. For example, fatalities and injuries can be expressed relative to: the total number of transits, the total passenger/crew-hours or miles travelled, the total tons or tons-miles of PDG, the total number of PDG shipments/packages – all these per unit of time. Some of these measures can also be employed for the property and environmental risks.

The purpose of the risk presentation is to reduce the large amount of information and provide a simple quantitative/qualitative risk description useful for decision-making. The forms of presentation vary depending on the objective and measures of the risks. Some risk presentation formats are: *single number index* (e.g.1/100,000), *table* (e.g. typical sizes or bands of fatalities are 1-10, 11-100 and 101-1000), *graph* (e.g. Frequency-Number (F-N) curve) and *map* (e.g. risk contour plot i.e. 'isorisk' lines expressing risk vs. distance.)

ETA can be used as an effective tool in exploring failures of packaging resulting in release and/or involvement of DG and how various factors and conditions affect the course of events. It can also be used to explore and, if possible, quantify hazards and consequences of DG.

Key steps of ETA consists: a) Identify and list (on the left side of the tree) and categorized the initiating events according to the lines of assurance: events as defined by IMO and Lloyd's Register of Shipping and other events, for example, toxic releases; b) Identify and list the lines of safeguards or assurance and physical conditions (placed across the top of the tree) – human and designed systems onboard and ashore for prevention, detection, response and mitigation; c) Determine events progression: identify the success (e.g. no spill, no cargo loss, no fire or explosion, or no fatalities) and failure (e.g. spill, cargo loss, fire or explosion, or fatalities) branches of each line of assurance and physical conditions; estimate frequency for each branch point; d) Estimate events sequence consequences and frequencies; estimated individual and cumulative consequences for each category of events; estimate the aggregated frequency by multiplying together the initiating event frequency and all probabilities from the branch points; order events from high frequency/low consequence to low frequency/high consequence e) Summarize results: employ F-N curve – plot cumulative frequencies (y-axis) of events causing N or more consequences (x-axis).

Step 9: Sensitivity Analysis

Sensitivity analysis is a step that has been performed in a number of recent risk studies. The risk index determines the risk level. Whereas, the management index provides further ranking for those risks that have equivalent index. This analysis may be beyond the risk analysis, which largely focuses on the technical aspects of the risks. The sensitivity analysis takes into consideration many other socio-economical aspects of the risks. The equations of the risk and risk management index are:

Risk Index = Likelihood*Consequence or Consequence*Exposure
Risk Management Index = Risk Index*Sensitivity

Management indexing may be employed in any type of risks. In marine environmental risk analysis the purpose of the sensitivity analysis is to identify areas that are sensitive to marine pollution. Together with the pollution risk analysis, the sensitive analysis is used, for example in the UK, as a basis to establish Marine Environmental High Risk Areas (DETR, 1999). The first step in this analysis is to identify and classify all protected, designated or sensitive sites. Classification is developed to meet the special needs and physical, ecological, social and economic characteristics of a country or region. Sites are, for example, classified based on wildlife importance, vulnerability of seabirds to pollution, fishing, amenity and economic benefit of the surrounding community, landscape and geology. This classification system is based on a variety of methods such as laboratory and field studies, case histories of the past pollution events, and judgements of specialized bodies in the marine environment. Marine environment sensitivity is then documented and, by using advanced technologies (e.g. geographical information system – GIS), an index mapping is created. The marine environment sensitivity mapping has recently become an essential part the marine pollution prevention program in a number of countries.

Stage 3: Conclusions and Recommendations

This is an important stage of the risk study. Based on the facts and the analysis provide key concluding statements or remarks concerning risk elements are stated – this is a synthesis of the entire risk study work. Synthesised information about the main elements of the risks should be provided, including: hazards and their causes and contributing factors, frequency/probability and major contributors of events involving PDG, consequences due to hazards of DG and the risks expressed in either qualitative or quantitative form. Estimated risks may be judged or evaluated against established risk criteria, if any, for example, whether the risks of PDG are negligible or non-negligible, acceptable or unacceptable. One objective of the risk analysis is to develop recommendations for a better management of the risks. In this context, it is necessary to suggest risk management strategies and measures. However, the results and recommendations form only one set of information considered by the decision makers. Recommendations do not make in themselves the decision, but inform it, as many other factors are often taken into account in the decision-making process.

Concluding Remarks

This study attempts to 'fill the gap' in the literature in the field of the risk methodology and to enhance the understanding and 'refine' concepts of the risk analysis, in particular in marine transport of dangerous goods. Based on empirical data, the literature review and personal research experience, a specific risk analysis framework has been adopted for application in marine transport of PDG. The framework relies on the essential principles of the risk analysis and management practices in the field.

The model (Figure 9.3) combines two elements: a) the framework structure which consists of five key steps of the risk analysis process, namely hazard identification, exposure and consequence analysis, likelihood estimation/quantification, and risk characterisation and presentation and b) the analysis techniques structure (i.e. FTA and ETA), which is the way in which risk-related data is analysed. The structure of the model is a combined reflection of the marine transport system of the PDG, the risk elements and the courses of marine events involving PDG. The framework provides a 'blue print' for preparing and performing the risk analysis in a more effective and efficient way. Whilst enhancing and maintaining human health and the marine environment protection through better-informed decision-making, the implementation of the framework in practice may, at the same time, yield savings in time and resources.

References

Alp, E. (1995), 'Risk-based transportation planning practice: Overall methodology and a case example', *INFOR*. Feb, Vol.33, pp.4-19.

American Chemical Society (1998), 'Understanding Risk Analysis. Guide for Health, Safety and Environmental Policy Making', *American Chemical Society.*

Batten, S.D., Allen, R.J.S. and Wotton, C.O..M. (1998), 'The Effects of the Sea Empress Oil Spill on the Plankton of the Southern Irish Sea', *Marine Pollution Bulletin*, Vol.36, No.10, pp.764-774, Pergamon.

Carol, S., Vilchez, J.A., and Casal, J. (2001), 'A new approach to the estimation of the probable number of fatalities in accidental explosions', *Safety Science*, Vol.39, pp.205–217.

CCPS (1989), 'Chemical Process Quantitative Risk Analysis', Centre for Chemical Process Safety of the American Institute of Chemical Engineers.

Dennis, S.M. (1996), 'Estimating risk costs per unit of exposure for hazardous materials transported by rail', *Logistics and Transportation Review*, Dec. Vol.32, No.4, pp.351-375.

DETR, Department of the Environment, Transport and the Regions (1999), 'Identification of Marine Environmental High Risk Areas (MEHRA's) in the UK', Report prepared by Safetec for the UK DETR.

Directorate General XI of the European Commission (1998), 'The Technical Guidance on Development of Risk Reduction Strategies', EC.

DNV Technica (1995), 'Feasibility Study For Safety Assessment of RoRo Passenger Vessels'.

Donk, J. and de Rijke, W.G. (1995), 'A risk-effect model for waterway transport of dangerous goods', *Conference proceedings Reliability and Maintainability Symposium*, pp.349-355, IEEE.

EPA, Risk Assessment Forum (1992), 'Framework for Ecological Risk Assessment', EPA/630/R-92/001, Environmental Protection Agency, Washington, D.C.

European Commission (1999), 'The Concerted Action on Formal Safety and Environmental Assessment of Ship Operations', The project conducted by Germanischer Lloyd and Det Norske Veritas and funded by the European Commission under the Transport RTD Programme of the 4th Framework Programme.

Fay, J.A., (2003), 'Model of spills and fires from LNG and oil tankers', *Journal of Hazardous Materials*, Vol.96, No.2-3, pp.171-188, Elsevier.

Fowler, T.G. and Sorgård, E. (2000), 'Modelling Ship Transportation Risk', *Risk Analysis*, Vol.20, No.2.

Gade, M. and Redondo, J.M. (1999), 'Marine pollution in European coastal waters monitored by the ERS-2 SAR: a comprehensive statistical analysis', *Journal of OCEANS '99*, Vol.3, pp.1239-1243, IEEE & Marine Technology Soc.

Gilfillan, E.S., Harner, E.J., O'Reilly, J.E., Page D.S., Burns, W.A. (1990). 'A Comparison of Shoreline Assessment Study Designs Used for the Exxon Valdez Oil Spill', *Marine Pollution Bulletin*, Vol.38, No.5, pp.380-388, Pergamon.

Giziakis, K. and Bardi-Giziaki, E. (2002), 'Assessing the risk of pollution from ship accidents, Disaster Prevention and Management', *An International Journal*, Vol.11, No.2, pp.109-114, Emerald (MCB).

Goulielmos, A.M. (2001), 'Maritime safety: facts and proposals for the European OPA Disaster Prevention and Management', *An International Journal*, Vol.10, No.4, pp.278-285, Emerald (MCB).

Goulielmos, A.M and Pardali, A. (1998), 'The framework protecting ports and ships from fire and pollution, Disaster Prevention and Management', *An International Journal*, Vol.7, No.4, pp.281-287, Emerald (MCB).

Haastrup, P. and Brockhoff, L. (1990), 'Severity of Accidents with Hazardous Materials: A Comparison Between Transportation and Fixed Installations', *Journal of Loss Prevention in the Process Industries*, Vol.3, pp.395-405.

Hall, A.J., Watkins, J. and Hiby, L. (1996), 'The impact of the 1993 Braer oil spill on grey seals in Shetland', *Journal of The Science of The Total Environment*, Vol.186, No.1-2, pp.119-125, Elsevier.

Health and Safety Commission (HSC) (1991), 'Major Hazardous Aspects of the Transport of Dangerous Substances', *Advisory Committee on Dangerous Substances*, HMSO.

HSE (1998), 'Five Steps to Risk Assessment', *Health and Safety Executive*, HSE Books, Sudbury, UK., INDG163.

HSE (2002), 'Marine risk assessment', *Offshore Technology Report 2001/063*, prepared by Det Norske Veritas for the Health and Safety Executive, United Kingdom, ISBN 0 7176 2231 2.

Hokkanen, J. and Pelline, J. (1997), 'The Use of Decision-aid Methods in the Assessment of Risk Reduction Measures in the Control of Chemicals', Nordic Council of Ministers, Copenhagen.

IMO (1996), 'Focus on IMO – IMO and dangerous goods at sea', *IMO May*.

Kaplan, S. and Garrick, B.J, (1981), 'On the quantitative definitions of risks', *Risk Analysis*, Vol.1, No.1, pp.11-27.

LaBelle, R.P. and Anderson, C.M. (1996), 'Offshore oil-spill occurrence rates', *Journal of OCEANS '96*, Conference Proceedings, Vol.2, pp.751-753, IEEE.

Miraglia, R.A. (2002), 'The Cultural and Behavioral Impact of the Exxon Valdez Oil Spill on the Native Peoples of Prince William Sound, Alaska', *Spill Science and Technology Bulletin*, Vol.7, No.1-2, pp.75-87, Pergamon.

Morgenstern, R.D. and Landy, M.K. (1997), 'Economic Analysis: Benefits, Costs, Implications in Economic Analysis at EPA', Assessing Regulatory impact, Resources for the Future, Washington D.C.

Mullai, A. and Paulsson, U. (2002), 'Oil Spills in Öresund – Hazardous events, Causes and Claims', prepared for the Sundrisk project, Lund University, Department of Industrial Management and Logistics, Lund.

Nicolet-Monnier, M and Gheorghe, A.V. (1996) 'Quantitative Risk Assessment of Hazardous Materials Transport System', Kluwer Academic Publishers.

NOVA Chemicals Corp (2001), 'The Chemical Accident Risk Assessment Thesaurus', *(CARAT) Database*.

OECD (2000), 'Risk Management. No. 13 Framework For Integrating Social-Economic Analysis in Chemical Risk', *Environmental Health and Safety Publications Series*, Management Decision Making ENV/JM/MONO(2000)5. Environment Directorate OECD Paris 2000.

Onyekpe, B. (2002), 'Response-predictive model of oil spills in aquatic environments', *Journal of Environmental Management and Health*, Vol.13, No.1, pp.66-70, Emerald (MCB).

Purdy, G. (1993), 'Risk assessment', *Hazardous Cargo Bulletin Dec.*, DNV Technica.

Reed, M., Johansen, Brandvik, P.J., Daling, P., Lewis, A., Fiocco, R., Mackay, D., Prentki, R. (1999), 'Oil Spill Modeling towards the Close of the 20th Century: Overview of the State of the Art', *Spill Science and Technology Bulletin*, Vol.5, No.1, pp.3-16, Pergamon.

Report of the Royal Society Group Study Group (1992), 'Risk: Analysis, Perception and Management', Royal Society.

Risk Assessment Forum (1992), 'Framework for Ecological Risk Assessment', EPA/630/R-92/001, Environmental Protection Agency, Washington, D.C.

Romer, H., Haastrup, P and Styhr Petersen, H.J (1995), 'Accidents during marine transport of dangerous goods. Distribution of fatalities', *European Commission, Joint Research Centre Ispra*, t.p. 650, 1-21020 Ispra, *Journal of Loss Prevention in the Process Industries*, Vol.8, No.1.

Ruxton, T. (1996), 'Formal safety Assessment of ships', *Trans IMarE*, Vol.108, No.4, pp.287-296.

Saccommanno, F. (1993). 'Transportation of dangerous goods: assessing the risks'. Paper presented by J.R. Spouge, Technica Ltd. UK. *Proceedings of the first International Consensus Conference on the Risks of Transport of dangerous Goods*, held April 6-8, 1992, Toronto. Reference ISBN 0-96966747-1-6.

Sii, H.S., Ruxton, T., Wang, J. (2001), 'A fuzzy-logic-based approach to qualitative safety modelling for marine systems', *Reliability Engineering and System Safety*, Vol.73, No.1, pp.19-34, Elsevier.

Stanners, D. and Bourdeau, P. (1995), 'European Environment: The Dobris Assessment'. *The European Environment Agency (EEA), Office for Official Publications of the EC, Luxembourg.*

UNEP (1997), 'Global Environment Outlook', *(GEO-1) United Nations Environment Programme (UNEP) Report.*

U.S. EPA. (1989), 'Risk Assessment Guidance for Superfund (RAGS)', *Human Health Evaluation Manual (HHEM) (Part A, Baseline Risk Assessment). Interim Final,* Vol.1, Office of Emergency and Remedial Response, Washington, DC. EPA/540/1-89/002. NTIS PB90-155581.

Chapter 10

Outsourcing Advanced Logistics: A Shipper's and Provider's Perspective on Risks

Dan Andersson and Dr. Andreas Norrman

Introduction

A practice more and more applied within logistics and SCM is outsourcing. A changing industry context and new demands on logistics are driving a trend towards outsourcing of more advanced logistics services; often called third-party logistics (Andersson 1997; van Laarhoven et al, 2000). Following this trend, the organizational relationships in the supply chain gets more complex and hence the risk situation changes both for the shipper and the service provider (Lalonde and Cooper, 1989). Uncertainty and risks have to be handled both before the outsourcing decision and during the outsourcing period. Many different kinds of risks are involved, which on a high level can be categorized as either strategic or operational risks. Before the outsourcing decision, the risks to be assessed are more of strategic kind. Risks can also be a key factor when deciding which logistics functions to outsource (Rao and Young, 1994). After and during the outsourcing, the operational risks have to be handled in different ways.

So far there has only been a limited research focus on *uncertainty and risks created by* 'third party logistics' and changes in the *risk situation and the risk management processes* for both the buyer and the provider in an *outsourcing situation.* This chapter focus is on how outsourcing of advanced logistics influences the risk exposure and how the buyer of the services and the provider respectively influence, as well as handle these risks. The following questions will be addressed:

1. What risks/uncertainties have to be managed when outsourcing logistics?
2. How does the risk/uncertainty situation between the ante and post situation *changes* for both the buyer and provider of advanced logistics services?
3. How *are the involved parties* using the risk management process and how has this changed?
4. How is liability transferred between the partners in *relation* to activities and control?

Due to the complexity and novelty of the topic the selected method has been a case study. So far interviews have been made with the shipper and one provider and in addition secondary written material has been obtained from the shipper. In order to create a platform for the rest of the chapter a theoretical overview of supply chain risk management is presented, followed by a case study of advanced logistics outsourcing. The case illustrates how both players are working with risk management and the chapter concludes with a discussion on the implications of the results and how the research will be continued.

Frame of Reference

In the frame of reference we will further elaborate on risk and uncertainty, based on the general discussion of Norrman and Lindroth (Chapter 2) but now more connected to logistics outsourcing. The steps of the risk management process will be discussed: risk analysis, risk assessment and risk management.

Risk and Uncertainty

Related to outsourcing in general, many strategic risks/uncertainties have been discussed. Walker (1988) for example, identified three different kinds of strategic risks related to supplier relationships: appropriation, technology diffusion and end product degradation. The appropriation risk is if a supplier takes advantage of his customers' dependence on him/her and thereby increases his/her part of the total end customer revenues. The diffusion risk is about protecting innovative product or process technology from being imitated. The risk that important product attributes will be distorted or impaired in distribution, marketing or technical service operations is called product degradation. Lonsdale (1999) points out two main risks with outsourcing in general: a) resources or capabilities outsourced in fact are very critical and responsible or crucial for present or future competitive advantage and b) companies can become dependent on suppliers. The latter could emerge in a number of ways: outsourcing into a limited supply market; poor internal alignment or contractual incompetence in the face of different degrees of assets specificity.

Risk Sources and Consequences/Impact

As discussed in previous chapters *risk (and uncertainty) sources* and *risk consequences* (similar to the term impact) could be separated. Jüttner et al (2002) divide risk sources relevant for supply chains into three categories: external to the supply chain, internal to the supply chain and network related. This last one is especially interesting from a supply chain perspective and for Chapter 4, as network related risks arise from interaction between organizations within the supply chain due to, for example, suboptimal interaction and cooperation.

Risk consequences/impact are the focused supply chain outcome variables like costs or quality (but also health and safety) i.e. the different forms in which the variance becomes manifest.

Risks and Uncertainties in Logistics Outsourcing

Only a few authors have mentioned risk in terms of logistics outsourcing. Rao and Young (1994) identify 'risk liability and control' as one of the key factors influencing the decision whether or not to outsource logistics. Lalonde and Cooper (1989) highlight a number of risks of a third party logistics relationship. From the buyer perspective they stress:

1. The loss of control – the management does not really control the flow of materials through some segment of the logistics channel – often interfacing with the firm's customer base.
2. The issue of continuity – the risk that the entrepreneur would disappear from the scene or that short-term financial reverses could severely impact the company's performance. This situation may put the seller's product at risk or even threaten some significant share of the seller's customer base.
3. The risk that the service provider cannot or will make major shifts in procedures, short run-changes, new programs or technology that the shipper asks for.

The level of risk tends to be proportional to the contractual nature of the relationship. The longer the contract and the less the number of providers used, the higher the risk. The risks tend to increase as the scope and nature of value-added services increase from a transactional base to a contractual base.

From the third-party service provider perspective Lalonde and Cooper (1989) stress the following risks:

1. Kinds and levels of investment required.
2. The willingness of the buyer to share the risks undertaken by the third-party.
3. The risk that accumulated expertise, personnel and machinery for value-added services may not be amortized or be transferable to other accounts if the buyer decide to cease or to shift its operations.

Risk Analysis and Assessment

Risk analysis (or risk identification) can be seen as a fundamental phase in the risk management process. It follows that by identifying a risk, decision-makers become conscious about events that may cause disturbances. To assess risk exposures, the company must identify not only direct risks to its operations but also the potential causes of those risks at every significant link along the supply chain (Christopher et al, 2002). The main focus of risk analysis is hence, to recognize future uncertainties and to be able to manage them pro-actively.

Risk Management

Generally used strategies for risk management are to *avoid, reduce, transfer, share* or even *take* the risk. To avoid is in principal to eliminate the types of event that could lead to the risk. To reduce applies both to the reduction of probability and the consequence. Examples of how to reduce the impact could be to have extra inventory, multiple sources, sprinklers in buildings, parallel systems and to diversify. Probability could be reduced by improving 'risky' operational processes, and to improve processes related to outsourcing (e.g. supplier selection and supplier development). Risk could also be transferred to insurance companies but also to supply chain partners by moving inventory accountability, changing delivery time of suppliers (just-in-time deliveries) and to customers (make-to-order) or by outsourcing activities. Furthermore, contracts could be used to transfer commercial risks. Finally, risks could be shared, both by contractual mechanisms and by improved collaboration.

According to a study made by CMI (2002) only 9 per cent of companies that have outsourced activities (not only logistics) insist on their outsource suppliers to have Business Continuity Plans (BCP). These plans consist of a priori written guidelines for recovering critical business functions after a disaster occurs, sometimes called contingency plans.

It could be argued that the contract can have an important role with respect to safeguarding (i.e. protect ones own interest and minimize risks) and operations support (definitions of processes, activities, roles and responsibilities, incentives/penalties) – see Pruth, 2002. The contracts for purchasing of more complex logistics system do contain more details due to the scope of services but they also contain a number of issues dealing with unknown future issues and how to handle them and how to ensure that the relationship develops and improves the performance.

Case Description: A Shipper's and a Service Provider's View on Risk Management Issues

The Changed Logistics System

A shipper in the high-tech industry, Company Alpha, has a relatively complex distribution system. They mainly deliver to new 'construction sites' both located in remote areas and in congested city centers and the deliveries are subject to very high service demands. Some years ago Alpha decided to minimize the in-house management of distribution activities as well as reduce the number of logistics service providers with a direct interface. Alpha contracted a very small number of first tier logistics service providers to let each take the management responsibility for physical distribution in a different region of the world. One of these providers is Provider Beta to whom reference will be made later. The first tier service provider manages and coordinates a layer of second tier providers and takes full responsibility for coordination of all activities needed in the distribution system for that region. They should also be active in developing the distribution system, not only running it. The second tier service providers provide operational services and assets necessary to operate the system.

Alpha has also partly changed the distribution structure to support the development of a new stockless supply chain. The past use of warehouses for integration of different material flows are gradually being replaced by a merge-in-transit-concept. Hence, there are a number of risks and uncertainties that need to be minimized. The incentives to do so are strong; in addition to the risks of loss of sales, the shipper may face severe penalties if the products are not delivered as agreed with the customer.

Some people at Alpha argue that much of the increased risk in the distribution area is due to the introduction of the new distribution concept with short lead times, direct shipments, no warehouses, and merge-in-transit. Several of the distribution related risks would increase regardless if the distribution is handled in-house or if it is outsourced. Others argue that the risks will be handled in a better way if the distribution is outsourced because by keeping in-house responsibility the risk management may be hampered by internal bureaucracy. If outsourced, problems are by necessity more focused, as they will appear in an inter-organizational context. It is also believed that there is a greater likelihood that contingency plans will be carried out if required in a commercial contract with a service provider, than if required in an internal policy document. Penalties (even if limited) will probably also create more focus towards problems than sending complaints to an internal organization member.

Company Risk Policies and Organizations

Company Alpha's opinion is that risk management is becoming increasingly more important within all areas, especially due to the increased number of outsourced activities. At Alpha a corporate risk management group coordinates the business interruption and loss control activities in order to reduce both costs and risks of losses for the company. This work encompasses the responsibility to issue corporate risk management directives, supporting documents and initiate audits. The heads of the different company units and companies ensure that the directives for risk are implemented.

Risk management in the distribution area has so far not been a focused area but it has been strongly influenced by other risk management efforts in Company Alpha. The outsourcing of distribution activities has, according to one manager, resulted in an increased focus on risk management. He believes that several of the procedures carried out, for example, workshops to develop contingency plans, would not have taken place if the operations had not been outsourced.

Provider Beta is of the opinion that when a supplier-customer relationship is begun this will initiate an interest in risk management issues. They argue that the business impacts of operational risks are greater for any kind of supplier to a manufacturing company (the risks may be greater than the profit or maybe even bigger than the revenues). This is a very strong incentive for a thorough risk analysis and efforts to reduce the risks. Beta argues that the risk management awareness has increased during the last three years, as a combined result of customer demands, increased scope of the business (more exposure to risks) and influences from the business community (e.g. presentations at conferences).

Alpha's Risk Analysis and Assessment

A risk analysis carried out by Company Alpha encompassed 11 different scenarios, and was based on three basic elements: *cause, effect and impact* (see example in Table 10.1). This work was based on a risk management methodology supplied by IBM. The 11 scenarios covered issues about lack of information (order information, delivery information), break down of different systems (ERP, order system, shipping system), broken communications to and from the service provider and reduced capacity in the physical operations system.

Table 10.1 Example of Risk Scenarios

#	Scenario	Cause	Effect	Business Impact
1	No order information available: Mail call-off, Auto call-off, Draft Invoice(Fakturaunderlag)/Delivery Request(Leveransuppdrag), Manual proforma not available. Shipping systems are running. Order systems are running.	OUTLOOK, printers etc not available. Telephone lines down. No communication with Logistics Department	No deliveries. No invoices. Excess of goods in the warehouses.	No cash flow due to lack of invoice. Dissatisfied client due to lack of delivery. Penalties. Loss of business. Inventory turns reduced.

The events that may *cause* a disturbance were to be identified in the internal as well as the external environment in the following categories: *Staff; Facilities; Machines; Data or Application Availability; Raw Materials Availability.*

The current general increase in outsourcing may also result in different types of distribution risks. In Alpha's case the outsourcing of manufacturing has for example, resulted in increased damages due to insufficient or wrong packaging. This is due to incomplete or non-existent transferral of packing instructions (from Company Alpha to the contract manufacturers) and the purchasing department not being aware of this issue or not interested in issuing additional specifications to the purchasing agreement. This has now to be solved by the logistics service providers.

The disturbances/events could result in a number of different types of *effects*. Alpha has considered: *Customers do not receive product; Product quality is unacceptable; Unable to order from suppliers; Product 'key' data lost; Impacts to product homologation; Unable to invoice.*

For each scenario Alpha assess the business *impacts* of the identified effects, such as: *Loss of revenue; Loss of image; Loss of competitive position.* The risks have been assessed in terms of their business impact and probability (Table 10.2) and these aspects have been categorized as high, medium or low.

Beta's Risk Analysis and Assessment

Provider Beta carried out the most important and comprehensive risk analysis before the contract was signed. Important issues to clarify in relation to different risks were the liability and the position of their insurance company. Regarding the risk analysis on an operational level Provider Beta has collaborated with his client, Alpha but also with competitors who also are providers to Alpha. The most crucial operational risks are according to Beta related to: *Data communication (to keep the systems running); Power supply; Fire; Sick leave.*

The collaboration was not limited to the risk analysis; it also included discussion about how the different organizations could support each other to reduce risks. Beta has made a risk assessment (by distributing points to different types of risks).

According to Beta the risks they generally face when taking over outsourced logistics operations are related to: *Information and transferral of information; Liability and economic risks; Risk of opportunistic behavior of clients regarding the business volume and scope; Financial risks; A drifting business scope; Operational risks (accidents, fires, sick leave, strikes); Client losing logistics competence.* Provider Beta believes that the most serious risks are linked to the data transferral between different IT systems (information is regarded as a crucial resource). There are two main groups of causes behind the *information risks*: the first is of technical nature, the second is relationship related. The first group involve interruptions in data communication between computers. The second group deals with risks of not getting relevant information (at the right time) about the development within the client's organization, e.g. about new markets or forecasts about volume changes (which may be subject to strict confidentiality, which the client cannot change)

The *liability risks* (and the connected economic risks) are caused by uncertainties about who is liable for what. This is due to the fact that there is no conventions or praxis applicable to more advanced outsourcing of logistics (including for instance logistics development). Liability will be further elaborated in the contract section below.

The risk of *opportunistic behavior* is of a more generic kind and Beta has not experienced that in the relationship with Alpha. Beta believes there might be a risk that some shippers may outsource part of the logistics operation as a way to get rid of problems and to facilitate a shut down of a certain business. If they do this without informing the provider and without giving him any guarantees the effect of this could be serious for the provider (i.e. they will then be left with all the costs but no revenues),

The *financial risks* have increased as a result of increased commitments to the clients. The provider asks themselves what will happen if they have financed a certain logistics operation and thereafter a client goes bankrupt.

The risk of a *drifting business scope* is related to the situations where personnel at an operational/tactical level agree on changes in the number and type of activities performed by the provider. These changes may (after a while) lead to a situation where the services performed are not covered by the contract.

The *operational risks* are not perceived to have changed in themselves but their business impact gets more serious when a provider takes an increased responsibility/liability.

Provider Beta regards the fact that the client may lose logistics *competence* as a result of an outsourcing, as a risk. They argue that if this happens they will for instance lose a crucial support in the development of new or redesigned systems. Beta also argues that a loss of competence will result in a decreased system performance, which eventually will also indirectly hurt the provider organization. Beta is of the opinion that Alpha has identified this risk and so far managed to avoid it. Beta also claims that through their close collaboration with the client they are also of assistance when it comes to competence development and maintenance at Alpha.

Alpha's Risk Management and Contingency Plans

Alpha has, in workshops with key stakeholders analysed the operational risks in the distribution system and developed contingency plans (for an example of their structure see Table 10.2) for the handling of these risks. Assessments and plans were made for each of the 11 scenarios mentioned earlier.

Table 10.2 Example of Risk Assessment and Contingency Plan (for scenario #1)

#	Description	Time Horizon to failure	Business Impact	Risk Probability	Cont. Strategy Level	Remediation Strategy	Contingency Plan and Triggers	Feasibility	Completion Date	Current Status	Resp.
Scenario			**Business Priority**				**Contingency Plan**				
1			High	Medium	1	OUT-LOOK	Call Logistics Dept according to the emergency list.	High		OK	Name
							Make sure emergency list is updated. Hard copy available.	High	Date	OK	Name
						Printers	Call Logistics Dept according to the emergency list.	H		OK	Name
							Check orders in Order Systems and Shipping Systems.	M		OK	Name
							Make sure mobile phones are available	H		OK	Name

The contingency plan is developed to prepare the organization for problems occurring despite ongoing preventive efforts. The contingency plan covers the following: a) the development of means to eliminate or reduce the impact of problems b) the definition of business resumption activities c) the needs of the stakeholders.

The contingency plan includes aspects such as: *manual creation of documents; fax to service providers; rules for prioritization of orders; manual information entry into shipping systems; use of mobile phones for communication etc.* The feasibility of these actions is assessed in terms of high/medium/low and linked to a completion date, as well as to a responsible person and organization.

Beta's Risk Management and Contingency Plans

Beta has discussed and collaborated both with his client Alpha but also with other service providers to Alpha (competitors), about how the different organizations could support each other to reduce the risks. Beta has also developed contingency plans and informed other service providers about them. A common agreement on their validity has been made. Beta used a project-based organization to work with risk management and included the following areas: *contingency plans, work instructions, corrective actions and back up systems.* These plans have been made available to the operational staff so that they could see what to do if something goes wrong. According to Beta the contingency plans have been used and found to be useful. Examples of the ways identified to handle operational disturbances are: *use a modem instead of a server connection; go home and work from there; go to a competitor and use their premises when serving the joint client Alpha (according to Beta this is a result of a very good collaboration between the different providers).*

Risk Management: Contracts

The contract plays an important role in the risk management, both at strategic and operational levels. An example of Alpha's more strategic considerations is that the contracts with the service providers are made on a corporate level, thereby securing commitment and availability of resources regardless of what happens in individual countries and business segments. The operational risks are handled by clauses, for example, stipulating that the logistics service provider shall at all times maintain a contingency plan to show measures to be taken in order to promptly restore full operational capabilities to perform the services, in case of possible major disasters or disturbances. In the case of a disaster or other major disturbance the service provider is obliged to use its best efforts to ensure that: a) performance of the services can be resumed promptly and as soon as possible b) performance of the services is returned to normal capacity without any undue delay.

Alpha argues that it may be better to focus the content of the contract on preventive measures, instead of focusing on claims and penalties. In order to avoid certain issues the contract contains directives on how service reviews and planning activities should be performed (an overview is presented in Table 10.3). These meetings should facilitate good communications between the involved parties, including a feedback loop regarding the current situation and discussions about what can go wrong in the future and how to avoid this. One manager at Alpha argues that from a total business perspective it is less productive to blame the providers for things that have gone wrong (and issuing penalties), especially since such discussions in many cases reveal uncertainties about which party actually caused the problems. Instead efforts should be made to have an ongoing dialogue to avoid risks in the distribution system. The experience from the collaboration with service providers have shown that a formalized service review (which is required in the contract) is working very well in comparison to traditional internal communications.

Table 10.3 Standardized and Documented Review and Planning Activities

Control level	Involved units	Frequency
Operational review and planning	Sales companies, Order fulfilment responsible unit, 1st tier provider	Weekly-Monthly
Performance review	Order fulfilment responsible unit, Corporate Distribution, 1st tier provider	Monthly-Quarterly
Service agreement review	Business unit, Corporate functional units incl Distribution, 1st tier provider	Yearly

Beta believes that the contract is of a great importance for risk management and that it may have two different functions. Firstly, it will provide an overview of the business risks and in order to protect oneself each party has to carefully review what they are signing, thereby giving incentives for risk analysis. Secondly, the contract may state certain demands on what should be done within the risk management area and how this work should be carried out. Thereby it will have a clear risk preventing function.

Risk Management: Liability

Company Alpha argue that even if the contract stipulates that the providers have a certain degree of liability for such things as product losses and damages, the industry norms and legal conventions are such that the providers only assume a very limited liability. The providers are also liable for any delays in the distribution but also in this respect Alpha regard this as a very limited liability, even if penalties that the shipper might suffer as well as bad will and lost business etc is disregarded, Alpha argues that they may have out of pocket expenses due to a delayed delivery that is bigger than the potential penalty the provider may pay.

Provider Beta finds an issue in the fact that there are no conventions or praxis applicable to who is liable for what in more advanced outsourcing of logistics (including for instance, logistics development). Beta believes this to be due to the type of relationships that have emerged during the last few years. The service providers have approached the problem by starting from the legal framework available for transports and amended this in certain areas and in others areas parts have been excluded.

Regarding liabilities, providers and shippers tend to have different opinions. The shippers perceive it as the provider takes a very small risk in comparison to the total product value. The providers on the other hand compare the risk with the revenues and profits from the business. Provider Beta makes the comparison that they may influence costs to the size of a couple of percent of the product value and their profit will in addition be a couple of percent of this sum. They argue this will be a very weak base to support any comprehensive liabilities, at least in comparison to the shipper situation. The economic consequences of one single incident could be devastating for a provider and this is one aspect of the risk. Another issue is that the involved parties get cautious, which may lead to inefficiencies and conflicts. In addition to direct economic consequences the provider also faces the risk of getting a bad reputation in the market and thereby losing potential future revenues.

Analysis

Risks and Uncertainties

Both the shipper and the provider have during the last couple of years increased their attention to supply chain risks and their management. At the shipper, there has been an overall development of supply chain risk management, mainly focused at 'manufacturing' activities (also outsourced) and this work has influenced distribution. The changes towards a more stockless distribution system, as well as the outsourcing have also created a higher risk awareness. In terms of risks discussed, the shipper seems more focused on operational risk sources, whilst the provider stresses strategic risks. However, in practice it may be that both the shipper and provider are focused on the same issues but they can have different implications for each party. What is only of an operational nature for one party could be of strategic significance for the other. Both the shipper and the provider stressed the risk sources connected to information and communication, since availability of information has now become so crucial. Problems in these areas could lead to delivery or invoicing failures, impacting business variables such as revenue, image and competitive position. Alpha did not think that the outsourcing influenced the risks in any major way, at least not in comparison to the risk increases caused by changes in the distribution system. Also, Beta did not see much change in the operational risks, except the impact they now could have on them as their responsibility had increased. At the same time Beta stressed a number of risks of a more strategic nature for them. The risk sources related to distribution and its outsourcing are mainly related to what Jüttner (2002) defined as internal to the supply chain. Information is a crucial risk element in this case, both due to the complex and information intensive distribution system but also due to the importance of the information exchange between the partners. The inter-organizational (or network) risks are dependent of the structure and coordination of the relationship, which will fail if one of the actors take advantage of the other's dependence in order to achieve benefits for themselves (Walker, 1988).

None of the risks that Lalonde and Cooper (1989) identified for the shippers have been an issue in the studied case. Those risks have most likely been addressed in the stage when the outsourcing was planned and providers were selected, which for this advanced service set-up was quite a long time ago and has therefore not been seen as significant now. However, the provider's risks that Lalonde and Cooper (1989) mention are corresponding to the issues at hand in our case.

Risk Analysis and Assessment

The shipper Alpha analysed potential risk causes, effects and business impacts for 11 different scenarios. The approach shows similarities with the ETA-analysis, as it starts with possible events and what their impact could be. Further Alpha assessed the risk by trying to evaluate probabilities and consequences. Risk analysis and assessment had not been undertaken with the same scope as before but was stressed partly due to the outsourcing and change of distribution structure and also due to a general increasing focus on supply chain risk management within the organization. An interesting aspect of Beta's risk analysis is the collaboration among the different parties, including competitors, which has lead to better results than individual efforts.

Risk Management

In the case studied the focus seems to have been on two of the generic risk management strategies: to avoid and reduce risks. This has been done in very close collaboration between all of the parties. When it comes to the risk strategies transferring or sharing risks, the picture is not as clear and in some aspects there seems to be grave problems in using these two means.

Both the shipper and the provide argue that operational risks management might be improved due to outsourcing, as operational risks get more attention and are explicitly handled as they occur in a commercial relationship, instead of inside a bureaucracy. For the provider, the outsourcing of advanced services has increased their risk exposure and hence, given incentives for improving risk management.

Both the shipper and the provider have developed contingency plans which are believed to have been useful. Alpha's plan means to eliminate or reduce the impact of problems, business resumption activities and what stakeholders need. Further actions are assessed in terms of feasibility. Beta has also in the development of contingency plans, involved both the shipper and their competing providers, which is an interesting approach from a supply chain management perspective.

Both parties find that the contract plays an important role in risk management. The most important role of the contract, may be as a risk preventive tool. It has been argued that it is more productive from a total business perspective, to focus on a dialogue to avoid risks in the distribution system instead of using penalties if someone has done something wrong. As the providers take increasingly larger responsibilities for the logistics system, the issue of liability will become a vital issue. The issue is both related to actually protecting against losses and also to ensure the best possible service. Regarding liability, we found great differences in the shipper and provider views. The shipper argues that the providers assume a very limited liability in comparison to their operational responsibility (and the risks the shipper faces), the reason for this is claimed to be tradition and legal conventions. The provider on the other hand perceives the risks as very big in comparison to their revenues and profits. In addition to the direct economic consequences the provider also faces the risk of badwill if something goes wrong.

It seems like the risk level for both shipper and service provider changes in an outsourcing situation but that the liability does not change in the same way, thus a gap is created (see Figure 10.1). In a situation with all logistics activities performed in-house, the shipper is responsible for all risk sources and is naturally accountable for all risk consequences. If the shipper outsources basic logistics services like transportation and warehouse management, they transfer the responsibility for these activities and hence, some risk sources to the provider. The provider must in this situation (2nd case in Figure 10.1) take measures to reduce the risk which previously were the sole responsibility of the shipper. Such measures could be choice of mode and carrier; multiple sourcing of transports; improve tracking and tracing; modify scheduling; streamlining the goods reception; stockpiling of input resources like fuel (Christopher et al, 2002). According to the shipper, the consequence of incidents will seldom affect the service provider to the full extent as they normally are only liable for a part connected to the value of the service. However, in this case the service provider only gets paid for performing basic services and this could suggest to them that their commercial risk exposure should not be higher.

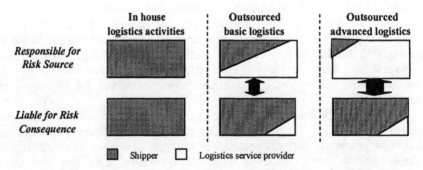

Figure 10.1 Gap in the Transfer of Risk Responsibility and Liability

In the third case (in Figure 10.1), the service provider has got even more responsibility as their role is to manage the logistics set-up, often consisting of sub-providers performing the basic activities. Further, they are responsible for developing and re-engineering the logistics systems when needed, thus the responsibility for risk sources has increased. Looking at the actions listed for reducing the risks of a basic transportation service, a shipper may transfer almost all of them to a service provider. However, when we look at the liability if something happens, the situation has not changed much. The contract between the two parties is more or less the same, due to the transportation industry tradition and conventions. The shipper still takes the risk, although the service provider now is the one who has the operational responsibility and can influence the risks. In this case we have a mismatch, i.e. the gap in Figure 10.1. However, even if the parties do not agree on how the liability should be divided they both agree on the fact that the liability issue is a big problem, due to uncertainties created by the lack of conventions or praxis applicable to the outsourcing of advanced logistics. It is this fact that creates a risk in itself.

Conclusions

In the case of outsourcing of advanced logistics services, both the shipper and provider increase their work in terms of analyzing, assessing and managing risks. This is due to their risk situation changing – not as much in terms of the pure operations but in who is responsible and liable. For the shipper it seems to be a matter of operational risks and for the provider the risks seem to contain more strategic elements. This might be due to activities being core activities for the provider and hence, the relationship is more strategic, than for the shipper who whilst outsourcing is critical, it is still a none-core activity. The provider is taking on more responsibility than they normally do and is also investing in specific assets for the client. In terms of operational risk sources, both the focus for the shipper and provider has been on information and communication transfer.

In terms of common risk management process, this has been more developed on the shipper side, which has started to use common tools for risk analysis and risk assessment. In terms of risk management, both parties have so far developed contingency plans. An interesting observation in this case, was the provider's involvement of both the shipper and competing providers in the process of operational risk analysis and developing contingency plans. The contract was seen as a major tool in risk management, both to handle risk ex-post but even more importantly ex-ante to point out risk sources and guide work to minimize risks.

The major gap between the two parties is the liability issue: who is responsible for a risk and its business impact? There seem to be a gap between how much operational/managerial responsibility is being transferred from a shipper to a provider and the subsequent increase in their liability. This issue is not really discussed in the context of supply chain management and logistics outsourcing and is hence, a topic for future research.

The outsourcing of logistics and the related strategic risks, has indirectly reduced the operational risks in the distribution system by creating incentives to focus on these risks. The move from an in-house operation into something more of a market situation has introduced what in transaction costs terminology, would be defined as strong incentives. However, when it actually comes to handling the risks the use of strong incentives are not regarded as effective at an operational level, instead cooperation and an open dialogue are favoured.

References

Andersson, D. (1997), 'Third Party Logistics–Outsourcing Logistics in Partnerships'. *Dissertation No. 34*, Dept of Management and Economics, Linköpings Universitet, Sweden.

Christopher, M., McKinnon, A., Sharp, J., Wilding, R., Peck, H., Chapman, P., Jüttner, U. and Bolumole, Y. (2002), *'Supply Chain Vulnerability'*. Cranfield University.

CMI – Chartered Management Institute, (2002), 'Business Continuity and Supply Chain Management'. Report available at
www.thebci.org/2809-01%20Bus%20Continuity%20Summ.pdf.

Jüttner, U., Peck, H. and Christopher, M. (2002), 'Supply Chain Risk Management: Outlining an Agenda for Future Research', in Griffiths J., Hewitt, F. and Ireland, P. (eds) *Proceedings of the Logistics Research Network 7th Annual Conference*, pp.443-450.

Lalonde, B.J., Cooper, M.C. (1989), *'Partnerships in Providing Customer Service: A Third Party Perspective'*, Council of Logistics Management, Oak Brook, IL, USA.

Lindroth, R. and Norrman, A. (2001), 'Supply Chain Risks and Risk Sharing Instruments – An Illustration from the Telecommunication Industry'. *Proceedings of the Logistics Research Network 6th Annual Conference*, Heriot-Watt University, September 13-14 2001, pp.297-307.

Lonsdale, C. (1999), 'Effectively managing vertical relationships: a risk management model for outsourcing'. *Supply Chain Management: An International Journal*, Vol.4, No.4, pp.176-183.

Mullai, A. and Paulsson, U. (2002), 'Oil Spills in Öresund - Hazardous Events, Causes and Claims', Lund University.

Pruth, M. (2002), Kontrakt som styrmedel i TPL samarbeten – Existerande funktioner och utveckling av nya principer, *Dissertation*: Department of Business Administration, School of Economics and Commercial Law, University of Gothenburg, Sweden.

Rao, K. and Young, R.R. (1994), 'Global Supply Chains: Factors Influencing Outsourcing of Logistics Functions', *International Journal of Physical Distribution and Logistics Management*, Vol.24, No.6, pp.11-19.

Walker, G. (1988), 'Strategic Sourcing, Vertical Integration, and Transaction Costs', *Interfaces*, Vol.18, No.3, May-June, pp.62-73.

Van Hoek, R.I., (2000), 'The Purchasing and Control of Supplementary Third-Party Logistics Services, *The Journal of Supply Chain Management*, November, pp.14-26.

van Laarhoven, P., Berglund, M. and Peters, M. (2000), 'Third-party Logistics in Europe-five years later', *International Journal of Physical Distribution and Logistics Management*, Vol.30, No.8, pp.425-444.

Chapter 11

Effective Practices and Tools for Ensuring Supply Continuity

Dr. George A. Zsidisin, Dr. Gary L. Ragatz and Prof. Steven A. Melnyk

Supply Chain Crises – The Challenge

Increasingly, firms and their management are coming to rely on lean supply chains to augment and enhance their own internal capabilities. These are also chains where waste and buffers in their various forms are actively identified, evaluated and attacked. The goal is to replace the traditional 'internal' factory (a system where the firm relied on its own capacities and capabilities to meet customer demand) with more effective and efficient supply chain systems.

As can be seen in the experiences of such as firms as Dell, Wal-Mart, Mothers Working and Calyx and Corolla, this new strategy can and does create significant competitive advantages for those firms willing to embrace it. Yet, there is a 'dark' side to this new supply chain based strategy. As firms become more reliant on the supply chain and as they seek to identify and eliminate waste by applying the lessons and tools offered by developments, such as Total Quality Management (TQM), Six Sigma, Just-in-Time Manufacturing and Lean Thinking, they are realizing that their supply chains are become increasingly 'fragile.' That is, their systems are becoming less able to deal with shocks that have a very low probability of occurring but that have significant, if not catastrophic, impacts for the firm.

Numerous examples of such shocks can be found in today's newspapers. On August 14, 2003, electrical power in the American Midwest and Ontario was disrupted, with the resulting power outages lasting anywhere from minutes to days (www.macnn.com/news/20654). The effects of this disruption were felt as far away as California, where Apple Computer was preparing to launch its much-anticipated G5 computer – the first mainstream personal computer featuring 64 bit processing. This launch was affected by the power disruption since Apple relied on IBM to supply its chips. These chips were manufactured in a factory located in upstate New York – a factory affected by the power disruption. On September 21, 1999, a magnitude 7.6 tremor struck Taiwan, killing over 1,500 people. From a supply chain perspective, this earthquake hindered the supply of computer memory chips, affecting many firms' ability to meet anticipated consumer demand for the upcoming holiday season. Finally, on Tuesday September 11, 2001, New York experienced the destruction of the World Trade Towers due to terrorism.

Companies such as American Express experienced significant losses in terms of their information databases.

As a result of these and other similar interruptions, firms and their management have become aware of the need to maintain and enhance inbound supply continuity. As discussed by Monczka et al (2001) the assurance of supply continuity is one of the nine primary objectives of Purchasing and Supply Management (PSM). Other leading textbooks in the field of PSM have provided similar perspectives (Burt et al, 2003; Leenders et al, 2002). However, none of these sources have provided specified guidance into how purchasing organizations can create or implement BCP, nor even provided guidance into the overall structure or key elements that constitute an effective BCP process for supply management.

These events have created greater awareness in society with regard to the problems that business organizations face from the external environment. Many firms have attempted to allay these fears from critical stakeholders and have created planning processes and structures to reduce the effects of business disruptions. For example, in a recent study by Digital Research Inc. (2002), it was discovered that 77 per cent of the survey respondents have business or disaster recovery plans in place. However, this study did not specify its application for inbound supply.

One system that has emerged in response to this challenge of managing and reducing supply chain risks and disruptions is that of Business Continuity Planning (BCP). This is a system intended to assist managers in identifying, managing, evaluating and ultimately eliminating risks within the upstream supply chain (i.e. that portion of the supply chain consisting of the firm and its supply net). This is a relatively new development. Consequently, little is known about it and its operation. One area in which this lack of knowledge is most pronounced involves effective practices and tools for ensuring supply continuity. This chapter will focus on addressing this lack of knowledge.

Specifically, the chapter will present the reader with several practices and tools that have been found to be effective in ensuring supply continuity. These findings are based on detailed case studies conducted with three purchasing organizations that have been recognized as being at the 'leading edge' in their ability to develop and implement effective BCP systems. The lessons contained within this chapter are targeted to both researchers and practitioners.

This chapter will begin by presenting the reasons for this increased awareness of risk within the supply chain and the BCP response. Next, the chapter will focus on the effective practices and tools needed for creating awareness, preventing supply discontinuity, remediating supply interruptions and managing knowledge. The chapter will conclude with examples of business continuity planning tools in action and conclusions drawn from the case studies, summarizing the key elements for ensuring supply continuity. Supply chain risk is increasingly a fact of modern supply chain management but it is a risk that can be identified and reduced through the appropriate application of the various practices and tools presented in this chapter.

Supply Chain Management + Lean Practices can Equal 'Fragility'

To understand the principles and practices of BCP, we must first understand the problems that are giving rise to it. Interest in BCP can be traced to the interaction of two major developments: (1) the emergence of and acceptance of supply chain management and (2) the 'leaning' of the supply chain through the application of lean principles and practices. It is the interaction that is important since either of these two developments by themselves does not provide a necessary, nor sufficient condition for the emergence of catastrophic risk – the major driver of BCP.

The Emergence of Supply Chain Management

Supply chain management began to surface in the late 1980s. It was the product of several independent developments that came together. The first was the emergence of the never satisfied customer (McKenna, 1997) – a customer who wanted more (more options, more flexibility, better quality, greater responsiveness) at a lower price and who was willing to move from firm to firm in search of a 'better' deal.

The second is the shrinking product life cycle. Products are introduced and disappear at an increasingly rapid pace, often driven by constantly changing technology. Whilst in the past a product such as a car may have had an effective product life (through its various incarnations) of close to 10 years, this life is now shrinking. In the microcomputer industry, for example, the authors have encountered products with life cycles of 14 weeks to nine months. Shrinking total life cycles bring with them some important implications. The first is that managers no longer have the luxury of correcting problems after a product has been made and delivered. In many cases, by the time that the product has been detected and a solution formulated, it is too late, the firm is onto a new replacement product. Furthermore, customers are less willing to wait for the firm to correct these problems after the fact.

A third factor contributing to the interest in SCM has been the emergence of newer, faster and cheaper computer hardware and software. This development has enabled management to link and coordinate not only internal activities but also the activities of its suppliers and supply chains with those of the customer.

Together, these three factors have forced managers to rethink their reliance on the 'internal' factory – the manufacturing system owned and controlled by the firm. They have turned to the supply chain in the hopes of being able to meet the demands of the 'never satisfied' customer while simultaneously coping with the challenges of shrinking product life cycles. Managers have been willing to give up the high control and visibility offered by the internal factor with the reduced cost and visibility (but lower costs and higher responsiveness) offered by the external factory – the upstream supply chain.

The 'Leaning' of the Supply Chain

As firms have come to rely more heavily on their supply chains, they have also begun applying the procedures and processes of lean manufacturing and lean thinking (Womack and Jones, 1996) to those supply chains. These procedures offer the promise of improved performance (shorter lead times, better quality, lower costs, enhanced flexibility) by identifying, attacking and reducing all forms of waste both internally (within the firm) and externally (between the firm and its supply chain partners). In part, these waste reduction activities have focused on reducing the presence of buffers. Most firms rely to varying degrees on three types of buffers: safety stock, safety lead time and safety capacity. All three types of buffer create costs and consume resources. By 'leaning' the supply chain, managers have hoped to create a new system characterized by lower costs, higher responsiveness and less waste.

The Interaction – 'System Fragility'

Once these two developments are combined, they can create a situation that is best described as 'system fragility.' That is, we find ourselves faced by a system over which we have reduced control and that is less able to respond to or to cope with the effects of a sudden, unexpected and catastrophic problem encountered within the supply chain. When faced by a catastrophic problem, we may find that our supply chain has become too lean. Without the buffers offered by safety lead time, safety stock or safety capacity, the firm may find itself immediately exposed to the effects of the disruptions.

If such a problem occurs, the purchasing function is unable to satisfy its primary objectives – that of providing the firm with an uninterrupted flow of goods and services from the upstream supply chain. BCP exists to enable management to recognize, evaluate and deal with such threats to its supply chain. The various practices and tools are intended to assist managers in containing these upstream threats.

BCP – Effective Practices and Tools

Barnes (2001) defines BCP as the integration of formalized procedures and resource information that firms can use to recover from a disaster that causes a disruption to business operations. This definition provides a general conceptual framework for the need to create formal plans that help firms minimize the time and cost of a supply disruption. However, for BCP to be successful, it must inherently facilitate identifying and providing a structure for eliminating known risk.

Consequently, in this chapter, we treat BCP not as one tool but rather as a system of tools and practices that focuses on four major activities (these four activities provided the needed structure):

1. Creating system awareness
2. Preventing supply discontinuity
3. Remediating supply interruptions
4. Managing knowledge.

The effective practices and tools are categorized into one of these four activities. These four major activities will form the structure for the subsequent discussion and exposition.

The Source of the BCP Insights

To better understand how organizations manage supply continuity, a study was undertaken at three purchasing organizations noted for their proactive engagement in supply management practices. The first case study was undertaken with a strategic business unit of an aerospace supplier located in the Midwest U.S.A. The second firm examined in this research was the corporate headquarters for a firm that provides telecommunication equipment and is based in Northern Europe. The third firm is a strategic business unit for a large multinational firm that manufactures electronic components. The findings presented in this chapter are based on the insights gained from these three case studies.

Effective Practices for Creating Awareness and Preventing Supply Discontinuity

Intra and inter-organizational awareness is required for firms to develop business continuity plans that provide guidance for taking appropriate actions if a supply disruption occurs. Disseminating the importance of ensuring business continuity, within the firm and its critical supply chains, is the first step in getting those key participants to 'buy in' to the plan and planning processes. The threat of supply chain risk is real. By creating awareness, purchasing organizations can obtain insight into the potential risk factors they may otherwise not address in their continuity planning processes.

Creating awareness of supply risk throughout the critical facets of the supply chain is not enough. When possible, firms should strive toward preventing the likelihood of supply discontinuity from occurring. By creating awareness of the threats and implications of supply discontinuity, purchasing organizations can elicit suggestions from different supply chain participants. For example, finance professionals can alert supply management professionals of poor supplier financial health. Production engineers can point to deteriorating trends in supplier quality performance. Sales and marketing professionals can forewarn purchasing of significant demand fluctuations that can have a detrimental ripple effect of shortages for critical purchases. Suppliers can notify their customers (purchasing) of potential problems with second-tier suppliers.

It is important to note that not all risk in the supply chain is controllable by purchasing organizations. However, by creating awareness and encouraging intra- and inter-organizational supply chain participants to communicate potential supply chain issues, purchasing organizations can place themselves in a better position to alleviate supply chain concerns when possible, create strategies for best dealing with risk, or modify business continuity plans in response to environmental changes.

Creating Awareness of Supply Risk

The risk of supply chain disruptions is real. This awareness needs to be created both internally and externally to the firm.

Internal Awareness

Even though the 'stories' of supply chain risk events are well known, the process of creating internal awareness of risk from supply sources can be a difficult task. Many firms have now focused on lean business processes that remove many of the buffers and organizational slack that used to be in place 'just-in-case.' The rationale behind these decisions is logical – when organizations can remove the 'fat' in their organizations, significant cost reductions follow, often leading to increased efficiencies and greater profitability. However, it also leaves the organization more susceptible to environmental conditions that can lead to significant losses. Therefore, it can be challenging to promote awareness of supply risk in this era of leanness. Purchasing professionals should consider several general guidelines for creating internal risk awareness throughout their organizations. These guidelines include communicating with key personnel that disruptions can have a serious financial and competitive impact on the firm, facilitating a systems view to business continuity planning, soliciting the viewpoints of operational personnel closest to the supply base and having top management support.

The creation of *internal awareness* of the need for firms to engage in BCP for supply management is the critical first-step necessary for structuring and managing these plans. There are several ways for purchasing professionals to create this awareness. The first is by communicating with key personnel the seriousness of supply risk and its potentially devastating effects on business profitability and survivability. Business functions that are not focused on inbound supply may see the message of supply discontinuity as not fitting within their job descriptions and see it instead as a nuisance. One technique to alleviate this organizational resistance is by providing examples of other firms and the problems that they had to face when confronted with supply failures. Examples such as the work slow-down in California during the summer of 2002 and the power outages throughout the Northern states in the USA in August, 2003 show the fragility of supply chains. Within these examples, it was not just the purchasing function affected but instead the events affected all business organization functions and their supply chains.

Arguments can be made by other business functions that appropriate buffer stock of inbound supplies can alleviate these concerns. However, these arguments have their limitations. For example, the work slowdown of California dockworkers in 2002 represented a significant risk of supply interruption for many firms. Some companies, such as Ralph Lauren and Tommy Hilfiger anticipated this risk, and began re-routing their shipments through the east coast months in advance (Wolk, 2002). Others, like Nummi, while aware of the potential for problems, continued using the West Coast ports but stockpiled an extra six days of inventory. Unfortunately, Nummi still ran out of parts and had to shut down for several days. Nummi is currently working with its supplier base to set up contingency plans to prevent this situation in the future (Jacobs, 2002).

Taking a systems view of supply chain management can also go a long way in helping create internal awareness of BCP. No organization is an island. In creating internal awareness of risk in BCP, it needs to be understood within the organization that the firm is dependent on its supply sources, especially with regard to critical direct and indirect purchases. A well known saying is that a 'chain is as strong as its weakest link.' This is true as well for most business organizations. Creating internal awareness in this vein becomes important for identifying organizational weaknesses. The optimization of one business function can result in other links having greater susceptibility to risk events. For example, if marketing and sales promotes a product, or over-promises order fulfillment to a key customer, the in-bound supply chain may not have the flexibility to meet such increased demand, resulting in stock-outs and poor customer service. When taking a systems view of the organization and supply chain, potential threats to business continuity can be addressed in advanced and potentially avoided.

By taking a systems view, operational personnel that are closest to the supply base may be able to serve as 'listening posts' when environmental changes take place. These personnel, often buyers, assistant buyers, or commodity managers, often have the greatest knowledge of their supplier organizations and changes that occur within their environment. However, these personnel may or may not have a macro-level perspective of risk from the corporate level. Therefore, it becomes imperative for firms to first have clear and open communication channels throughout the organization, to include those of the operational personnel with their supervisors and eventually with top-level management. One problem that may arise is the fear that operational personnel may have of reprisals when reporting 'bad news.' Therefore, managers and directors need to ensure that they do not 'shoot the messenger' when that individual presents problems that can have detrimental effects on inbound supply assurance.

From these discussions, it becomes clear that the role of top management is critical for organizations to successfully engage in supply management BCP. Without top management support, it becomes very difficult for supply management to dedicate the time and resources required for developing and managing BCP. Creating top management support and buy-in should start from the Chief Purchasing Officer or its organizational equivalent (the highest ranking purchasing professional in the organization). Once top management buy-in is secured, it becomes much easier for purchasing professionals to drive internal awareness to the importance for ensuring supply continuity.

External Awareness

The creation of internal awareness is an important first step in BCP for supply management. However, internal awareness is limited because it only provides one perspective of business continuity. Creating external awareness, especially with critical first-tier supplier organization, provides an additional and potentially clearer view of the risk factors organizations face in their upstream supply chains. Suppliers normally have greater awareness of the problems they individually encounter. However, most supplier organizations are guarded of the information they provide to some of their customers. There is an inherent fear, often with valid reasons, of sharing with customers the threats to supply that exist. To best address this fear, it is incumbent on the purchasing organization to first establish open lines of communication with their supplier organizations and a willingness to work with those suppliers to manage problems and issues. Then, with those open lines of communication, derive appropriate mechanisms for motivating supplier firms to be proactive in understanding, sharing and providing insight for managing supply risk and creating plans for the risks that cannot be eliminated.

The communication of critical information is necessary for effectively managing supply chains and networks. It is also essential for creating awareness among organizations to the sources of risk that exist that can stop the flow of inbound products or services. Creating an awareness of risk sources allows firms to work together towards preventing risk when possible and quickly remediating it if it does occur. Even though the message may be clear to suppliers that the threats with supply can be damaging to both firms, most suppliers are unwilling or hesitant to bring up potential problems due to a fear of reprisal and for protecting their image. Therefore, discussions with suppliers need to emphasize that the reporting of potential problems is highly encouraged and that the relationship with the supplier will not be jeopardized at any time when discussing potential supply threats.

One method for motivating suppliers to identify and manage risk in their firms and supply chains is through the metrics in their evaluations. Further, prior to selection, potential suppliers can be evaluated on the extent they implement BCP within their organizations and supply chains. This provides an initial grounding for where they currently stand on managing risk and how they can improve to continually meet the organization's future requirements.

Preventing Risk Occurrence

BCP is critical when dealing with the uncertainty of supply, especially with regard to events that could not be seen in advance. However, there may be circumstances where risk can be identified *a priori*. When a threat to supply continuity is identified, such as when the competitive market of a supplier becomes a sole source of supply, the management of that risk may be better handled through its prevention instead of expending resources for remediation. It was observed in the cases conducted for this study, as well as other industry observations, that well-formulated BCP addresses prevention as well as creating 'what-if' scenarios and supply options in the event that a supply disruption occurs. There are four effective practices that were discussed for preventing supply disruptions. The first consists of prioritizing suppliers and commodities for focusing attention to risk. The second practice consists of considering the full spectrum of resources and flows managed within the supply chain. Risk consists of two dimensions – probability and impact. Therefore, the third practice examined in prevention, is having organizations understand both dimensions of risk. The knowledge attained in understanding probability and impact facilitates helps in the creation of appropriate strategies for either eliminating risk when feasible or implementing buffers when elimination is not possible. Since business and supply chains are not static, the fourth and final practice identified monitoring and revisiting these issues on a regular basis.

Prioritizing Suppliers and Commodities to Focus Attention

All business organizations have limited resources. Therefore, decisions need to be made with regard to the activities that purchasing organizations engage. It is not realistic to prevent all risk from occurring. In addition, the impact of risk events in terms of cost and duration significantly differs according to the type of product and supply market that exists. For example, Kraljic (1983) and Steele and Court (1996) among others, have described supply risk in terms of market complexity, which involves supply market factors such as the existence of monopoly or oligopoly conditions, the pace of technological advancements and entry barriers to supplier markets. In circumstances where the threats of supply risk and its ramifications in terms of supply discontinuity are minimal, it does not make sense to focus managerial resources on preventing the likelihood of risk disruptions. However, when significant risk is identified and the purchasing organization can exercise some control of that risk in a cost-beneficial manner, it is often in the best interests of the purchasing organization to engage in activities that can prevent supply disruptions from occurring in the first place. Therefore, suppliers considered 'at risk,' and commodities that are characterized by having a significant extent of market complexity, should be targets for engaging in risk prevention activities such as creating a second supply source, better managing relationships, or developing supply substitutes.

Considering the Full Spectrum of Resources and Flows Managed within a Supply Chain

Business organizations have a wide scope of resources and flows that must be managed. Resources can include management and employees, capital equipment, inventory, money and information. Many of these resources flow within the organization, as well as throughout the supply chain. For example, money flows through the supply chain as customers pay suppliers, those suppliers pay their suppliers and so forth. Information, strategic as well as tactical, flows through supply chains as well.

When purchasing organizations identify risk, they need to consider the resources available within and external to its firm for preventing supply disruption occurrence. One of the critical resource flows is information. It is through information that many supply chains today have shifted from focusing on buffers such as surplus inventory to that of communicating information such as anticipated demand volumes and customer orders. The sharing of information from suppliers and internally within the organization can also serve as a method for preventing risk. For example, if the purchasing organization anticipates surges in demand from its salesforce, it needs to notify its critical suppliers in a timely manner so they can better plan for meeting future requirements. If product changes are imminent, the purchasing organization should also notify suppliers of these changes and work together with them to minimize the chance that the supplier cannot ramp-up in time to meet these new requirements. From the supplier perspective, it is also their responsibility to notify their customers of market changes and internal supplier-specific changes that can affect the timely shipments and cost structures of products. This information can include cash-flow problems, over-capacity and issues associated with second and third-tier supply sources. The information exchanged among adjoining supply chain firms can help 'buy time' for creating alternative strategies that serve to avoid supply disruptions.

Understanding Both the Probability and Impact of Supply Chain Disruptions

It is imperative that firms differentiate between probability and impact because the efficient management of risk differs according to the severity of each dimension. Under circumstances where the probability that supply discontinuity is high and firms can exercise some degree of control over the circumstance, the use of process improvement techniques may be the most cost-beneficial way to address risk. Techniques such as developing suppliers and forming key alliance relationships with critical suppliers can create more robust supply chains. In other circumstances, it may be more efficient for firms to expand its supply options through multiple sourcing or having contingent supply sources.

Monitoring and Revisiting Issues on a Regular Basis

Supply risk, similar to business today, is not static. The actions that purchasing organizations take to prevent risk and supply discontinuity today may become obsolete tomorrow. Products, suppliers, customer requirements and supply chains change. BCP in supply management needs to be reassessed on a regular basis. This reassessment should be done on a periodic basis, at least once per year and include representation from all affected business functions.

Effective Practices for Remediating Risk and Organizational Learning

Awareness and prevention are two important facets to address for ensuring supply continuity. However, even with creating awareness and implementing measures to prevent risk occurrence, the risk of supply discontinuity cannot be completely eliminated. Therefore, purchasing organizations need to create plans in advance for quickly remediating supply shortages and stoppages. In addition, if risk does manifest and detrimentally effects inbound supply, firms need to foster a learning environment from the event to reduce the likelihood of its future occurrence. This will provide insight for remediating supply interruptions and learning from those events.

Remediating Supply Interruptions

The third task in the continuity planning framework is *Remediation*. While the firm takes steps in the *Prevention* stage to reduce its exposure, risk cannot be completely eliminated and disruptions to the supply chain cannot always be avoided. Thus, firms need a course of action to follow in order to recover from a disruption when it occurs. The firm should consider how it might shorten the duration of the disruption, minimize its impact on the business and identify in advance the resources that will be needed to carry out this plan. The two practices identified in remediating supply interruptions were planning for and managing the impact of supply disruptions.

Planning for Supply Disruptions

It is impossible to totally eliminate the risk of supply chain disruptions. However, it is critical to have a plan in place to deal with the disruptions when they occur. The process of planning for supply disruptions provides firms with several benefits. Firstly, it provides firms with an incentive for better understanding the supply chains in which they participate. Subsequently, garnering greater knowledge of the inbound supply chain allows firms to identify the threats that exist with supply. Secondly, having plans already established provides firms with a 'blueprint' of the appropriate actions to take in case business disruptions occur with supply. Alternatives would already be laid out ahead of time. Instead of firms operating in a panic mode, they will be better able to handle supply disruptions more quickly and efficiently. A third benefit concerns the reduced reliance on key personnel. In case a supply disruption does occur, the established plans are not dependent on one key contact person but instead if the designated point of contact is gone, other organizational leaders can quickly jump in and work toward remediating the business disruption.

Managing the Impact of Supply Disruptions

The impact of supply disruptions has two key elements, cost and duration. These two elements are related to each other. For example, the longer the duration of the supply disruption, the greater the overall cost will be to the firm, as shown in Figure 11.1. This figure shows that there are four stages to a supply disruption.

Once the disruption occurs, purchasing organizations need to first respond to the crisis, then recover as quickly as possible to reduce its impact.

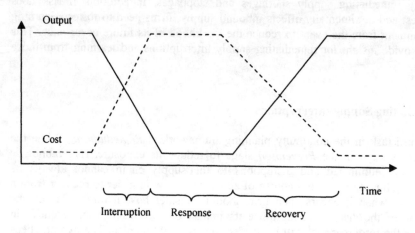

Figure 11.1 Stages of a Business Interruption

Effective Practices for Organizational Learning

The last task in the framework is *Knowledge Management*. When supply chain disruptions occur, it is important that the firm *learn from the experience*. That requires a post-incident audit that identifies important lessons learned, things gone right, things gone wrong and the results of the remediation effort, along with feedback to the earlier stages in the continuity planning process. The purpose for managing knowledge is to learn from supply disruptions, since they are an indication that something went wrong and that the existing plans and contingencies in place may not be adequate. Even if the plans were adequate and the effects of the disruption were minimal, management must review what happened and improve current BCP processes by carrying out a 'post-mortem.'

Take a Continuous Improvement View of Supply Chain Continuity Planning

The exposure to supply chain disruption cannot be fixed overnight. Further, the risk that purchasing organizations encounter that can disrupt business operations can never be completed eliminated. Purchasing organizations need to focus on continually improving internal and interorganizational processes that reduces the likelihood of supply disruptions from occurring. In addition, supply chain structures frequently change, whether it is for a new product, new supplier, or new production process. Therefore, protecting the supply chain is not a one-time activity but instead requires on-going attention and effort.

Make a Post-event Audit of Supply Chain Disruptions Standard Operating Procedure

Organizations need to learn from inbound supply failures in order to prevent their reoccurrence. A supply disruption indicates that something went wrong, whether it was the supply strategy pursued, supplier selected, or changes that occurred in the supplier marketplace which were not detected beforehand. A post-event audit should become a standard operating procedure so firms can learn from their mistakes, make appropriate changes to the BCP and provide guidance for future organizational managers. Further, actions and activities that worked to reduce the duration and impact of the supply disruption should also be noted to disseminate to other organizational members and divisions the learning lessons for managing supply risk, and considered for adoption throughout the firm itself. Therefore, it is imperative to share what was learned and avoid 'reinventing the wheel' in BCP.

Summary of Effective Practices

Effective practices in BCP for supply management have been discussed with regard to the stages of identification, prevention, remediation and knowledge management. Most of these practices have been discussed in general terms for providing managers guidance for managing supply risk with BCP. The following section provides some specific tools that organizations can implement or modify for creating BCP processes.

Business Continuity Planning Tools for Supply Management

A variety of tools can be used to assess and monitor the risk of disruptions in the upstream supply chain. These tools help to highlight the buying firm's exposure and also provide a structure for taking preventative action to deal with those exposures.

One useful tool for building awareness of business continuity issues in the supply base is the supplier audit. Tables 11.1 and 11.2 below illustrate a portion of a supplier audit that focuses on supply chain continuity issues. Consistent application of an audit of this type will create awareness of the importance of this type of preparedness in the supplier base and encourages attention to such issues on the part of suppliers. Further, this tool helps the buying company develop a clearer picture of its risk exposure.

Table 11.1   Material Supplier Quality Audit Section Relating to Supplier's Disaster Recovery Planning

Element: Disaster Recovery Program				
Requirements	Status	Evidence & Location	Action Plan Y/N	Score 0/10
Is there an emergency Disaster/Business Recovery/Business continuity plan established in the Supplier Company?				
Is this plan deployed according to all existing sites?				
Is this plan addressing management succession and identification of key staff?				
Is this plan identifying all 'strategic' materials and equipments and their identical sources of replacement?				
Is there an off-site storage of vital records?				
In case of disaster are there procedures to restart minimum service level and to organize transport to a back-up site?				

Table 11.2   Material Supplier Quality Assessment Scoring Method

Description	Score
Supplier is not familiar with the requirements of the element and has no relevant source documentation (flow charts, forecasts, plans, procedures, strategies, etc) in this area.	0
Supplier is familiar with the requirements of the element but there is not evidence of source documentation, planning or implementation.	1
Supplier is familiar with requirements of the element and has preliminary source documentation with incomplete plans for implementation.	2
Source documentation is available. Implementation (with assigned responsibilities) has just started (0-30% complete)	3
Source documentation is available and implementation is in progress (30-60%). Deficiencies have been identified but improvements are not quantifiable.	4
Implementation has progressed (60-80% complete) and there is preliminary evidence of relevant results.	5
Implementation is nearly complete (80-95%) and documented evidence of implementation effectiveness exists.	6
Full implementation of source documentation for the requirement and complete confirmed evidence of implementation effectiveness. The supplier has met minimum requirements.	7
Analysis of results and on-going continuous improvement can be demonstrated in key areas linked with customer satisfaction.	8
Supplier has reached world-class performance and is able to show growth beyond QS-9000 requirements and continuous improvement in all areas.	9
Supplier is best-in-class and is able to demonstrate significant innovation in new ways to show relevant results beyond the customer requirements. The supplier sets the industry benchmark.	10

A minimum score of seven is required on every applicable question.

Another tool in BCP is the *Purchasing Risk Register*. The example shown in Table 11.3 includes fourteen categories for identifying, assessing and managing supply risk. This tool provides a structured approach for the buying firm to identify and evaluate risks in the upstream supply chain, assign responsibility for managing each of these risks and track progress on eliminating or minimizing the risk. Various personnel are responsible for assessing each of the fourteen identified risk categories, each of which relates to a specific business process. For example, purchasing directors are responsible for categories such as supplier financial distress and market imperfections that result in uncontrollable price movements. Each category is evaluated for its probability and impact in qualitative terms of high, medium, or low. Table 11.4 provides an example of the scales used to assess probability and impact in each of the exposure categories. Business processes that may be affected are listed, as well as the individual responsible for addressing the risk. Actions for managing and controlling the risk are then identified and tracked. After management/control measures are established, a residual risk effect is again qualitatively estimated for probability and impact. Table 11.5 provides additional detail on how one of the risk categories might be treated.

Similar in principle to the 'Risk Register,' purchasing organizations can conduct risk assessments for specific products and suppliers. An example, provided in Table 11.6, also includes a diagram, contrasting the probability and impact dimensions of risk and how that risk is quantified.

The *Purchasing Risk Register* can be further augmented with the *At Risk Register,* which documents specific suppliers that are identified as posing a risk to the buying firm. Risk factors include financial problems such as the filing of Chapter 11, dependency on the supplier firm, business consolidation and location issues. Information in the *At Risk Register* is provided for specific supplier organizations and by the group. Criteria evaluated in the *At Risk Register* include if a dual source exists, if there is a planned exit of the relationship, if an acquisition of the supplier is planned, the date of when the supplier was identified at risk, lead time for the purchased items, if engineering drawings are available, and if engineering approval was completed. An example of an *At Risk Register* is provided in Table 11.7.

Table 11.3   Purchasing Risk Register

Risk No.	Title	Initial Risk Prob	Initial Risk Impact	Business Process
1	If suppliers are in financial distress then delivery will be impacted	H	M	Supplier Network
2	If suppliers have quality problems then delivery will be impacted	H	M	Supplier Network
3	If key suppliers become totally incapacitated then delivery will be affected	L	H	Supplier Network
4	If there are volatile movements in base materials and alloys then cash will be affected	H	M	Manage Cash
5	If there are market imperfections then there will be uncontrollable price movements	H	M	Supplier Network
6	If key suppliers fail to generate sufficient cost reduction then FYC profit and cash levels will not be achieved	M	H	Dev. Support Chain Performance
7	If SAP/ERP data is incorrect, then we will be unable to manage our tasks and meet our commitments	H	H	Fulfil Orders
8	If there are skill shortages within purchasing then the FYC will be impacted	H	H	People & Knowledge
9	If we do not pay suppliers on time then the FYC will be affected	H	M	Manage Cash
10	If there are sudden changes in load then supplier performance will be impacted	M	H	Plan the Business
11	If the supply base is not restructured and parts transfers not correctly managed then the FYC will be impacted	M	M	Create Customer Solutions
12	If design changes are not implemented correctly then supplier cost reduction performance will be impacted	H	H	Create Customer Solutions
13	If we fail to align reward to business and personal performance then objectives will be less likely to be met	M	M	People & Knowledge
14	If supplier diversity goals are not achieved, we will not be awarded government contracts	H	H	Manage Cash

Table 11.4   Example Structure for Assessing Probability and Impact of Exposure (Purchasing Risk Register)

Probability	
L	<5% chance
M	5% - 25% chance
H	> 25% chance

Impact	
L	< $8 million
M	$8 - $16 million
H	> $16 million

A critical risk area, especially in a weak economy and especially for smaller suppliers is the danger of smaller suppliers' financial failure. If a supplier is having cash flow problems, it can result in either poor performance or even the loss of business. Supplier financial health can be tracked in many ways.

One approach is the use of financial appraisal reports. These reports provide financial information about suppliers such as growth and profitability ratios, dependency ratios, liquidity and working capital management, gearing and an overall financial rating of the supplier. An example of the summary report from such an analysis is shown in Table 11.8.

Another method for identifying suppliers with potential financial difficulties is a 'Media Review.' This periodic review, based on a review of press releases, announcements and news reports appearing in a range of media outlets can provide an 'early warning system' regarding supplier financial difficulties. An example of this form can be found in Table 11.9.

Table 11.5   Risk Action Example

Risk 1: Actions		
Risk Description – If suppliers are in financial distress then delivery will be impacted.	**Probability:** **Impact:**	
Background – Changes in economic factors, supplier capability, or in workload from our firm or other key customers, may increase the risk of suppliers becoming insolvent. This may expose us to ransom demands or disruption should the supplier go into receivership/Chapter 11.		
Actions/Control Measures	**Owner**	**Date**
Identify high risk suppliers (using D&B ratings and intelligence from supplier visits).	Supplier Intelligence	Ongoing
Supplier risk assessments of top 100 suppliers, private companies and suppliers difficult to switch.	Purchasing Executives	Ongoing
Bi-Annual financial appraisals of top 100 suppliers plus ad-hoc as needed.	Supplier Intelligence	Ongoing
Consolidation of supply base.	Purchasing Director	Ongoing
Quarterly Risk meeting.	V.P. Supply Chain	Quarterly

Table 11.6   Risk Assessment Process Example

Classes of Risk Exposure:

- Class 1: The product is currently sourced from more than one approved source.
- Class 2: The product is currently sourced from one approved source. Other sources are approved and available, but not used.
- Class 3: The product is currently sourced from one approved source. Other sources are available and approved, but tooling and/or equipment is limited.
- Class 4: The product is currently sourced from one supplier. No additional source is available.

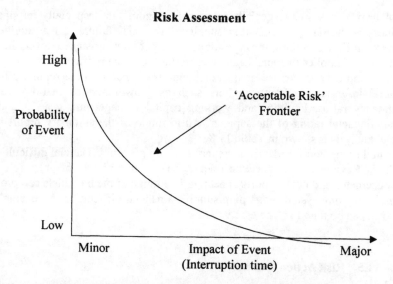

Diagram 11.1 The Probability and Impact Dimensions of Risk

Measurement scales for Probability and Impact:

Impact (Interruption Time)
- Class 1: ≤ 3 months to get deliveries from alternate source
- Class 2: $3 - 8$ months to get deliveries from alternate source
- Class 3: $9 - 12$ months, redesign only alternative
- Class 4: > 12 months, redesign of a complex unit or product

Probability
- 0 – 25   Very unlikely
- 25 – 50 Unlikely
- 50 – 75 Likely
- 75 – 100 Very likely

Table 11.7 At Risk Register

Supplier	Risk	Dual Source	Planned Exit	Brokered Acquisition	Date	Lead Time (Weeks)
A	Chapter 11	✓	.	.		22
B	Chapter 11	.	✓	.	1 Aug 02	36
C	Vol dependency/ Financial			.		18
D	Financial (Chapter 11)	✓	.	.		4
E	Financial	.	.	.		26
F	Financial	.	.	.	31 Dec 02	10
G	Vol dependency		.	.		.
H	Vol dependency		✓	.		1
I	Vol dependency		✓	.		26-52
J	Business Consolidation		.	.		.
K	Location	✓	.	.		32
L	Location	✓	.	.		12
M	Location	✓	.	.	.	12
N	Exiting Business		✓		2 Dec 02	6

Table 11.8 Financial Appraisal Example

Date:	
Ref: Fin App 784	
FINANCIAL APPRAISAL	**Fly-Right Corporation**
REASON FOR REQUEST	
Various Global sourcing strategies	
PRINCIPLE ACTIVITIES	
Fly-Right corporation is a leading supplier of innovative products and services to the aerospace, defence and space industries around the globe.	
NOTES	
The financial year-end for this company is December and financial statements to December 200X have been analysised.	
SIZE, GROWTH & PROFITABILITY	
The company has revenue in the region of $735m and has been growing rapidly for the past five years. A major consequence of this increased growth has included increased interest commitments and poor cash flow as capital has been injected into the business infrastructure and R&D activities. Over the same period profitability has dropped from 13.5% in 1996 to 9% in 2000; however, it should be noted that absolute profits have risen from $22m to $38, in the same period. During 1999 Fly-Right increased its capacity through various minor acquisitions and major investment in capital equipment. The fixed asset base rose from $163m to $358m in this period.	
LIQUIDITY	
Liquidity refers to whether the company has enough cash to pay its short-term debts if they all become due at once. Firm A prefers suppliers to have a current ratio of no less than 1.4 and a quick ratio, which excludes stock, of no less than 1.0. Fly-Right's liquidity is poor and over the past two years has worsened. This is generally in relation to increased interest charge on debt used to fund the above mentioned capital investment. The company is reliant upon an overdraft in the region of $62m; it would appear that this credit line has also increased dramatically over the last two years. Current and quick ratios are 1.2 and 0.5 respectively.	
LEVERAGE	
Leverage refers to how far the company is financed by debt rather than shareholders. If there is too much debt, then a business may not be able to borrow enough extra capital to expand. Firm A prefers its suppliers to have debt to asset rations of less than 40%. Fly-Right is leveraged at around 34% however, this does not take into consideration the overdraft and credit facilities they have with their bank. It is unlikely that they would be able to access a great deal more debt finance at present until their cash flow and current debt levels improve.	
CONCLUSIONS	
Fly-Right has grown their business well and as an ever-increasing presence in the aerospace industry is beginning to reap the rewards of aggressive investment and acquisition activities. The company's cash management is poor and the over-reliance upon an overdraft has the obvious consequences on profit and liquidity. From a negotiation point of view, Fly-Right is still making pre-tax profits of around ten per cent, if we are to have nay degree of buying power over this supplier, this fact could be a leverage point in negotiations. As both business units are interested in this supplier it may be advisable that both businesses negotiate with this supplier together. This may achieve greater cost reduction and contractual concessions, as our buying power would appear to be greater. Can I therefore suggest that, if feasible, the two businesses 'join forces' when entering into further negotiations with Fly-Right?	
ACTIONS	

Table 11.9 Media Review Example

Supplier Q

- Supplier Q has completed the disposal of a business unit to an electronic firm. The move is part of a major strategy to organize the business around their aerospace and defence businesses. Supplier Q has not confirmed what it intends to do with the cash generated from the sale of this business but it is likely that it will be used in further capital investment or to repay outstanding loans.

Supplier Q Press Release

[*By selling part of their industrial business, Supplier Q is further reliant upon the aerospace market. Supplier Q may be more receptive to our demands due to their exposure to Aerospace markets, this may be of strategic advantage.*]

Significant Supplier Appraisals Completed this Week

- Alloy supplier [*This company is a rising star and looks set to take the number one position from a major rival*]
- Supplier X [*Looking good and indications are that the company will be able to manage itself through the next couple of years*]
- Energy Supplier [*mainly an Energy supplier. They have been doing well, but liquidity and debt are a concern.*]

If you require a copy of these appraisals please contact Mr. 'Brown'

Significant Supplier Appraisals Completed this Week

Risk is a Fact of Supply Chain Life, But it can be Managed!

Managers and researchers must recognize that lean supply chains are a fact of life for business. The potential benefits offered by such systems are too great to be ignored. Yet, as managers continue to lean out their systems in search of more responsive and lower cost systems, they must recognize that these systems are increasingly becoming 'fragile' – more sensitive to the effects of potential changes and unanticipated disruptions. In the past, the commonly accepted prescription for dealing with such disruptions was to rely upon buffers in the forms of safety stock, safety lead-time and safety capacity. Such buffers are no longer as attractive as they were in the past.

What is needed is a different approach. This chapter has explored the effective practices and tools of one such approach – Business Continuity Planning. It has shown that these tools not only make logical sense but that they also work, if applied correctly. We have shown that the management and reduction of supply chain disruptions and risk is both feasible, effective and cost efficient. Risk is a fact of life but one that can be managed.

References

Barnes, J.C. (2001), *A Guide to Business Continuity Planning*, John Wiley & Sons, New York, NY.

Burt, D.N., Dobler, D.W., and Starling, S.S. (2003), *World Class Supply Management: The Key to Supply Chain Management*, 7th Edition, McGraw-Hill, New York, NY.

Digital Research, Inc. (2002), Business Continuity & Disaster Recovery Planning, Report Prepared for AT&T, Kennebunk, ME.

Jacobs, D. (2002), Wakeup call, *Supply Chain Technology News*, Vol. 4, No. 9.

Kraljic, P. (1983), 'Purchasing must become supply management', *Harvard Business Review*, Vol.61, No.5, pp.109-117.

Leenders, M.R., Fearon, H.E., Flynn, A.E., and Johnson, P.F. (2002), *Purchasing and Supply Management*, 12th Edition', McGraw-Hill Irwin, Burr Ridge, IL.

McKenna, R. (1997), *'Real Time: Preparing for the Age of the Never Satisfied Customer'*, Harvard Business School Press, Boston, MA.

Monzcka, R.M., Trent, R.J. and Handfield, R.B. (2002), *Purchasing and Supply Chain Management*, 2nd Edition', Southwestern, Cincinnati, OH.

Steele, P. and Court, B. (1996), *Profitable Purchasing Strategies: A Manager's Guide for Improving Organizational Competitiveness Through the Skills of Purchasing*, McGraw-Hill, London, UK.

Wolk, M. (2002), 'Behind the West Coast port lockout', MSNBC, October 8, www.msnbc.com/news.

Womack, J.P. and Jones, D.T., (1996), *Lean Thinking: Banish Waste and Create Wealth in Your Corporation*, Simon & Schuster, New York, NY.

Chapter 12

Conclusion

Prof. Bob Ritchie and Dr. Clare Brindley

Introduction

In every chapter the case is made that in differing industrial sectors in differing countries supply chains are becoming increasingly vulnerable to total breakdown, dislocation, disruption or simply failure to deliver the value added required by the final consumer. Zsidisin et al (Chapter 11) discuss the increasing fragility of supply chains and their inability to sustain even mild shocks resulting from strategies designed to make them leaner and more efficient. The text has addressed the reasons underpinning this increased vulnerability and examined the consequential changes in risk exposure both in terms of incidence and consequences. Each chapter has explored either conceptually and/or empirically approaches to managing such risks. As stated in the introductory chapter, the key aims of the text are to consolidate the current research in the field of supply chain risk management, in order that the knowledge and experience gained can be shared and equally importantly to generate synergy from a more informed evaluation of the research within the field. This concluding chapter seeks to draw together some of the key themes and developments presented in the text, although it would not claim to be a comprehensive synthesis of the entire research presented.

Diversity of Definitions

It is perhaps not surprising that each of the authors presenting chapters in the text have adopted, either explicitly or implicitly, differing definitions of risk, supply chains and risk management. Examining each of these in more detail demonstrates that the differences are marginal rather than substantive and result primarily from the differing perspectives taken. These differences in perspective contribute a richness and depth to the text, which helps to establish risk management in supply chains as a valid and valuable emerging field of study. It is also indicative of an emerging discipline that research is grappling with definitional issues.

Definitions of risk and uncertainty have been explored in different parts of the text and whilst variations in emphasis appear from author to author, there is a common understanding that the key issue being addressed is the exposure to risk. The management of risk typically subdivides this issue into two elements, the incidence or likelihood of occurrence and the consequences when an event does occur. Risk management is seen to be the structures and processes designed to tackle either or both of these elements.

The field of supply chain management has itself spawned a variety of definitions of the term the supply chain. As was demonstrated in the chapters in Section 1 of the text, these various definitions are not necessarily incompatible, more precisely they are simply differing perspectives on the same phenomenon. For example:

1. *Dyadic* focuses on the relationship between only two partners in the supply chain, sometimes referred to as the basic supply chain.
2. At the other end of the spectrum, *ultimate* would represent a view of the total supply chain from primary raw materials through to consumption of the final product or service.
3. The term *network* captures the reality of the extensive dimensions of any supply chain dealing with many organizations which may have no direct contact or even awareness of the full membership of the supply network. Hallikas and Virolainen (Chapter 4) provide an interesting concept of the virtual enterprise, defined as the connection of certain members of the network to deliver value for a specific product/service offering.
4. The term *amorphous* was employed by Ritchie and Brindley (Chapter 3) to reflect the complex, dynamic and often ill-defined structure of many supply chains that resulted from ICT developments.

Supply chains are by their very nature multi-dimensional and multi-functional, involving the interaction of every function in an organization and dealing with information exchanges etc. Assumptions are often made that the supply chain is concerned with tangible products and logistics in the sense of production, warehousing distribution etc. However, what the studies reveal is that many of the non-tangible dimensions (e.g. information flows, relationship building) of the supply chain offer the greatest potential to add value or improve efficiency.

The literature review by Paulsson (Chapter 6) supports the view that the primary focus of much of the previously published research in the field of risk management in supply chains has addressed the dyadic relationship between the organization and the immediate upstream supplier with the emphasis on the more conventional approaches to risk management (i.e. insurance, buffer stocks, service level agreements). The research presented in this text demonstrates that the research field has widened considerably beyond the more tactical and operational perspective of purchasing to the technical, operational and strategic considerations and their impact across the entire supply chain and the final consumer. Future research will need to address increasingly complex and dynamic structures and relationships within supply chains.

A further perspective on the supply chain is that of the supply chain as the vehicle for the delivery of added value. This view focuses primarily on the effectiveness of the supply chains and arguably, each stage in the process should add value towards the final product/service consumed at the final stage. In many respects this perspective is implicit in the supply chain management approach, although often the increased efficiency goal may prove a more important parameter in dictating the decision making than adding value.

Emerging Frameworks

Two frameworks were presented to provide a conceptual mapping of the field and the research being undertaken. Norrman and Lindroth (Chapter 2) present a three-dimensional model encapsulating degrees of risk, unit of analysis within the supply chain and a graduated scale of risk management activities. This was developed into a second contingency framework by Ritchie and Brindley (Chapter 3), providing a more extensive framework to capture the diversity of contexts within this field. An appropriate and more simplified framework to structure the conclusions from this text is presented in Figure 12.1. This figure represents the four sets of factors which impact on supply chain risk and its management. These factors are interlinked in a complex and dynamic manner, as will be explained later in this Chapter.

Risks within the supply chain have been categorized as inherent in the sense that some are generic to all business organization (e.g. economic and political climate) and others are intrinsic to the particular supply chain context. Ritchie and Brindley (Chapter 3) captured the essence of this in their contingency framework identifying the differing levels of contextual variables. Most of the authors (e.g. Zsidisin et al in Chapter 11) make reference to the impact of competitive pressures on supply chain risks. Figure 1 represents these as twin pressures resulting from the drive to increase efficiency of the supply chain and hence the business and improvements in effectiveness. Paulsson (Chapter 6) identifies four efficiency-related developments that enhance the risk exposure in the supply chain, making the supply chain leaner (i.e. stripping out unnecessary stages); improving the agility (more responsive to new developments); outsourcing operations and services and the development of single sourcing arrangements. Each of the four developments and variations within these may result in increasing uncertainty and risk for many of the partners in any supply chain, as certain key partners (i.e. those with significant commercial or economic influence) seek to achieve cost reductions to remain competitive. Arguably, for some partners in the supply chain particular developments may potentially reduce the risk exposure. For example, a single sourcing agreement may resolve some of the commercial risks associated with the business relationship, albeit in the short to medium term that the agreement covers.

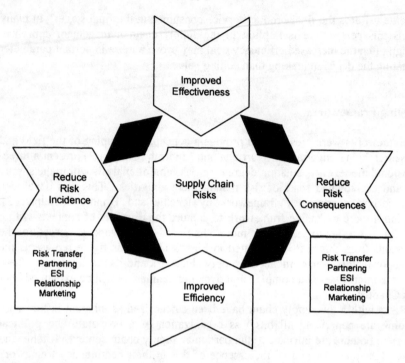

Figure 12.1 Managing Supply Chain Risk and Performance

Improvements in the effectiveness of the supply chain may similarly increase and reduce risk exposure. Enhancing reliability in the delivery of goods or services, improved quality, better design and greater exchange of information are all developments that may enhance the effectiveness of the supply chain and reduce the risks involved. However, the process of achieving the improvements in effectiveness may generate increased risk exposure, through for example the sharing of commercial and technical knowledge or the reliance on other partners to deliver what has been agreed. Burtonshaw-Gunn (Chapter 7) identifies risks emanating from the relationships themselves as well as from the competitive environment and the specific project parameters.

Risk management strategies have been a major focus of many of the research studies represented in the text. These have tended to address approaches to the reduction of either the incidence of the risks (i.e. reducing the likelihood of a particular event occurring) and/or the reducing the severity of the consequences should this occur. A number of authors (e.g. Zsidisin et al in Chapter 11) have recognized the limitations of the more conventional approaches to supply chain risk management in the current competitive climate of enhancing effectiveness and improving efficiency. The use of buffer stocks still provides solutions to risk exposure in particular contexts but not to the variety of complex inter-relationships that constitute most supply chains. Buffer stocks are also a significant impediment to improving efficiency in terms of cost reduction.

Much more imaginative solutions are being developed in every sector. Butonshaw-Gunn (Chapter 6) demonstrates the success of Partnering within the construction industry, a development that is not unique to the UK but one which is being paralleled in many other developed markets (e.g. USA and Australia). Such developments enhance the understanding and confidence between the partners and arguably generate benefits in terms of reducing the incidence of potential risks and the severity of the consequences should they occur. Zsidisin and Smith (Chapter 8) examined the approach of ESI (Early Suppler Involvement) as a means to managing the risks in terms of incidence and consequences. This involvement may operate at strategic and tactical levels, engaging a variety of functions such as engineering, marketing, production and finance. The extent of the engagement may vary from the simple sharing of information and knowledge to more significant strategic developments of new products etc. Andersson and Norrman (Chapter 10) investigated the transfer of risks from the client organization either to the supplier or alternatively to a third party logistics organization. Transferring responsibilities in this way helps to focus attention on specific risks removing some exposure for the consequences though perhaps not eliminating totally these. Brindley (Chapter 5) evaluates another dimension of this interaction between partners in the supply chain through the engagement of relationship marketing principles and practices.

Emerging Themes

Two themes emerge from the overall evaluation: knowledge sharing and confidence building. A key feature to building and sustaining resilient and robust supply chains is the ability not only to share information but more importantly the knowledge base (i.e. ensuring that partners have the capability to interpret and utilise effectively the information provided). It is important to ensure that this is a two-way process of information and knowledge generation. All of the risk management developments discussed in the text have either explicitly or implicitly recognized this requirement. The fields of knowledge management and the learning organization provide pertinent areas for future research and development in relation to supply chains and managing their risks. The second theme of confidence has information implications for the developing relationship in terms of trust, openness, honesty and sharing etc. These are all features associated with developing deep and enduring relationships. The emergence of studies into how organizations, as opposed to individuals might achieve these attributes provides further opportunities for research and development in the supply chain field.

Metrics

The issue of measurement and metrics represents a further issue underlying a number of the supply chain and risk management developments outlined in the text. A key challenge to participants in this and many other fields of management activity is demonstrating the benefits to the 'bottom line.' The issue of metrics and a possible means of developing an approach was developed by Ritchie and Brindley (Chapter 3). The fact that risk is difficult to quantify in numeric terms given that we are often relating to risk perceptions of the partners in the supply chain rather than objectively measurable risks, provides an additional problem. However, Mullai (Chapter 9) in examining risks associated with the marine transportation of dangerous goods, developed an approach to disaggregating the various components of this risk and developing measures for these. We need to establish some basis on which reduction in risk exposure, either through reduction in the likely incidence or through amelioration of the potential consequences, may be measured as a benefit not only to the individual organization but to the supply chain as a whole. The field of Utility Theory and choice may provide one direction for future research and development work in this respect.

Supply Chain Risk Management – the Way Forward

The issues explored in the text have illustrated that supply chain risk management is an emergent research field that is rich conceptually, offers empirical challenges and provides a research platform for academics from a variety of subject disciplines, such as engineering, operations, marketing, logistics and supply chains. The multi-disciplinary background is likely to feed the definitional debate until the research field matures. However, this is not to be viewed as a negative issue rather one that is indicative of the richness of debate. It is hoped that the frameworks and emerging themes explored in the text inspire and motivate readers to conduct their own research. As practitioners face the increasing pressures of dynamic, volatile and vulnerable supply chains and demand metrics to support their risk management decisions, it is critical that research is able to support them.

Index